The Representational
Theory of Capital

The Representational Theory of Capital

Property Rights and the Reification of Capital

Leonidas Zelmanovitz

LEXINGTON BOOKS

Lanham • Boulder • New York • London

Table 1.1: Austrian treatment of capital from Menger to Lachmann (Endres and Harper, 2011: 364), in Endres, Anthony M. and David A. Harper. "Carl Menger and his followers in the Austrian Tradition on the nature of capital and its structure," Journal of History of Economic Thought, Volume 33, Number 3, September 2011. (Reproduced under license of the publisher)

Table 2.1: Anthony M. Endres & David A. Harper, Carl Menger and His Followers in the Austrian Tradition on the Nature of Capital and Its Structure, Journal of the History of Economic Thought, Vol. 33, Issue 3. Reproduced with permission.

Zelmanovitz, Leonidas. "The Fiscal Proviso," in Criterio Libre, Volume 11, Number 19, July–December 2013, pages 23–49, Bogota, Colombia, 2013. (creative commons)

Zelmanovitz, Leonidas. "Designing Capitalism," posted on Law & Liberty on September 8, 2015. Available online at: - https://www.lawliberty.org/book-review/designing-capitalism/ (2015). (creative commons)

Zelmanovitz, Leonidas (2016) The Ontology and Function of Money—The Philosophical Fundamentals of Monetary Institutions. Lanham, MD: Lexington Books.

Zelmanovitz, Leonidas. Editorial Review of "Rethinking the Theory of Money, Credit, and Macroeconomics: A New Statement for the Twenty-First Century," by John Smithin, Lexington Books, 2018, (2018a).

Zelmanovitz, Leonidas. A model for a Representational Theory of Capital, in Perspectivas en Inteligencia, 10 (19): 141–161, 2018, 2018b). (creative commons)

Zelmanovitz, Leonidas. Review of "Time, Space and Capital" by Åke E. Andersson and David Emanuel Andersson. Journal of the History of Economic Thought 41 (2), 2019, (2019a). (Reproduced under license of the publisher)

Zelmanovitz, Leonidas. "The Baleful Consequences of Robert Skidelsky's Keynesianism," March 12, 2019, Law & Liberty, available online at: - https://www.lawliberty.org/2019/03/12/the-baleful-conse quences-of-robert-skidelskys-keynesianism/ (2019b). (creative commons)

Zelmanovitz, Leonidas. Modern Monetary Theory and the Moral Equivalent of War, in Law & Liberty, posted on November 20, 2019, available online at: - https://www.lawliberty.org/2019/11/20/modern-monetary-theory-and-the-moral-equivalent-of-war/ (2019c). (creative commons)

Zelmanovitz, Leonidas. "What Would the Treasury View of the Libra Be?," Law & Liberty, posted on July 51, 2019, available online at: - https://www.lawliberty.org/2019/07/31/what-would-the-treasury-vie w-of-libra-be/ (2019d). (creative commons)

Zelmanovitz, Leonidas. "Liberty in the Political Institutions of the 21st Century," Laissez-faire, Number 50–51, March–September 2019, pages 36–52, Guatemala City, Guatemala, 2019e. (creative commons)

Zelmanovitz, Leonidas. "A representational theory of capital," in Procesos de Mercado. Madrid, Spain, Union Editorial, Volume 17, number 1, Primavera 2020, pp. 267 a 294, 2020. (creative commons)

Zelmanovitz, Leonidas. "The Pandemic and the Roman Foundation of Property," Liberty Fund

Zelmanovitz, Leonidas. "The Representational Theory of Capital and Its Model," Liberty Fund

Published by Lexington Books
An imprint of The Rowman & Littlefield Publishing Group, Inc.
4501 Forbes Boulevard, Suite 200, Lanham, Maryland 20706
www.rowman.com

6 Tinworth Street, London SE11 5AL, United Kingdom

Copyright © 2021 The Rowman & Littlefield Publishing Group, Inc.

British Library Cataloguing in Publication Information Available

Library of Congress Cataloging-in-Publication Data Available

Library of Congress Control Number: 2020948468

ISBN 978-1-7936-0500-9 (cloth : alk. paper)
ISBN 978-1-7936-0502-3 (pbk : alk. paper)
ISBN 978-1-7936-0501-6 (electronic)

∞ ™ The paper used in this publication meets the minimum requirements of American National Standard for Information Sciences—Permanence of Paper for Printed Library Materials, ANSI/NISO Z39.48-1992.

This book is dedicated, in memoriam,
to my father, Leão Zelmanovitz

Contents

List of Figures and Tables

FIGURES

TABLES

Preface

This book proposes a "representational" theory of capital according to which there is a relation between capital goods in the real side of the economy and certain instruments representative of property claims on those goods in the abstract side of the economy. Financial instruments are treated herein as a kind of property claim, and a particularly liquid form of property claim.

The relation that I propose between these two things is not, let me stipulate at the outset, a direct one. Readers will not find me using the metaphor of a mirror image to describe it. The relation is a loose rather than a direct one, and the causes for (and consequences of) the looseness are explored in the chapters that follow.

My aim in writing this book is not to simplify our understanding of the relationship between "things" and "claims to things," but to make explicit and precise what many current researchers assume implicitly and, consequently, imprecisely. This book will, I hope, be a tool that researchers can apply to their own research, in the form of a standard by which inconsistencies in the literature on Capital Theory can be identified.

This work is not exclusively a piece of economic, legal, or social ontology scholarship; it is an interdisciplinary study, since more and more I am skeptical that we can understand social phenomena without the concurrence of all social sciences relevant to the matter at hand.

Understanding what capital is requires delving into its nature on both the real and the abstract sides, and this I undertake to do. In regard to capital goods, what they actually are, or at least one aspect of them, is made clearer by the thesis that they exist on a spectrum with respect to consumer goods. A number of inconsistencies or contradictions in Capital Theory that currently exist may be resolved with the use of this thesis.

It may be argued, I realize, that this study attempts to cover too much. In going back to the philosophical and economic basics, I make no claim to writing something profound, or something that goes deeper in most if not all of the details; however, that is not what I am aiming at with this work. My argument is that a crucial idea for our understanding of what capital is—and researchers ignore it at their own risk—is that actual capital goods (and processes, and knowledge) are represented in financial instruments and other property claims. A formal treatment that lays out the philosophical and economic basics is necessary, I believe, for me to put this idea across, and the model I am proposing for understanding these matters is, with all its limitations, a first step in that direction.

Further, by laying out the philosophical and economic basics of the theory I hope to offer to the reader the reasons why having a clearer concept of capital is an important tool for wealth creation, and why wealth creation is, more than never, necessary for our wellbeing and flourishing in our civilization.

The book is divided into five parts. The first is introductory. I begin by discussing how capital theory matters for our society, with a review of the relevant history of economic ideas, with emphasis on the Austrian School of economics. The second lays out my proposed model. It begins with a discussion about the relation between capital theory and property rights, the concept of representation, and the formal model proposed. The third part describes the classification of goods on the real side of the economy, as presented in the proposed model. The fourth describes property rights and other claims on the abstract side of the economy, and expands on one kind of property rights in the abstract side, namely financial instruments. The fifth is the book's Conclusion, where the consequences of the theory are made clear by its application to concrete questions in regard to capital allocation and economic performance. It also contains an Epilogue, where current applications of the theory are discussed.

Once I expound, using common language, my concept of representation in the abstract side of the economy of capital goods and processes in the real side of the economy, I will delve into my formal model of what this "representational theory of capital" consists of.

Granted, the idea that financial instruments are property titles representing claims over real goods is commonsensical if considered at microeconomic level (especially from a legal perspective). What I am arguing in this book is that this concept of representation aids our understanding at a macroeconomic level, as well. Such a claim, to my knowledge, is a novel one.

Acknowledgments

This book would not be possible if not for the institutional support of Liberty Fund, and the Mercatus Center at the George Mason University, where I began researching for this project during the Fall semester of 2016 as a visiting scholar of the F.A. Hayek Program for Philosophy, Politics and Economics. Neither would it be possible without the support of Miguel Angel Alonso Neira, Daniela Becker Cheffe, Helio Beltrão, Maria Blanco, Mauro Boianovsky, Nicolas Cachanosky, Gabriel Calzada, Ramon Paul Degennaro, Anthony M. Endres, Roberto Fendt, Daniel Fernandez, Juan Javier del Granado, Chris Guzelian, Khalil M. Habib, David A. Harper, Stephen Hicks, Steve Horwitz, David Howden, Jesus Huerta de Soto, Clynton Lopez, Ferdinando Meacci, Bruno Meyerhof Salama, Leonidas Montes, James B. Murphy, Jerry O'Driscoll, Emilio Pacheco, Maria Pia Paganelli, Danilo Petranovich, Douglas B. Rasmussen, George Selgin, Daniel Shapiro, Daniel Smith, John Smithin, Virgil Storr, Eugene Tan, Lauren Weiner, and Larry White (and two anonymous referees, one of the *Journal of Prices & Markets* and the other of *Procesos de Mercado*). However, the usual disclaimer applies, all errors are my own.

Part I

Chapter 1

Introduction

There are many different angles from which we can depict the building of Capital Theory, to use Sir John Richard Hicks's epigraphic image "Capital . . . is a very large subject, with many aspects . . . ; wherever one starts, it is hard to bring more than a few of them into view. It is just as if one were making pictures of a building; though it is the same building, it looks quite different from different angles (Hicks, 1973: v)." Professor Ferdinando Meacci, in a message to me, listed the following "angles":

> Capital: grounds for its being vs. being as it is; Individual vs. Social Capital; Money vs. Real capital; Circulating vs. Fixed capital; Circulating capital vs. Capital of circulation; Material changes (of matter) vs. Formal changes (of property) in the process of circulation; free vs. Invested capital; Variable vs. Constant capital; True capital vs. Capital goods vs. Capital value (Clark, Knight, and Fisher); Durable goods vs. Goods in process; and Instrumental vs. Working capital.

All of these offer valuable insights to the understanding of what capital is. However, many would lead us far from the perspective developed in the present work. To the extent that some "angles" may help us more than others in developing our theory, it is these that have been incorporated herein—for instance, Individual versus Social Capital as derived from the distinction between positive, relative and compound profits in Adam Smith and James Steuart (Meacci, 2020).[1]

Professor Meacci of the University of Padua describes the twofold notion of capital in Smith: that is, capital from the point of view of the individual and from the point of view of the society as a whole, the locus classicus of which is Smith's discussion of "dwelling-houses" and "profitable buildings" in *The*

Wealth of Nations (book II, chapter I, "Of The Division of Stock," Paragraphs 12 and 15, Smith, 1981: 281–282). A rented house may be a capital invest-ment for an individual, since he may derive some income from it, but that investment does not generate new wealth for society as a whole. By con-trast, a rented building used for a commercial or industrial activity not only produces income for its owner but is part of the capital structure of society, helping to generate the services and products produced or performed in that building. That is to say, not every claim to a stream of revenue corresponds directly to the production of new goods and services, but requires for its satisfaction the appropriation of some wealth produced elsewhere. Therefore the likelihood of satisfying those claims derives indirectly from the existing capital structure, of which they are not part. That is an important insight for my project in writing this book and should be kept in mind.

THE STRUCTURE OF THE FIRST TWO CHAPTERS

As a way into the matters under examination in this book, we might best begin with some discussion of the history of capital theory (with emphasis on the description, by Böhm-Bawerk and others, of the relation between capital and property rights); the light shed by this body of theory on different concep-tions of the good life, and hence on the proper political arrangements for a society of free and responsible individuals; Capital Theory's current exposi-tors; and the unsolved controversies in Capital Theory.

At the beginning of this introductory discussion of different approaches to Capital Theory, it seems necessary to add another disclaimer. This work is one of "speculative theory"; it is not empirical or historical. The purpose of the survey of the literature on which we embark with these first two chapters is only to illustrate some of the problems raised in this book and to give a context for examining those problems. It is not, as I trust that readers will understand, meant to be exhaustive.

THE SOCIAL RELEVANCE OF CAPITAL THEORY

The social relevance of Capital Theory lies in the fact that representation of the real side of the economy in the monetary side has consequences for economic performance. Even acknowledging pervasive government intervention in our lives, we live in an open society, one in which most eco-nomic relations are impersonal, in which exchanges happen under the legal and moral framework of more or less free markets, but still, mostly guided by the price system.[2] For those who consider individual human flourishing as the ultimate justification of the political order, the open society and the market economy supporting it are extremely important instrumental moral goods.

I am convinced that a better understanding of the philosophical fundamentals of money may help us to come to more adequate monetary arrangements in the real world. In the same way, I am convinced that a clear understanding of what capital is and how it is represented in (among other modalities) financial instruments, is a necessary condition for creating institutional arrangements under which most, if not all, individuals can prosper and accomplish their goals in life.

The relevance of Capital Theory can be perceived in the practical application of that theory: It makes a difference, not only for the economic performance of society as a whole but at an individual level as well. For instance, knowing what the different kinds of financial instruments represent is useful for choosing which ones are better for a given individual to invest his own savings in.

In regard to society as a whole, significant economic growth (measured in terms of fast growth in income per capita) is, I argue, following Tyler Cowen,[3] the greatest source of legitimacy of the open society and the market order under a limited and representative government, all of which are at the core of what we understand as liberal democracy. A clear understanding of what each kind of financial instrument represents is crucial, I argue, for the proper functioning of that society and order.

Allowing individuals to pursue their own ends is what permits all of us to benefit from the advancements of applied science and to enjoy the refinements of culture and the arts. A well-balanced life worth living is one that requires action in this world; and the productive capacities we enjoy today, thanks to the capitalist system, result in the wonders that are available to us, whatever our personal preferences may be, to try live the life we aspire to live.

The link between the institutions of the open society, capital accumulation, and human progress cannot be more eloquently stated than von Mises stated it:

> Saving, capital accumulation, is the agency that has transformed step by step the awkward search for food on the part of savage cave dwellers into the ways of modern industry. The pacemakers of this evolution were the ideas that created the institutional framework within which capital accumulation was rendered safe by the principle of private property of the means of production. Every step forward on the way toward prosperity is the effect of saving. The most ingenious technological inventions would be practically useless if the capital goods required for their utilization had not been accumulated by saving. (Mises, 2008: 39)

It is generally understood in the specialized literature, for instance in Jones and Vollrath, that the modern examination of economic growth began in the 1950s with two papers by MIT's Robert Solow that "helped to clarify the role of the accumulation of physical capital" and highlighted "the importance of technological progress as the ultimate driving force behind sustainable economic growth" (Jones and Vollrath, 2013: 2). Later, Paul Romer and Robert Lucas from the University of Chicago acknowledged the importance of human capital, and Harvard's Robert Barro made theories of growth quantifiable and testable.

Some of the limitations of many current treatments of Capital Theory come into view when, in the same work, Jones and Vollrath argue for the relevance of Capital Theory by asking three questions. The first two are: Why are some countries rich and others poor? and What is the engine of economic growth? They answer both with the phrase, "technological progress." The third question—how do we explain economic miracles—leads into their treatment of the basic neoclassical model and the "social infrastructure" of the economy. That is the entire extent of their concession to institutional economics (Jones and Vollrath, 2013: 18).

We find in the specialized literature that the Misesian notion that the main determinant of economic growth is the accumulation of physical capital, often referred to as "capital fundamentalism," has often been attributed to "Harrod's and Domar's proposition that the rate of growth is the product of the saving rate and of the output-capital ratio" (Boianovsky, 2018: 477).

However, in the mainstream economics literature in the 1950s and 1960s we also find discussions of whether society could profitably invest a larger fraction of the national income. There were doubts about the extent to which that would be possible without the "concomitant growth of the labor force and of technological progress" (Boianovsky, 2018: 478). Those discussions, we may note, do not mention the institutional environment most conducive to capital formation and to economic activity in general. Actually, except for a mention by Hirschman of the "elimination of obstacles to investment," there is no other reference to institutional arrangements, to the enforcement of contracts and private property rights, to free trade, to sound money, or to independent courts of justice in the literature reviewed by Boianovsky (2018). Although the author states that other economists reject the "mechanical application of the model," the reasons for such rejection do not involve institutional considerations, just questions of labor and technology (Boianovsky, 2018: 481).

As for Harrod's model, some have criticized it as tautological, such as Higgins (Boianovsky, 2018: 488). Without a doubt, the static model is just an identity, serving merely to present the proposed relation in a formal way. But that is not without significance. It opens, for example, the possibility of measuring the Incremental Capital-Output Ratio (ICOR). As pointed out by Boianovsky (2018), Easterly concludes that "the *ICOR* is not an independent causal factor but just a ratio between two variables (investment and growth) loosely related, echoed the 1960's literature." Such approximation, it is important to recognize, is the best that a model created at this high level of abstraction can do. Yet there is no way to make from that approximation a model from which predictions could be extracted.

These highly abstract models, and the mechanistic approach that was in vogue at the time, led many economists to conclude that it was not only possible to supplement entrepreneurship with planning but that planning would actually raise the rate of savings and therefore increase the natural rate of growth (Boianovsky, 2018). Sadly missing from their reasoning, due to the limitations of knowledge in society as pointed out by Hayek (1945), was that "planning" actually reduces the profitable opportunities for investment. But to understand this, different theoretical tools than the ones they were using would be necessary.

ON WHETHER ECONOMIC GROWTH CAN OR SHOULD BE A POLICY GOAL

Let us not, however, get ahead of ourselves in discussing the relation between Capital Theory and economic growth. Perhaps we should not assume that the latter can or should be a policy goal, or that Capital Theory can or should be an instrument to achieve that goal. It is well at this point to step back and engage with some of the criticisms of economic growth as a unifying public policy goal for those interested in the betterment of the human condition. To do that, we may bring in Robert and Edward Skidelsky and a recent discussion I had with my good friend Professor Jim Murphy of Dartmouth College about the Skidelskys' arguments against the value of economic growth, put forward in their book *How Much Is Enough? Money and the Good Life* (Skidelskys, 2013).

The Skidelskys open their book with the following passage about capitalism, writing that it

has exalted some of the most reviled human characteristics, such as greed, envy and avarice. . . . Our call is to chain up the monster again by recalling what the greatest thinkers of all times and all civilizations have meant by the "good life.". . . In doing this, we will be challenging the current obsession with the growth of Gross Domestic Product (GDP) as the chief goal of economic policy. . . . The extent to which further GDP growth will improve welfare is therefore moot. It surely does so for very poor countries, but it may be the case that rich societies already have too much GDP. Our view is that, for the wealthy nations of the world, GDP should be treated as a by-product of policies aimed at realizing the good life. (Skidelskys, 2013: 3)

Although my comments about *How Much Is Enough* are centered on this passage, they reflect my general impression of the entire book. And be it noted that their Keynesianism was not a problem for me; in fact, I think I give more credit to Keynes than they do when it comes to his predictions in his 1930 essay, "The Economic Possibilities for Our Grandchildren."[4]

The first thing to keep in mind is that the good life is "agent-relative." That is to say, my conception of it might not be yours. If we think about a "pizza chart" in which each slice represents a different component of the good life—such as job, family, health, spiritual life, leisure (which the Skidelskys emphasize), education—different people will have not only different components (race cars, professional wrestling, or gambling may be included in their definition of the good life although they are not part of mine) but also different proportions assigned to those components. Even if we might doubt that someone could have a good life without a family component altogether, that component will vary in size among the people who do include it.

So, my first objection is to the Skidelskys' idea that it would be possible to assign a price tag to the good life. It is impossible to know how different individuals would divide their individual pizza pies, and some forms of self-perfection may require more money than others. I think, for instance, that the figure of 66,000 USD per year in today's money, which they attribute to Keynes in a footnote, would probably enable anyone to have an honorable life "in principle," but it would not meet the cost, for example, of the education and training of a neurosurgeon.

It seems to me people often err in what they think is good for them; and from the perspective of Adam Smith's "impartial spectator," I would consider that many things a lot of people value do not contribute to their happiness. It is not just any kind of life that ought to qualify as a good life, but still, that is a matter of individual choice. The relevant point here is that you cannot price out what a good life would cost in dollars and cents, and therefore you cannot declare "how much is enough" unless it is your particular case that is being considered.

The Skidelskys are arguing that wealthy countries should impose policies that will likely curb economic growth. My problem with their approach is based on the assumption that the GDP per capita of wealthy nations today is not enough to pay for a plethora of "real" needs, regardless of the share of that income that is distributed through the political process. If the sum of everything that is produced by 350 million Americans is a GDP of 17.5 trillion USD, their GDP per capital is 50,000 USD, regardless of how that income is distributed. At the current level of income, the United States can afford to educate only so many people as neurosurgeons (or any other profession that requires substantial investments). It is not that the Europeans, who have a GDP per capita somewhat lower than the Americans, can pay for more education, health care, or any other service just because those services are funded by taxes. The fact is that they can pay for less of those services, since they do not produce as much as the Americans produce. We can discuss the wisdom of how money is spent at an individual level and at the level of the polity here and there, but my essential qualm with this analysis is that I do not believe that any level of income will ever be "satisfactory" given that "essential" needs are limitless.

To give an example, let's suppose that at the price of a million dollars per capita it would be possible to do even better than in Huxley's *Brave New World*, and provide a health care system that would permit to everyone to enjoy a teenager's health well beyond age seventy (that is, beyond the limit in Huxley's novel). How long would it take for that to be perceived as a "need" in the same way that indoor plumbing, air-conditioning, vaccines, and emergency care are perceived today (perhaps I should exclude vaccines from this list, since so many flat-earthers are now denying the value of that)? "Need" is a moving target. That will continue to be a strike against the Skidelskys' argument regardless of how wealth is distributed in a society.

Parenthetically, I am not much concerned about how to distribute the 50,000 USD per capita of current annual income in the United States; I am concerned about the curbs that these authors want to impose on growing that income out of a conviction that they think we already have "enough." In the particular life of any individual, in the abstract, I agree that there is, at any given moment, an amount adequate to live a decent life in the context of the society in which that person lives. We shall see a demonstration in my Athenian example below. But who wants to live today like he used to live? My concern is not to impose limits on what (some) individuals may want to achieve, even if, for my own part, I am content with what I have and prefer to devote my time to other pursuits than making more money!

Let us move to the Skidelskys' claim that "GDP (increase) should be treated as a by-product of policies aimed at realizing the good life." My objection to this is based on the same premise, that human flourishing is an "agent-relative" pursuit.[5] If we accept that self-perfection is something to be achieved by individuals, any "policies aimed at realizing the good life" could only be legitimate if those "policies" were governmental arrangements operating at a meta-normative level. That is, if we understand any political institution as designed to create the best possible environment for individuals to flourish, each one pursuing his or her ideal of what the good life is. In this sense, it is possible to accept that changes in the GDP would be a "by-product" of those policies. But if, contrariwise (as I think the authors have in mind), they are saying that the government should define normatively what the good life is for all the citizens, and then enforce it, no matter what the consequences in terms of the aggregate production of wealth—that to me would be objectionable. That may be in line with a strongly collectivist understanding of what *eudemonia* is, not with the more individualistic view I hold.

If all they want is a social-democratic liberal regime, I am fine with that. I agree that there are "essential goods" and that those goods are of higher moral value than "empty pleasures," and that it is thus reasonable to expect that society will support the supply of the former, likely at the expense of the supply of the latter. We may discuss different ways to provide those goods in a more efficient way or a more fair way. For instance, I think that vouchers to pay for education is a better arrangement than having public schools—incidentally, like they do in many European countries, in which many students attend religious schools paid for by the government. I also think that individual health accounts coupled with health insurance for extraordinary health care expenses is a better arrangement than the public provision of (and public meddling in) health care that we have today.

These opinions of mine are about how best to provide these services to the majority of the population; I am not disputing that the services are essential. However, my impression is that the authors want to go further than that. It seems they want to do industrial policy to redirect economic activity, to regulate working hours in ways that hamper people who may want to work longer hours, and the like. It does not seem they would be content only with creating conditions for people to enjoy a more complete life; really they want to nudge, and if necessary, to coerce, people to live the way they think is best.

Not surprisingly, the authors are willing to declare outright that "rich societies already have too much GDP." Here I only have a problem if the statement is to be taken literally. At a deep anthropological level, I think human beings have a different relation with nature than our "original" or "natural" relation. For instance, *homo sapiens* interact with nature using fire, which allows them to extract pure metals from rocks—something that did not exist "*in natura*." We can travel long distances, we can communicate long distances, we can fix our teeth, we can print our thoughts, we can transmit our knowledge—all of that because we changed our relation with nature from what it was when our species came into being. That Pandora's Box was open when the first fire was lit; so, there is no such a thing as "a proper life" according to an immutable "human nature," since what we consider proper to human beings today is the result of a lot of human action changing what our original condition was.

This is not to dispute that there are basic truths about a good human life; these have been acknowledged in all places at all times. But note that when we talk about "cultures," even if we go back to the Bronze Age, we are already talking about a kind of human life that was radically different from the hominids who had no fire, or from the Stone Age humans who had no metals. It seems safe to say that family, education, health, and leisure are essential elements of the good life today as they were in Ancient Mesopotamia and will be in the future while human beings exist. Again if we take literally the notion that "rich societies already have too much GDP," I think that in order to have a family life today—and to have education, health, leisure—one might well be able to afford adequate instrumental goods without needing to work more than 40 hours per week, 200 days per year on average in a Western society.

What is missing from the picture is that, in the same way that what we consider adequate today would be unthinkable by the nineteenth century's standards, what may be adequate by the twenty-second century's standards is unthinkable for us today. But the progress we need in the applied sciences in order to improve our health, our communications, our education, our availability of the arts, will only materialize if we allow continued economic growth at the pace that results from the sum of all individual evaluations. That is, not at the pace determined by the Skidelskys.

If we accept that as true, we can see that a "proper human life" becomes a moving target. Edward Gibbon considered the period between "the death of Domitian and the accession of Commodus" as the "period of the history of the world, during which the condition of the human race was most happy and prosperous" (Gibbon, 2010). Well, the Romans living in that time did not have indoor plumbing, electricity, anesthesia, X-rays, vaccines, or many of the things that are accessible to most people today, even many living below the "poverty line." So even if, for the sake of the argument, we consider what is not the case, that there is "too much" production in wealthy societies today, that completely misses the point that perhaps in fifty years, a much higher GDP will allow better education, better health, longer and happier lives for more people than it is possible to conceive of today. That is, of course, if subjectivists like the Sidelskys do not prevail in the arena of public debate.

To the extent that it is true and statistically relevant that the life expectancy of middle-aged men is a good proxy for a nation's living standards, we should wonder how it is possible that, in spite of being so productive, our society has made it difficult for many individuals to live a productive and fulfilling life. That is the conclusion drawn in a recent article on "Life Expectancy and Mortality Rates in the United States, 1959-2016" (Woolf and Schoomaker, 2019). However, the culprits identified in the article as having reduced the life expectancy of middle-aged Americans in the three last years of the authors' sample are drug overdoses, alcohol abuse, and suicide—symptoms of social and cultural problems to be sure, but not that people are getting poorer while the GDP is growing. Trying to address these problems seems to me the right

thing to do. Only it seems highly unlikely that the circumstances which lead
to falling life expectancies among middle-aged men will be improved by
restricting anyone from engaging in productive endeavors. Quite the opposite. If we could unleash more productive capacity, we would see wealth not
trickling down, but Niagara Falling down, even to the most uneducated and
unproductive individuals in society—be that directly, through opportunities for paying jobs they can do, or through government transferences and
subsidies.

The question may be illuminated by considering jobs with the same level
of productivity in a wealthy and in a less wealthy society: the job of shining
shoes, for example. Why does a person who shines shoes for a living in the
United States earn more than a person doing the same thing in Brazil? Well,
because American society in general is more productive, even if that person is
not. The same logic may be applied elsewhere. If you consult a person with a
job outside the Ivory Tower, that person will tell you how life is constrained
by scarce resources. And I am not referring to things that perhaps in the minds
of the Sidelskys are frivolous, such as repeated trips to Disney World. I am
talking about important things, such as how many units of blood transfusion
(each 6 ounces cost about 2,000 USD if you compute all the associated costs)
should a public hospital administer to a patient with internal bleeding before
giving up on him; or how much to pay for better body armor for our combat
soldiers.

I disagree with the Skidelskys that financial incentives somewhat hinder
technological development; but even if we accepted that as true, there would
still be some advances that require a lot of wealth to materialize. It is not
enough to develop the technology of mag-lev transportation; you need to
have the capital to build the mag-lev trains. If you impose restrictions on
growth, you retard the arrival of the moment when those advances will be
seen in our daily lives. The ancient Egyptians knew how to use steam to open
"automatically" the doors of their temples, but lots of capital was needed to
create the intercontinental railroads and the steamboats that increased international trade many fold in the nineteenth century and accelerated the increases
in human productivity that we enjoy today. Even if the Egyptians had thought
about applying that knowledge in order to increase human productivity, they
would have been required, like the British in the eighteenth and nineteenth
centuries, to generate a lot of wealth and invest that wealth in productive
endeavors before any result would show up in the lives of average people.

Someone who decided, as I did, to give up a well-paid business career to
pursue intellectual interests is likely to be sympathetic to the idea that the
incessant pursuit of money above other good things in life is not the best
route to human flourishing. And I am sympathetic. However, it was not the
absence of financial incentives that determined me to change course. I did so

in spite of the existing financial incentives. Consider that I enjoy the freedom to go back to business if I choose. To others who have the freedom to devote as much time as they want to what suits their fancy, I might say (if asked, and if they devoted all of their time to making money) that perhaps there are better ways to live their lives—think about the time away from their kids, for example. But using the powers of the state to impose on others what we value as the good life—that I cannot condone.

This is a question that must be understood in context. At the time of Aristotle, an Athenian citizen who owned a sizeable farm and perhaps a dozen slaves, an orchard, and some dozens of heads of cattle, instead of devoting himself to commerce might devote himself to politics and philosophical inquiry. He could afford to do this; it would make him a more well-rounded person than if he were only bent on working so he could buy another silver plate for his table. (In that society, it would not make sense to save to buy health insurance, since there was not much in terms of health care, anyway.) And even that proud Athenian would be a much poorer person than most Americans living below the poverty line today. His life would not be deemed exactly a good life by anyone today—whether ethically, considering his slave-owning, or materially, given his inability to purchase, for example, penicillin to save his children from common infections. How much happiness would the prevention of the death of a son or daughter bring to our proud Athenian if he and his society could afford that?

How much happiness, by the same token, could a cure for cancer bring to us today if we could afford that? It is hard to imagine the advancement of knowledge, which is underwritten with expensive research, or the dissemination of that knowledge to the public at large, without economic growth. Even if magnetic resonance scans had been developed in the 1950s and not in the 1990s, how much of their use would be limited either to the wealthy or to the well connected (as with the *nomenklatura* of the old Soviet Union) if we had continued to live with the GDP per capita of the 1950s?

Another objection one could raise to the Skidelskys' thesis has to do with the reason I think we do not have even more people working fewer hours and enjoying more leisure than what has been observed.[6] One possibility, as I said, is that different people have different conceptions of what a good life is and, even if an "impartial spectator" would agree with them that their particular form of individual flourishing is indeed a good one, there is still room for hard work and monetary gain, whether as an end in itself or as a way to pay for the health care or education of one's family, for a comfortable retirement, or whatever else one desired.

At one level, I agree that income transfers through the political process may attenuate some incentives to work harder, and we could debate if that would be a good or a bad thing. Perhaps in some cases, it is a good thing; I can think of a number of cases in which it seems not to be so to me. But the relevant question is based on my (possibly wrong) interpretation of their main claim. It seems to me they would impose low growth, whereas for me, low growth would be acceptable but only if it came as a consequence of changes in cultural values by the individual agents. It is the authors' "static" view of what is enough that leads them astray. It might indeed be possible to have a good idea of how much is enough in a static state in which society does not evolve technologically. What I reject is the idea of deliberately hindering future advances in the material resources that could potentially become available to mankind.

Just as a thought experiment: Let's suppose that scientists had just announced that, twenty-five years from now, a massive shower of asteroids would hit the earth and that only an investment of the equivalent of ten times the global GDP could save humanity from oblivion. Would it not be the moral thing to do, in that case, to increase production in every way we could so as to be able to foot that bill? Well, behind the veil of ignorance about such a future, I argue that the limits to state action be set at creating the conditions under which each and every individual can work and save as much as that individual wants. I would continue to resist the impositions of others as to how I must live my life, and reciprocally, I would not try to inhibit others' pursuits, even if I found them to be low pursuits—not, that is, beyond what we as a society are already doing in the realm of "sin" taxes.

If, alternatively, we interpret the Sidelskys as saying that the institutional conditions must change to allow individuals to flourish, instead of taking a "one number fits all" approach—this might be good policy advice on their part, for it would imply the need to find ways to have more productive economic activity (that is, more growth). Enlarging the amount of income that can be redistributed, whatever the method of distribution, and creating more options about the quality of the essential services available (in this example, education and health care)—these are desirable ends. Somehow one doubts this interpretation is accurate, though.

If the size of the labor force were bigger as a percentage of the total of the population, more workers could be tempted to work less, which is what Keynes predicted in the aforementioned "Economic Possibilities for Our Grandchildren." In the end, Keynes was right: On average, we are working much fewer hours to pay for a lot more things we have today. But some people do a lot of work while many others are just consumers. One does not need to look further than to pensions to realize this: In the 1930s, life expectancy was around sixty years; today it is north of eighty, and most people older than sixty-five, who at the time Keynes wrote would be dead, are now enjoying retirement.

The bottom line is that the Skidelskys' calling attention to the fact that "money can't buy happiness" merits praise. It's just that they have not considered all of the implications of their thesis.

THE BALEFUL CONSEQUENCES OF ROBERT SKIDELSKY'S KEYNESIANISM

Or perhaps they have.[7] At the risk of prolonging this digression, it seems apt to consider Robert Skidelsky's more recent book *Money and Government: The Past and Future of Economics* (Skidelsky, 2019). It helps us to understand the intellectual influences and the real-world consequences of the attitude displayed by *père et fils* in their 2013 effort. *Money and Government* has a laudable goal: to explain the monetary and financial problems that today preoccupy not only specialists but also many members of the general public. It contains a profound but easy-to-follow discussion of monetary theory, along with a compelling and entertaining history of the evolution of the financial arrangements that collapsed in 2008. It comprehensively details the financial crisis that began in the late 2007 and lasted until 2009, and it is a useful guide to understanding that episode. Furthermore, it prescribes what should be done to prevent future financial crises and to lift the political and economic malaise of current Western democracies. Yet, it is a very problematic book.

In the first of its four parts, "History of Economic Thought," Skidelsky, emeritus professor of political economy at Warwick University and honorary fellow of Jesus College, Oxford, covers the evolution of ideas about money, with some attention to philosophical discussions about the nature of money and value, the main schools of thought about money, and how the latter, along with historical experience, led to the establishment of the gold standard during the century of liberalism (1815–1914). On the cusp of the Great War, according to Skidelsky, there was consensus, by and large, on what he calls the "Victorian constitution," despite some fissures among Western governments. Its main economic components: (1) sound money embodied in the gold standard, (2) free trade, and (3) a small government footprint, kept limited by budgetary discipline and faith in the self-regulating nature of the market as proclaimed by Jean-Baptiste Say's law that supply creates its own demand.

The second part, "The Rise, Triumph and Fall of Keynes," covers the period following the end of the Great War, in which the United Kingdom followed misguided economic policies that led to high unemployment, stagnant incomes, and low growth even before the beginning of the Depression. The Depression, writes Skidelsky, came to shatter the confidence among economists and the public that free markets would result in an equilibrium with full employment. They came to believe that only the establishment of a "Keynesian constitution" would be able to increase aggregate demand, by governmental intervention through active monetary policy (monetary expansion) and active fiscal policy (a program of public investments funded by public debt).

According to Skidelsky, this period is basically divided in four parts: (1) the Keynesian response to the Depression; (2) Full Employment Keynesianism, from 1945 to 1960; (3) Growth Keynesianism, from 1960 to 1970; and (4) Stagflation Keynesianism, from 1970 to 1976. When two afflictions hit simultaneously—inflation and unemployment—Keynesianism was discredited and abandoned. The old "Victorian constitution" came back as the guide for monetary and fiscal policy. Under this alleged return to fiscal austerity, monetary restraint on the part of the government allowed the banks to take the lead in money-creation, and there was deregulation of the economy and a reduction of the size of the state, all of which supposedly set the stage for a repeat of the crisis of the 1930s.

Part Three, "Macroeconomics in the Crash and After, 2007," offers a description of the economic policies adopted in the United States and Europe to fight the Great Recession with particular attention to quantitative easing (QE) and the alleged importance of income inequality in explaining the crisis. This section contains an excellent description of the different forms of financial innovation and of global imbalances that, in the minds of many commentators, are the mechanisms through which the financial crisis came about.

The book concludes with "A New Macroeconomics," in which the author offers his prescriptions to prevent the problems of unemployment, slow growth, and financial weaknesses that Western democracies are still experiencing in the wake of the crisis of late 2007 to 2009. These prescriptions can be summarized as a recommended return to the "Keynesian constitution."

A Keynes Biographer's Lament

As we assess the accuracy of the foregoing, it is useful to zero in on a major premise laid out by Skidelsky: that "the omnipresence of uncertainty makes money and government essential features of any market economy."

What does he mean by this? It is inconceivable to think of a "market economy" without money or government. Market economies are monetary economies by definition and operate inside a legal framework provided by the state. Even private international law, which regulates foreign trade in essence, is national public law, since it deals with the enforcement, inside the borders of a given country, of agreements with subjects of other jurisdictions.

However, the need for money and the rule of law for markets to operate does not seem to be what the author is driving at. He offers in this book a rationale for greater state intervention in markets, either by regulation or by the state's use of its monetary prerogatives. This policy prescription is what his interpretation of economic history is directed to. By his account, except for the blip of the Keynesian episode, "the dominant view" has been that "money and government should play only minor roles in economic life," and that even after the Great Recession of a decade ago (when, allegedly, a reassessment of that view was in order), the response has been only "punishing austerity and anemic recovery,"

Recall that this celebrated economic historian is most celebrated for his three-volume life of Keynes, published in 1983, 1992, and 2000. In the preface to *Money and Government*, the author says: "I have been chiefly influenced by Keynes, whose biography I have written. However, as the book progressed, I became increasingly drawn to the insights of Karl Polanyi, with his insistence that, to be viable, a market order has to be 'embedded' in a framework of rules, policies and institutions. This insight has been somewhat neglected by the dominant school of Anglo-American economics."

What Skidelsky advances here is his narrative that the "dominant" view in economics nowadays is not concerned with "rules, policies and institutions." It is difficult to understand what he means by that. The neoclassical synthesis which corresponds to the "dominant" view in economics has an integral part composed by Keynesian economics, giving a key role to the manipulation of monetary and fiscal policy by political institutions specially created for that purpose—that is, central banks—in order to achieve the political objectives of the respective governments. To say that that has been neglected is an odd interpretation of the recent history of economic thought.

Some Curious Contradictions

Skidelsky starts by stating: "Macroeconomics is about money and government, and their relationship." After arguing that the dominant view in economics for the last 250 years has been one in which "money is of no importance," and "government interference with the market usually makes things worse," he specifies that such a view implies that "a competitive market economy . . . has an automatic tendency to full employment," and that government's meddling with the money supply induces people "to trade at the wrong prices."

Next, he argues that Keynesianism was the "dominant macroeconomic policy until the 1970s," and that the Keynesians deny that a monetary economy would have an automatic tendency to full employment, since people may reveal their preference for holding money given the "omnipresence of uncertainty." As we can see, at the very beginning of his text, Skidelsky downplays the role of the price system in conveying the information that economic agents need to coordinate their actions and also assumes that "uncertainty" would necessarily lead to the famous Keynesian "liquidity trap."

Those conclusions would not seem so obvious had Skidelsky applied Friedrich Hayek's insights from his 1945 article on "The Use of Knowledge in Society," or David Laidler's insights into the factors driving "the demand for money," the subject of his 1997 book of that title. However, those two texts are not in the bibliography and I can only wonder why he does not even mention them.

First, if he had considered the coordinating role of prices in a free society, as explained by Hayek in that article, he would understand why most economists would acknowledge that governmental manipulation of the money supply and other forms of interventionism would induce people "to trade at the wrong prices."

Second, if he had given the proper consideration to Laidler's reasoning about the elements informing the demand for money and the implications of that, he would not have jumped from the statement about the existence of uncertainty in a market economy to the supposed inevitability of an "inherent instability" in the economy, leading to a position of "underemployment equilibrium." Instead, he concludes that "therefore" it is necessary for the government to manage money as part of the management of the economy as a whole, in order to regulate supply and demand and insure full employment.

Such "necessity" has the same justification that Keynes himself found to develop his theories; and Skidelsky describes how Keynes became convinced that a paradigm shift was necessary, once his suggestion of simply asking the Bank of England (BoE) to lend the treasury the money needed to fund the road-construction projects proposed by David Lloyd George in 1934 was resisted by economists in general and the treasury in particular. That is why Keynes wrote "The General Theory." Skidelsky does not consider that perhaps asking the central bank to lend money to the treasury would be really inflationary, regardless of the "opinion" of businesspeople about the policy, or even if they had not been aware that that was going on.

The chapter on how Keynes developed his monetary theories is at the center of *Money and Government*, as it is at the center of Skidelsky's intellectual project. This book labors to restore respect for the Keynesian approach to monetary and fiscal problems. Hence the author's constant evocation of the supposed similarities between today's accepted wisdom in economics and that of economists in the 1920s and 1930s, which prompted Keynes to propose his "new" approach to macroeconomics. At the conclusion of this chapter, the author attributes the accomplishment of having undercut the cases for both "state socialism" and fascism to Keynes's theory, although he concedes that it opened the road for governmental intervention to "ensure at least a quasi-optimal equilibrium."

Oswald Mosley and Jeremy Corbyn, Keynesians

Skidelsky's earlier work and his political views are relevant here. In 1975, the economic historian, then a militant in the Labor Party, wrote a biography of the British fascist leader Oswald Mosley (1896–1980). In that hagio-graphic biography, Skidelsky cast himself not as Mosley's "prosecutor" but as a "counsel for the defense," one "able to view his life and the causes he espoused with both detachment and sympathy." Mosley partook of the British political class's pathetic response to the Great Depression in his sympathy for lax monetary and fiscal policies. These later became known as Keynesian, but were advanced by Mosley as early as 1925. All of which might explain why Skidelsky decided to write sympathetically about an authoritarian, inter-ventionist anti-Semite who had Adolf Hitler attend his wedding, hosted by Joseph Goebbels' wife, in Berlin, and who was a German agent (he spent most of World War II in prison).

In his 2015 article on "Corbynomics," Skidelsky made waves by praising Labor's Jeremy Corbyn for proposing the creation of a national investment bank in the United Kingdom, to be financed with increased taxation, and a program of investments in infrastructure to be financed by money-creation. It is not that Skidelsky thinks that any of those is a particularly a good idea, but his belief that "austerity" policies and private "speculation" must be replaced by government investment would trump any other concerns that arise with that political figure. According to Skidelsky: "Some of his posi-tions are untenable, but his remarks on economic policy are not foolish and they deserve proper scrutiny."

Apparently, the fact that a political leader is an apologist for totalitarian-ism, a supporter of anti-democratic regimes of both the Right and the Left and an unashamed anti-Semite is something that Baron Skidelsky is willing to gloss over, so long as the person adheres to the Keynesian formula to "save" the open society. One might wonder how much there would be left to save, if political power were given to a fascist like Mosley or a socialist like Corbyn, being the latter supported by Skidelsky in his bid to head the Labor Party, which he led to a crushing defeat at the hands of the Conservatives in late 2019.

INEQUALITY OF INCOME AND REDISTRIBUTION

To return to the notion that Western societies already produce "too much": This is used not just by the Skidelskys but by many others on the Left when they urge having the state dictate what to produce and how to better distrib-ute what is produced. It has considerable appeal to those worried about the effects on the environment of industrialization and affluence. And it is not the only basis for advocating policies of redistribution of wealth. Two other underlying convictions are generally at work here. One is that the existing distribution of income is the result of unfair or even illegal advantages reaped by certain groups in society. Another is that the spontaneous interactions that take place in the market by their nature lead to the concentration of income, and that redistribution must take place to rectify this. These two views have been well-represented in Capital Theory for generations. What is said on the subject of property rights in this literature seems to me to be based on misconceptions about how capital is created and traded in society. Let us focus on recent contributions by Katharina Pistor (and have her contribution contrasted with Hernando de Soto's) and Thomas Piketty to draw a bead on these misconceptions.

The Code of Capital

Columbia Law School Professor Katharina Pistor, in her recent book *The Code of Capital* (2019), offers a simple thesis: that goods may be the object of different forms of property claims. This relation between goods and the property titles over them she calls their "coding." Implicit here is the idea that the attributes of different property claims vary, giving their owners differing degrees of *priority*, *durability*, *universality*, and *convertibility* (Pistor, 2019: 3). Furthermore, she argues, the advantages that certain forms of property claims possess are responsible for part of their relative value in comparison with other goods, and therefore, that they are instruments by which wealth becomes unequally distributed in society (p. 19).

Of course, there are other matters raised in Pistor's book, such as the relation between the state and the enforcement of property rights, and the use that private individuals make of the legal system to enhance the value of their assets. However, the essential idea is that of the "coding" of some assets by "dressing" them in certain forms of property claims, and the supposedly unfair advantages that this coding gives to the claimants.

There is much to like and much to dislike in Pistor's analysis. On the one hand, she assumes the truth of the idea of representation that is at the heart of this work (though she uses different terminology from mine). "Fundamentally," she writes, "capital is made of two ingredients: an asset, and the legal code" (Pistor, 2019: 2). On the other hand, precisely because she fails to grasp the nature of the relation between things in the real world and the way in which they are represented by property claims, she ends up seeing that relation through a conspiratorial lens.

Her interest—and it seems to be an ideologically driven one—is not so much in explaining the relation between goods and claims on goods, as in blaming the fact that that relation exists for the inequality she sees in modern Western society: "Through this book I hope to shed light on how law helps create both wealth and inequality" (p. 3). As Professor Pistor herself acknowledges, groups with political power throughout history have been using the coercive powers of the state to create privileges (as the breakdown of its Latin root indicates: *prive+leges*)—that is, special legal statuses—for particular groups (usually themselves), be they tax immunities (p 3) or censitary suffrage, for example. What she fails to recognize is that some forms of property claims generate a more efficient economic allocation of resources and are open, in principle, to anyone to use.

She assumes a "zero sum" form of relation—in which a benefit that is granted to one part is taken from the other parts—rather than a Pareto Superior relation, in which everyone is better off because they can interact in ways that would not have been possible before the use of the new forms of property claims. Examples would be the right of landowners to sell their land if they wanted to, or the abolition of serfdom, which pinned the peasants to the land. When these two developments took place at the end of the Middle Ages, they contributed in no minor part to a better allocation of land in Europe, bringing together the lands and the people more inclined to put them to the most productive uses.

To view capital through the lens of the privileges extracted from society by special groups of interests that exercise state coercion, without taking into account the development of new legal technologies that have allowed for more efficient uses of scarce resources, is negligent to say the least; but it is exactly what Pistor does.

She mentions how legal institutions are "combined and recombined" in order "to code capital" by using elements of "contracts, property, collateral, the law of trusts and corporations, as well bankruptcy law" (p. 13)—that is, the spontaneous evolution of private law in order to regulate voluntary exchanges—as if this were no different from using public or administrative law to extract wealth from one segment of the population and give it to some privileged group, such as the pensioners of the public sector or the beneficiaries of agricultural subsidies.

In short, she conflates voluntary exchanges with involuntary ones. To analyze capital and capital instruments without making that distinction is to approach reality with an inadequate theoretical toolkit, which can only lead to a misapprehension of reality and, in turn, to ill-advised prescriptions about how to correct the mistakenly perceived problems.

The Mystery of Capital

Before moving to Piketty, let us contrast Pistor's approach to the idea of legal representation of capital to that of the renowned Peruvian economist Hernando de Soto. For de Soto:

> Capital is born by representing in writing—in a title, a security, a contract, and other such records—the most economically and socially useful qualities

[associated with a given asset]. The moment you focus your attention on the title of a house, for example, and not on the house itself, you have automatically stepped from the material world into the conceptual universe where capital lives. (de Soto, 2000: 50)

In his 1989 book *The Other Path*, de Soto presents the conclusions reached by his team of researchers on the informal sector of the economy in Peru. What they found was that "Peruvians' decisions to conduct their activities informally are in large measure the result of a rational, though less detailed, evaluation of the cost of formality" (de Soto, 1989: 133." Paraphrasing this insight, one that well deserves a Nobel Prize in economics: "The cost of formality is what determines the size of the informality."

From this powerful conclusion, and after years of further research to test its validity, de Soto developed his understanding of the idea of representation in property titles of existing assets, and the importance of formal recognition of property claims in order to give them additional features and greater value:

A formal property representation such as a title is not a reproduction *of* the house, like a photograph, but a representation of our concepts *about* the house. Specifically, it represents the nonvisible qualities that have potential for producing value. (de Soto, 2000: 50)[8]

In discussing de Soto's thesis in the Introduction to *The Mystery of Capital and the Construction of Social Reality*, editors Barry Smith, David Mark, and Isaac Ehrlich claim:

As those who live in underdeveloped regions of the world well know, it is not physical dwellings that serve as security in credit transactions, but rather the *equity* that is associated therewith. The latter certainly depends for its existence upon the underlying physical object: but there is no part of physical reality which *counts as* the equity in your house. Rather, as de Soto emphasizes, this equity is something abstract that is *represented* in a legal record or title in such a way that it can be used to provide security to lenders in the form of liens, mortgages, easements, or other covenants in ways which give rise to new types of institutions such as title and property insurance, mortgage securitization, bankruptcy liquidation and so forth. (Smith et al., 2008: xi)

I think that contrasting Pistor's and de Soto's approaches to the relationship between private property rights and capital, and analyzing that relationship as Smith, Mark, and Isaac do, using the theoretical tools provided by John Searle, sufficiently demonstrate the shortcomings of her claims.[9]

Piketty and Capital in the Twenty-First Century[10]

Let us assume that social justice requires that social rewards be distributed not on the basis of inherited position but on the basis of individual ability and contribution to society. Following the Rawls difference principle, inequality is permitted if it relates to merit; equality is respected in making opportunity available to all. That, anyway, would be the most benign interpretation of Thomas Piketty's thesis in his book *Capital in the Twenty-First Century* (2014).

Although the idea of social power rightly belonging to the most able has roots going far back in human societies, for example in ancient China and Greece, the term "meritocracy" was coined the day before yesterday, comparatively speaking. It first appeared in a book by Michael Young called *The Rise of the Meritocracy, 1870–2033* (1958). Let us use that 1958 work, and the ideas of Friedrich Hayek, to launch a discussion of modern meritocracy and its implications for political and economic life. Although Young's sociological satire may or may not be understood as a leftist complaint that the principle of merit has overridden socialist ideals of egalitarianism, *Capital in the Twenty-First Century* argues that the really important driver of inequality today is neither merit nor political favor, but the inheritance of private wealth.

Given the major impact that Piketty's book has had since the middle of the last decade, it seems appropriate to look at his views on inequality, and their relation to Capital Theory, especially when it comes to the matter of social mobility, and whether it exists in the countries of the West. What we want is to glean for ourselves whether there are institutional arrangements that lead to inequality of income, whether these involve merit, inheritance, or political favor.

For some not familiar with Hayek's thought, it may be surprising to see in the Austrian economist's work an acknowledgment of a natural inequality among men (Hayek, 1978: 85). This is but an acknowledgment of a fact; he is not expressing a value judgment. The concept of inequality that Hayek recognizes is an individualistic one, in which each individual can prove his or her value. Hayek is only pointing out the *inequality* that exists in order to defend the only *equality* he sees as possible among men: equality under the law. The reason he so strenuously defends the market order is that this is the framework that allows individuals of differing skills, and different levels of skill, to contribute to their own and others' benefit.

It is doubtful Hayek would ever have achieved such significance in the United States (he was awarded the Presidential Medal of Freedom in 1991) if there had not been a kinship between his ideas and the concepts of equity and equality under the law that are present in the U.S. Constitution. This common understanding of the realities of social life informs similar prescriptions for the social order. For America's Founding Fathers, as well as for those who amended the Constitution with the equal protection clause of the Fourteenth Amendment in 1868, it was assumed that we should be politically equal; it was not assumed that we were equal in our capacities to earn income. Whether Adam Smith (an influence on the American Founders) was right or not in his strong egalitarianism—expressed in his statement that at an early age, there are no perceivable differences between a street porter and a philosopher—we might debate. But the more essential point is that equality under the law helps every man, whatever his individual merits, to make a material contribution to society, and therefore to be able to earn material rewards. Hayek followed the Founding Fathers in grasping this.

Be that as it may, it is true that Hayek was interested in liberty for utilitarian reasons (it would increase social wealth), but his ethical views should more properly be understood as "Rule-utilitarianism." That the market order maximizes production and the satisfaction of individual needs also highlights, it may be said, the problem of the distribution of knowledge. If too much redistribution of wealth is effected by coercion, the spontaneous order is disrupted by removing the incentives for the use of dispersed knowledge. The problem is not how to be equally poor; poverty is the natural state. The problem is how to create wealth, and that is at the core of Hayek's argument for the need for a free market.

In the end, legal equality is the solution he proposes for the problem of factual inequality among men, and their need for liberty to enable each individual to do what he can, to the degree he can. It is possible, however, for legal equality to lose its legitimacy. It does so when material inequality leads to legal inequality. That is precisely what happens when income distribution becomes political.

When income is politically distributed, money does not matter, as Young suggested in his dystopia. A concrete example: the Soviet Union (1917–1991), where the range of remuneration was nominally narrow but benefits were plenty, and were distributed to those who manned the one-party state and/or who readily fell in line with its requirements. Wherever the power to redistribute income politically is considerable, the distribution of income becomes skewed in favor of the wealthy and well-connected. If there are few limits on a government's power to redistribute wealth, that is not surprising; more and more resources will be allocated to lobbying the state and extracting rents. That is, incidentally, how redistribution through the state politicizes economic life. The only known way to correct the problem is to limit legal protections as much as possible to just negative rights (like property rights), not positive rights (like entitlements).

At this juncture we might try to define to what extent any distribution of income through the state is legitimate. Of course, that depends on the conceptions of the good that one may have, and since they are many, it is almost impossible to reach agreement about what a fair solution to the problem of coercive redistribution is. A good point of departure may be to recognize that the United States is a welfare state, a place where, as in the European countries, the political system is gamed. Elites manage coercive redistribution for their benefit here, and we have ended up like the Germans, with bus drivers sending tax money into the public coffers so that lawyers may send their kids to college with subsidized tuitions. It could be argued that the main source of inequality in the United States today is not merit but abuses of political power.

The meaning of "meritocracy," let us be clear, is not only that merit is rewarded but that it is rewarded with power; it is supposed to be government by merit. In our day we tend to translate this as rule by the expertise of science. Letting the experts rule is a seductive notion, and it tends to erode the public's awareness of the importance of accountability and even of the principle of self-government. The idea that the governing elites do not need the consent of the governed because they know better than the people do what's best for them is, to put it mildly, not the American solution to the problem of what the proper role of government should be. Paraphrasing Wilfredo Pareto, in a free society, the elite circulate; one of classical liberalism's aims is to stop the elites from trying to freeze the circulation of power through political channels. If you maintain open access, you stand a chance of keeping the elites circulating instead of the tendency toward a mandarinate that we see today.

What, then, is the cause of social inequality? Possibly it is not to be found where Young was looking, in the bureaucratic design of the regime; perhaps it is a result of market processes, as argued in Piketty's *Capital in the 21st Century*. Piketty's main concern is the "rentier" and not the super-manager; he has a different emphasis, say, from Cowen,[11] and different prescriptions. For Piketty, capital includes real estate but not human capital.

The professor at the School for the Advanced Study of the Social Sciences in Paris and the London School of Economics is engaging, it may be said, in oversimplification and overstatement. Piketty does not give enough consideration to the saving of real resources to promote growth. He seems oblivious to the fact that taxes on capital will slow economic growth, while capital concentration, even if it exists, is not an economic problem.

Perhaps a cynical reading of Piketty would be to say that his political agenda is to lend legitimacy to European bureaucrats' avoiding austerity policies, to nudge them to use the European central bank as an agent of inflation, to increase the taxation of capital gains, and to tax wealth in order to induce people to do the "least" wrong, which is inflation. Although such an understanding of his agenda may be reasonable, it is not sufficient to point that out. It is necessary to engage with his work, and outline his grave methodological mistakes, such as his assumption that what is not wage is income from capital, or his treatment of capital gains not net of taxes already in existence.

There are even some important historical inaccuracies, such as his claims that the nineteenth century was a period of stagnant growth, and that there was not much wealth-creation at that time.[12] In accepting Harry Frankfurt's book *On Inequality* (2015) as correct in stating that international inequality is going down, and that this is what matters in the end, Piketty may be perceived as presenting a "prosecutorial brief"; he knew his desired conclusion in advance, and arranged his evidence and arguments to lead his readers there.

If that is the case, how to explain the success of his book? Let me begin to account for it with the following distinction: It is one thing for a rich man to give his offspring every possible advantage in finding a professional career; it is quite another if the rich man's son avoids jail after killing a poor man. The public perceives the problem of inequality in political power as derived from inequality of income, and not the other way around. This we can see from the high level of income inequality in Latin America resulting from cronyism. Such a perception makes Piketty's narrative easy to accept, and it ends up reinforcing this wrong perception.

Meritocracy, Inheritance, and Piketty's Prescriptions

Contrary to Young, Piketty thinks that inherited wealth is more important than merit in explaining inequality in the twenty-first century; that the inequality that exists is detrimental to society; and that it therefore should be eradicated. In trying to understand the chapter on public debt, let us restate the "cynical" reading of the book: It could be he promotes inflation in order to menace society with increased taxation. Piketty acknowledges how bad inflation is for small investors, but that does not bother him much. He could well have been trying to reinforce the European economic agenda at the time he wrote. On this reading, Piketty does not so much want to reform the state as to show support for Greece's not selling the Port of Piraeus.

Admittedly, that is speculation, and an alternative speculation regarding the book's treatment of public debt might be that Piketty realizes public debt is part of the claims on a real wealth that does not exist anymore. That is another possibility if you take him at his word. The fairest way to solve this problem (in his opinion) would be to expropriate the creditors of the public debt. Is not inflation already doing the work of expropriating the income of the owners of the public debt? He does not want to engage in austerity because he does not want to destroy the welfare state. There is, therefore, a fourth solution to the problem of certain EU members' crippling public debt:

repudiation. Yet this he does not discuss; there are creditors of the public debt whom he does not want to contradict.

It looks for many observers as if Piketty's views influenced Mario Draghi, the former president of the European Central Bank, who promoted QE in Europe to finance debt on the cheap and to incentivize even more public debt. Because following Piketty's prescriptions is sure to slow (to say the least) economic growth, it is worthwhile to question his motives. Because taxing capital is actually taxing consumers, his solution is just to confiscate wealth, similar to the prescriptions of Modern Monetary Theory, as we will have an opportunity to discuss next.

At this point, one has to ask how far down this road policymakers could go in a democratic regime. For Piketty, democracy means labor's participation in the running of companies—including seats on boards of directors—but this, I would argue, is just a smoke screen. It is like the racial or ethnic tokenism that is sometimes cynically used by American corporations. Worker participation was tried, for example, in Yugoslavia under communism, but Josip Broz Tito could never solve the moral hazard problem that labor would take the wages now and forget about the future. In the end, the best way to understand Piketty in that regard is to replace the word "democracy" with "smart people like me"; it is a pretense of democracy, when in fact it is a proposal that can be implemented only by an autocratic and elitist regime.

Inequality in the distribution of property was something the American Founders took into account. It would be disquieting if their ideas, which enjoy worldwide appeal, had been overtaken in the age of Piketty and Senator Bernie Sanders. It is a given that every time people have power, they will abuse it in their own interest; "Publius" figured this out long ago in Federalist No. 10.[13] The solution the Founders thought of was, of course, the establishment of checks and balances, of accountability. Inequality in the distribution of property leads people to try to capture the government (either by the majority or by a minority), and the solution is to break, or at least severely limit, the government's power to redistribute income. It seems to me, as it did to them, that the greatest danger to avoid is the use of government to promote unfairness and injustice. They sought to reduce this danger by neutralizing the powers of faction. It seems to me that in Federalist 10, Madison worked in an Aristotelian framework of virtues, and a modicum of virtue is still necessary, even in the best designed of the constitutional regimes.

Functional Finances and MMT

Let us address[14] with this section the most recent restatements of the "State Theory of Money" that is associated with Georg Friedrich Knapp (1842–1926), otherwise known as the chartalist school. Today the neo-chartalists call what they do "Modern Monetary Theory," or MMT—a sort of inside joke, since they claim the theory that Knapp set forth actually goes back 4,000 years. This introduction to our treatment of capital will benefit from an exploration of the "State Theory of Money," and the arguments of its advocates, to provide a contrast between the totalitarian conceptions of the relation between private property and the monetary and fiscal prerogatives of the state held by MMT, and other understandings of money and public finance as they evolved from the conception of limited government advanced by the American Founding Fathers.

This has in fact become a pressing issue given that leftwing politicians in the Western world have started to refer to MMT policies as the potential source of resources for their big spending proposals—notably, the ones intended to address environmental concerns, such as the "Green New Deal" in the United States.

Neo-chartalism has been aptly summarized as a theory under which "the issuer of a currency faces no financial constraints. Put simply, a country that issues its own currency can never run out and can never become insolvent in its own currency. It can make all payments as they come due. For this reason, it makes no sense to compare a sovereign government's finances with those of a household or a firm. . . . [S]overeign currency issuers . . . can always afford anything that is for sale if it is priced in their own currency" (Mitchell et al., 2019: 13). Such a stance is not new, as has been pointed out by Sebastian Edwards among others.[15] MMT has its origins in the "functional finance" proposal of Abba P. Lerner, a proposal inspired by Keynesian economics.[16]

One claim made by MMT advocates is that their policies have never been tested and therefore should at least be given the benefit of the doubt. Edwards and coauthor Rudiger Dornbusch disagree, asserting that MMT is another term for the economic policies of populist regimes that have plagued Latin America for decades. They write:

> For us "economic populism" is an approach to economics that emphasizes growth and income redistribution and deemphasizes the risks of inflation and deficit finance, external constraints, and the reaction of economic agents to aggressive nonmarket policies. . . . The purpose in setting out this paradigm is not a righteous assertion of conservative economics, but rather a warning that populist policies do ultimately fail; and when they fail, it is always at a frightening cost to the very groups that were supposed to be favored. A central thesis we advance is that the macroeconomics of various experiences is very much the same, even if the politics differed greatly. (Dornbusch and Edwards, 1991: 9)

So, one way to understand MMT is to position it in contrast with the market-oriented theory that money has evolved spontaneously in society, in which

"Money is . . . a system of mutual trust, and not just any system of mutual trust: money is the most universal and most efficient system of mutual trust ever devised" (Harari, 2019: 11). However, a different perspective, one that invites a difficult question to answer, would be to identify what distinguishes MMT from the high levels of public spending, public debt, and money-creation-by-fiat engaged in by virtually all Western countries for decades now. As noted by Kevin Dowd, "Keynes's proposal illustrates that helicopter money can be used to finance 'worthwhile' projects, however those might be defined. More precisely, it shows that helicopter money can be used to finance projects that somebody important regards as worth financing, but that presumably would not otherwise obtain finance" (Dowd, 2018: 9).

Here we might ask, is MMT an adequate tool to finance a governmental response to existential threats such as, allegedly, climate change—or is it, again, just a rebranding of discredited economic populism? In which respects might MMT proposals differ from what has been the orthodoxy in monetary and fiscal policies in Western countries since about the mid-twentieth century? Is it possible that MMT advocates are more conscious of real resource constraints than is usually understood? And flowing from that question, we would want to know: Are their proposals in effect aimed at transferring real wealth from society to the government once the government's agenda—say, the "Green New Deal"—is accepted as the moral equivalent of war?

In a 2019 article on "How to Pay for the Green New Deal," Yeva Nersisyan and Randall Wray mimic Keynes's 1940 "How to Pay for the War" in order to explain how the State Theory of Money, today's MMT, could be used to underwrite the interventionist proposals advanced in the U.S. Congress under the pretense of environmental concerns that have come to be called the "Green New Deal."

Professors Nersisyan and Wray are to be commended for their scholarship and intellectual integrity. Dispelling previous equivocations about the capacity of their fiscal and monetary proposal to "pay for itself" (which triggered criticism that MMT disregards real resource constraints[17]), they clearly spell out what their scheme amounts to. Their internal logic is unassailable, yet I disagree with their factual premises about impending environmental doom and their understanding of how the market economy works by giving individuals incentives to engage in productive activities.

If their premises about the environment and human psychology were correct, and if governments had the capacity to coerce people that they think it has, indeed, the Green New Deal could be financed by using their favored fiscal and monetary tools. That would represent an immense transfer of real wealth from all Americans, depriving people of resources now used for those Americans' own ends, such as paying for their homes or the education of their children. About this, the authors are actually quite candid. I assume that their argument will not in any way please the politicians who are using the Nersisyan/Wray research to advance their political agenda, and would much prefer to hide from voters the real consequences of implementing the Green New Deal.

The cornerstone of our authors' argument is the concept of the "Moral Equivalent of War" that William James assayed in 1906 and that President Jimmy Carter made famous in his 1977 speech on energy. They reason that, if we accept climate change as being as much an existential threat as were the fascist regimes of the Axis powers during World War II, the United States ought to recur to the same tools used back then to harness society and extract from individuals the resources necessary to meet the threat.

It would be morally acceptable to Nersisyan and Wray to deprive individuals of the real resources they currently use in their daily lives and divert them to fighting climate change, if that is as real and present a danger as the Axis powers were. The heavy taxation and greater public indebtedness that MMT advocates would impose on the public, and the purchasing power they would take away, would be put toward retrofitting the American economy on the scale proposed by the Green New Deal.

Starting in the early 1940s, and extending years beyond the Allied victory in 1945, Americans accepted a drastic reduction in their consumption, and not only continued to produce but increased what they were producing during 1941–1945, which made available to the government the resources necessary to wage war. Why would they not do the same if convinced that climate change posed a similar, or even a greater, risk than the nation faced eighty years ago? My disagreement with their analysis begins here.

First, and foremost, I disagree that "climate change" is a danger in the same sense that Nazi Germany or Imperial Japan were. Even if we accept for the sake of argument that the climate is changing, and that human activity has something to do with that, it does not follow that the Green New Deal idea of eliminating quickly and radically the use of fossil fuels is technologically feasible without a drastic reduction in Americans' standard of living. The authors accept this idea without question and move directly to how to pay for its implementation. It is worth mentioning that other initiatives—such as nuclear power, or the development of technologies for carbon capture, just to give two examples—once the proper incentives are in place, could actually reduce net carbon emissions faster and cheaper than what is contemplated in the Green New Deal.

Second, Nersisyan and Wray ignore the strong relationship that exists between the distribution of income in a society and its level of production. They believe that people will continue to produce whatever they are producing even if their earnings have been reduced by taxation, or forced savings. In a market society, both input and output prices guide people to continue to do, to do more of, or to stop doing, whatever economic activity they are engaged in at any given moment. It is as simple as that when there is no one coercing people to act against their best interest.

It is one thing to say that, in the case of an emergency, people would accept temporary sacrifices; it's another to say that, in a spirit of "permanent mobilization," people will continue, for life, to be productive even if no allowance is made for (for instance) depreciation or other costs of production. That is a second limitation imposed by the reality of scarce resources that MMT theorists need to face. You can consume the existing stock of capital in an emergency, but you should not expect that that stock will be maintained or expanded if no resources are used to pay for depreciation or new investments.

The reason is simple: In an open society, the existence of profitable opportunities is what drives investments, and taxes place a cost on that. When you tax people, you render some investments unprofitable, so you should not expect people to continue making those investments. As the disincentives caused by taking income away from people grow, production will plunge, as is happening nowadays in Venezuela. To be clear, even if economic agents are convinced that they need to consume all their capital in order to continue to produce at a loss, eventually they will run out of capital and will need to desist. As Herbert Stein propounded in 1976, "If something cannot go on forever, it will stop."

A parallel can be seen in government-run health care. It is demeaning for Americans to be told not to eat red meat or drink sugary sodas (because these things are not good for them), and that since the state is footing the bill, this entitles self-righteous politicians to dictate to the populace on these matters as they see fit. The problem, however, is not that the alternative to free markets is paternalism, or less subtle forms of bondage such as slavery or indentured servitude. The problem is that, unless one lives under a totalitarian regime, the absence of profitable opportunities for investment will reduce investments and production. The limits are real, and it is impossible to know better than each economic agent his or her conditions (as pointed out by Hayek), as the information about the most economically efficient uses of assets is not even possessed by the economic agents ex ante but is generated by their interactions. When they are free to interact, that is.

Even if Americans at large became convinced that manmade climate change was a real and present danger, and that eliminating the use of fossil fuels was the correct policy to follow, if there were no ways to make a profit in their economic activities under current levels of technology, production would be disrupted.

What Nersisyan and Wray are admirably frank about is the sacrifices that would be required, in terms of living standards, to enact the Green New Deal's radical environmental agenda. They concede that MMT's fiscal and monetary tools will not create wealth out of nothing, but are only a way to extract from society the real resources necessary. Even so, they fail to plumb the depths of the Green New Deal's ramifications. For all their straight talk, they fail to acknowledge that people are not pawns on a chessboard but autonomous agents with their own motivations.

A government like the British and the American governments during World War II, if the public believes in them, may count on the valor of the citizenry to sacrifice life, limb, and treasure to meet and overcome a grave danger. Even these sacrifices, however, are limited by what it is possible to do with a profit or, in extremis, consuming existing wealth over the longer term.

While it may be acceptable in theory to equate these two dangers, it is still a political gamble. Unless and until the public is convinced of this equation, it is preposterous to expect that people will commit to the grim course that the authors lay out (partially lay out, as I say). Moreover, what if the voters preferred an alternative green solution or solutions? Leftist politicians risk discrediting themselves here. It seems doubtful they have studied the failure of the Carter administration to regiment the American people behind its misguided energy policies in the 1970s; this history should give them pause.

CAN CAPITAL THEORY BE ABOLISHED?

John Smithin (Emeritus Professor of Economics at York University) made an important point when he wrote me a few years ago that "research on the ontology of money leads on to a re-consideration of capital theory." He agrees with the basic premise that the ultimate objective of such research is "the justification of the open society, the market economy, and a political order maximizing liberty." For Smithin, economic growth is the vehicle for maximizing liberty; but he questions which lessons we should take from our research about money and capital, and also "what economic ideas should be adopted to achieve these goals."

The commodity theory of money (or metallism), explains Professor Smithin, is held in common by Marxists, classical economists, and Austrian economists (let us accept the Austrians' membership in this group for the sake of argument). But while all "put a lot of store in the notion of capital," it is his view that "none of these ideas will conduce to achieving [their] political objectives."

He declares that "the notion of capital is bogus (as is the idea of a natural rate of interest), and that the credit theory of money (money as a social relation) is correct."

For Smithin, "The enterprise economy, commercial society, and everything that flows from that, socially and politically, would not be in existence at all unless money itself, in this precise sense, was already invented (cf. the founding of the BoE). This view of money and capitalism requires realism in social theory, which is something quite different from either materialism or idealism. It avoids this dichotomy."

In *Rethinking the Theory of Money, Credit, and Macroeconomics: A New Statement for the Twenty-First Century* (Smithin, 2018), he addresses most of these questions.[18]

In spite of Smithin's modest claim to the contrary, this is the culmination of a lifelong research program on the relation between economic theory and the social reality that that theory supposedly helps us to understand. Drawing from many different intellectual influences, he offers an alternative model for us to make sense of monetary phenomena, one that would serve as an important guide for policymaking if taken seriously.

It is refreshing to read Smithin and be surprised by the policy prescriptions to be derived from his descriptive project. It is impossible to plot his work on the political spectrum, although it is safe to say that, in his open-mindedness and epistemological skepticism, Smithin may be considered a truly classical liberal.

In this definitive statement about the ontological, epistemological, and ethical foundations of money and finances, Smithin allows himself to focus on the core constituents of the entrepreneurial method of production, such as profits, money, and private property, and to draw lessons from this breathtakingly wide interdisciplinary effort. His ecumenism allows him to generously acknowledge the contributions of Keynes and even Marx to a proper understanding of the role of money in the economic activity of a market society.

Macroeconomics must, according to Smithin, be practiced with a truly macroeconomic method if it is ever to help us prevent economic downturns. He rejects a "radical" methodological individualism in favor of a mild form of realism, one in which "money" is taken into account as a social reality in interpreting economic processes. Such a project is not without its risks, but the value of Smithin's contribution cannot be overstated, even by researchers who may find some elements of his methodology, or some of his applications of it, not wholly convincing.

Central to Smithin's alternative monetary model is that a market society must have a supply of money that is endogenous in nature. From there, using sophisticated but ultimately elegant mathematical formulations, he proposes the targeting of real interest rates as the optimal instrument of monetary policy if macroeconomic stability is the policy goal.

First, though, he must reckon with the confusions of Capital Theory, which so often result in incoherent policymaking. By way of demonstration, he points his readers to a semi-satirical picture of this by Joan Robinson (as quoted by Cohen and Harcourt, 2003: 201):

The production function has been a powerful instrument of mis-education. The student of economic theory is taught to write Q = f (L, K) where L is a quantity of labour, K a quantity of capital and Q a rate of output of commodities. He is instructed to assume all workers alike, and to measure L in man-hours of labour; he is told something about the index-number problem in choosing a unit of output; and then he is hurried on to the next question, in the hope that he will forget to ask in what units K is measured. Before he ever does ask, he has become a professor, and so sloppy habits of thought are handed on from one generation to the next.

To avoid the epistemological problems caused by a methodology that requires considering capital as homogeneous, Smithin proposes avoiding Capital Theory altogether.

For him, "The most important question to be answered is whether or not it is possible to construct a relevant and useful macroeconomic theory, without recourse to the dead-end of capital-theoretic reasoning, yet one that at the same time is well able to cope with important long-run questions such as growth, development and technical change, as well as the more frequently posed questions of short-run stabilization policy" (Smithin, 2018). His purpose in *Rethinking the Theory of Money, Credit, and Macroeconomics* is to show that "such a project is wholly viable, and that Keynes did much to point the way, even ultimately he was not able to deliver such a theory."

Smithin, in his personal note to me, claims that my discussion of capital's being ambiguous—for instance, how a car could be thought of as either a consumer good or a capital good—and how markets are not subject to Cartesian analysis, "reinforce the above conclusion."

In the end, Smithin believes, "it all boils down to whether we write the production function as: (1) Y = AK, or: (2) Y = AN." He believes that "it is not possible to derive a sensible growth theory from (1), but that it is entirely possible to do this with (2). So, it is entirely possible to explain growth without any recourse to capital theory." He thinks that there must be macroeconomics without Capital Theory. On this bold statement let us reserve judgment for now, but as I have mentioned above, a mild realism that takes into account both physical and social realities (among them, the need to save real resources from immediate consumption in order to apply them to productive endeavors and, with that, to generate growth) suffices for the observer wishing to engage in macroeconomic musings. The idea of representation I offer in the present work facilitates this, by allowing that observer to more clearly define the context in which the term "capital" is being used.

Smithin, for his part, would not even subscribe to the idea of financial instruments' representing capital goods. For him, "Financial instruments are always merely claims on money." I think, however, that the difference between debt claims and equity claims suffices to distinguish instances where a financial instrument is a form of direct property claim over some actual capital good and processes (such as shares in a publicly traded company) from instances where they are simply claims on streams of revenue (such as bonds issued by the same company). I understand that some critics of giving shareholders primacy in corporate governance consider shareholders to be, not the "owner" of the corporation, but just one more stakeholder like any other. I think they are ontologically mistaken—and it would seem Smithin should agree with me on that.

Smithin also thinks that my classification of the different monetary arrangements along several dimensions "actually confuses the issue too much." In the good company of Schumpeter, Smithin argues that "there are only 'two monetary theories worthy of the name,' commodity theory and credit theory," and that "in order to understand what 'capitalism' is we need a pure credit theory, and this necessarily entails a central bank and hence a relationship between the central bank and commercial banks."

Here I think Smithin neglects a crucial factor: that there are many different possible institutional arrangements for the provision of an instrument fulfilling the social functions of money. That money may be provided without a central bank is a matter of historical record, not opinion. We may argue, as I have done elsewhere,[19] that a sovereign government must retain its monetary prerogatives, which in modern parlance means the institution of a central bank, if it aims to remain sovereign; but that is not a sine qua non condition of a market economy. My point about varying monetary arrangements makes it possible to untangle threads of Capital Theory which, ignoring that variety, can lead to confusions such as deeming money either endogenous or exogenous when, in our modern arrangements (beginning with the founding of the BoE), what we have almost everywhere is a hybrid system.

THE HYBRID NATURE OF THE MONETARY SYSTEM: HISTORICAL ORIGINS, AND IMPLICATIONS FOR CAPITAL THEORY

Having made the case for economic growth, and having established how crucial a proper understanding of Capital Theory is for promoting that growth, let me turn to the historical origins of the financial and monetary arrangements we have today.

Since 1694, when the establishment of the BoE began the monetization of public debt, the monetary system in modern economies has been a hybrid one. Part of the money supply is provided "exogenously" by the government, and part is provided "endogenously" by the banks. A schematic description of the operations of the BoE at its inception will help here.[20]

The stockholders of the BoE initially received a charter from William III authorizing them to incorporate as a bank in exchange for giving a loan to the British Crown in perpetuity. That loan would be serviced by the revenue generated by a new tax, and among the privileges accorded the "Governor and Shareholders of the BoE" were: (1) that their notes would be accepted as payment of taxes owed to the Crown; (2) that they would be incorporated with limited liability; and (3) that they would be allowed to receive tax revenues on behalf of the Crown. So, although the Crown retained a monopoly on the striking of coins—that is, the prerogative to provide "external" money to the economy—the banknotes issued by the BoE soon started to circulate in parallel with the coins. This was the beginning of what came to be called "inside" money.

To be even more schematic, the stockholders of the BoE raised bullion equivalent to 1,2 million sterling pounds among themselves, and then loaned that amount to the Crown, thus adding to the assets side of their balance sheet the bonds issued by the Crown to formalize—that is to say, to represent—that loan. Next, they created banknotes in their books in the same amount of 1,2 million sterling pounds, and loaned them to private individuals, who accepted them as money.

The Crown and the bank were both subject to natural limits: The Crown was constrained in how much external money it could create (the government needed first to have the bullion to strike coins). The bank was constrained in its ability to create inside money, since it was only its capacity to make profitable loans and to convey a perception of financial strength that would prevent the money-holders from coming to the bank and cashing their notes for coins.

Although the cost of issuing the banknotes was low (just the paper, ink, and other costs associated with printing them), the cost for a private bank to actually generate profitable loans was not. Furthermore, the floating generated by the Crown business, aside from the regular operations that the bank started with the private sector, would limit the amount of cash the bank would have on hand and the ratio between the amount of coins in its safes and the amount of banknotes that it might safely put into circulation. In economic jargon, the amount of inside money that can be created by private banks is limited by the marginal costs incurred by those banks.

Still, at the beginning of our story, there was the equivalent of 1,2 million sterling pounds in bullion, which generated an equivalent amount in external money, to the extent that the Crown coined all of the bullion it received as a loan, and another 1,2 million sterling pounds in inside money represented by the banknotes issued by the BoE and lent to private individuals.

Starting with 1,2 million sterling pounds in equity, the BoE soon had a balance sheet of 2,4 million in assets (represented by the bonds issued by the Crown and the private loans it generated) and 2,4 million in liabilities, half of which was the equity raised among the bank's shareholders, the other half being the obligations for the banknotes redeemable in coins on demand (which were kept in circulation in the hands of the money-holders).

Everyone knew that the Crown used most of the money it borrowed from the BoE to rebuild the British navy after the defeats it suffered in sea battles with France. So it was only the future revenue expected from the imposition of an import tariff and a tax on beer and other liquors—and the arrangements made to segregate such revenue in favor of the creditors of the government organized and incorporated as the BoE—that gave the bank's officers the confidence to lend the bank's money to the Crown. And yet, not a penny was added to the capital stock of the country on the real side of the economy when those 1,2 million pounds were added to the stock of financial assets in the country (the shares of the BoE whose equity was 100 percent invested in the perpetual bonds issued by the Crown, having as collateral the revenue from the new taxes established by the initial Bank of England act of Parliament, which was the Tonnage Act of 1694).

The puzzle is this: Where did the real resources that the government used to pay for the military build-up come from? We know the government paid for it with coins struck from the bullion it received from the BoE as a loan. However, if on one hand this added external money to the total stock of money in circulation in the country, on the other hand, it did not change the stock of capital in existence in the economy. The bullion, after all, had been there already, at the beginning of our story.

Nonetheless, the historical record shows that the government, the bank, and the money-holders were right in believing that the arrangements made to segregate the new tax revenues, along with the British economy's capacity to generate those revenues, were sufficient to service that loan—and many more that came later. We should pause to consider that, had the Crown succeeded in monetizing a greater amount of debt than its capacity to service the debt, the entire edifice of modern finances established at that moment would have crumbled.

This may be understood as an example of an institutional change, the establishment of a legal and political new "technology" creating a "credible commitment" that the loan would be repaid—and repaid in spite of the awful track record of the British Crown at that time as a debtor. What markedly differentiated England from other countries at the time, we may note, was the political representation that the creditors of the Crown had in Parliament and the procedural avenues open to them to claim their rights. (This is shown, for instance, in the "Case of the Bankers" Desan, 2014:

281). This new "technology" in effect made available an amount of liquid resources in the economy greater than what had been available before. The capacity to segregate the tax revenues in favor of the BoE was perceived by the market as if new wealth had been created. Thus a private appropriation of that wealth (the present value of the stream of revenue of the 1.2 million sterling pound perpetual bonds paying 8 percent in annual interest) became possible.

In regard to the issuance of banknotes, the history is easier to understand. The BoE lent the banknotes to private individuals who offered sufficient evidence to the bank that they would employ the money in such a productive and profitable way as likely to be able to repay the loans with interest. In that way, the existence of the stock of banknotes in circulation matched approximately the wealth generated with those loans.

In our day, the production of external money is no longer limited by the gold standard. (The government can create, by fiat, reserves with the central bank or print paper money—the two components of the monetary base, or M0, as it is known.) This means the private banks are not limited in their capacity to create inside money, to the extent that they may get access to high-powered money produced by the government. The private banks may create inside money simply by crediting the checking accounts of their borrowers, if they can get access to reserves created by the government by fiat—and this they may do instead of being forced, in their effort to generate a portfolio of profitable loans, to incur costs in a competitive market for funds.

Granted, private banks still need to make a profit on top of the cost of getting fiat money from the government. But if the government is willing to create external money and lend it to the banks at a lower cost than the banks would spend in obtaining liquidity in the market, this creates the potential for inflationary expansion of inside money by the banks.

The possibility of inflationary expansion of the money supply is thus ever-present, given the supply of external money or the supply of internal money under the current hybrid arrangements of fractional reserve banking and fiat money. This is what has evolved from the arrangements initiated with the establishment of the BoE. The elasticity of the money supply under this regime (which was the purpose of its introduction in the first place) is, alas, much higher than would be the case under a system of commodity money and limited creation of money substitutes.

What have been the consequences for capital formation? It seems clear that the endogenous creation of money has become an instrument to mobilize existing savings in an efficient way to foster production; in that regard, it has made society more productive. On the other hand, to the extent that the endogenous component of the money supply operates by the adoption of fractional reserves—that is, of the multiplication of claims over a limited quantity of exogenous money—it has made the entire system dependent on state coercion to survive external shocks.

The bargain reached with the creation of the system begun with the BoE in 1694 has given an opening to governmental abuse. The state has been enabled to the point of repression—it has, down the centuries, been determining the allocation of resources in the real economy for political purposes. This symbiotic relation between bank and state has produced, at the same time, the instruments for a more efficient mobilization of savings and an instrument for their use for political purposes, often causing a disconnect between the claims over real wealth that financial instruments represent and the existing stock of capital in the community.

THREE BANKING VARIABLES, AND HOW COMPARING THEM PLAYS OUT IN CAPITAL THEORY

The first dimension along which we can distinguish monetary arrangements one from another is whether the base money of the community is a commodity money or fiat money. A second important dimension is whether the banks operate under 100 percent reserves, or whether fractional reserves are admitted. A third is whether or not there is a central bank.

There are many other dimensions to consider—for example, whether there is legal tender or not, and whether there is free banking or the banks are regulated. But if we consider just these, we find a three-dimensional matrix (a cube) with eight possible arrangements, as listed in table 1.1.

Before drawing conclusions about which monetary policy will best achieve the goal of having good money, one ought to consider the context. For instance, in a regime with commodity money, the opportunity cost of using the commodity for monetary purposes constrains the creation of

Table 1.1 Classification of Monetary Arrangements along Three Dimensions

	Nature of Money	Bank Reserves	Central Bank	Historical/Theoretical Examples
1	Commodity	100%	Yes	Bank of Amsterdam
2	Commodity	100%	No	JHS proposal
3	Commodity	Fractional	Yes	English System 1694–1932
4	Commodity	Fractional	No	Scottish System 1995–1848
5	Fiat	Fractional	Yes	Current arrangements
6	Fiat	Fractional	No	Hayek's money denationalization proposal
7	Fiat	100%	Yes	Cochrane's proposal of narrow banking with monopoly of external money
8	Fiat	100%	No	Narrow Banking without money monopoly

money. Also, it explains why certain banking arrangements are developed. If you have a money proper that is expensive, it makes sense to design a banking architecture with fractional reserve banking, so as to economize in base money.[21]

Why did the BoE come into being with the particular features it had? Because bullion was expensive, and creative ways to leverage whatever gold or silver they had for monetary uses made sense. In fact the above discussion of the BoE serves to illustrate historically a fundamental idea that can be divided in two parts:

(1) What is going on in the real side of the economy is not directly connected to what is going on in the monetary side of the economy, given that changes in prices caused by the inflationary creation of external money and of money substitutes may mislead economic agents into thinking that the relative prices of some goods have changed—until they realize that what is happening is a change in the general price level; and

(2) Government debt may distort investors' perceptions. They might mistakenly believe that new wealth has been created when the government issues new public debt while the prospect of being repaid is still credible.

Information about what is happening in the real side of the economy is always going to lack precision. It is not that the information does not exist, but rather that such information has not been created yet.

MONETARY THEORY LEADS TO CAPITAL THEORY—OR AT LEAST IT SHOULD

It was from my studies of monetary theory that my interest in Capital Theory arose. The former leads us to consider what monetary and other financial instruments represent; and, in turn, a good understanding of money and banking seems a logical prerequisite for developing a good understanding of Capital Theory.

Different varieties of monetary and banking arrangements abound, in practice. To be able to classify them in a coherent theoretical framework is crucial not only for discerning the best modalities to achieve the purpose of having good money, but also to understand each of these modalities in relation to the representation, formation, accumulation, and distribution of capital.

What emerges is a need for further clarification of a key aspect of Capital Theory: namely, the relation between capital and private property. This relation I intend to illuminate from an interdisciplinary perspective of philosophy, law, and economics. On monetary matters, my main guides have been

Simmel, Menger, and Mises; in much the same way, with regard to capital, I sit on the shoulders of Searle, Böhm-Bawerk, and Rueff.

When it comes to representing the capital structure in property titles, there are issues that, if better understood, might solve some of the most important problems economists face regarding the concept of capital. Moreover, insights about how the physical and the social reality interact—and, specifically, about the legal doctrine of property—may be the tools needed to move forward.[22]

So, unlike the parable that Nobel laureate Amartya Sen (1974) wittily used in one of his articles on Capital Theory—in which the Buddha tries to persuade one of his disciples to stop wasting his entire life trying to measure capital—my project is less than all-encompassing. It is modest in the sense that I am not claiming to have developed a big new idea. My aim is a "repackaging" of certain concepts in Capital Theory—but a repackaging that might really be useful, with practical consequences for our understanding of finances today. That, at any rate, is my hope for what follows.

SOME HEURISTIC CONSIDERATIONS RELEVANT FOR THIS WORK

Before we move forward with epistemological discussions, it seems appropriate to address the constants that we find when examining the links between costs, profit, and production—those elements that are evident and do not need to be proved every time out.

For the producer of any good or service, taxes are costs, and we may expect the impact of variations in the tax burden of doing business to be similar to any other variation in costs. If they go up, the business becomes less profitable, either because the unitary margin has been reduced if prices cannot be raised, or the total margin of profits is reduced if an increase in the unitary price of the merchandise results in a reduction in the quantity demanded by the consumers.

Likewise, any regulation reduces profits if it indirectly raises costs or directly forbids some exchanges from happening (in the latter case, by mandating businesses to not supply their products or services with specifications different from the ones spelled out in the regulations).The inverse relationship between economic activity, on the one hand, and taxation and regulation, on the other, should be no surprise.

Another postulate we can stipulate, without the need to restate it throughout this text, is that not all investments made by economic agents with their savings are done through instruments representative of capital formation—that is, through instruments representing the addition of new capital goods and processes to the structure of production in the real side of the economy. The savings of the investor may well be spent by the borrower on consumption, be that a vacation taken by an individual person who borrowed, or the current outlays of a government that borrowed. In either case, repayment of the principal plus the expected positive return to the lender will depend on the existing capacity of the borrower to generate income for such repayment, since no additional productive capacity was created with that "investment."

Yet another postulate is that the level of productivity in society is determined by the technology applied to production embodied in the "tools" economic agents use to produce—that is, by the capital structure of society. Those "tools," however, are not limited to physical capital; we also need to take into account human capital and, critically, social capital. The legal institutions of society, for instance, the precision with which property rights are defined, the instruments for their enforcement, the level of regulation, the tax burden (as mentioned)—all that may be understood as the "quality" or the "level" of institutional technology undergirding the exchanges among the economic agents, and therefore, determining their efficiency (in other words, their level of productivity).

The amount of productive activity in society depends on the existence of profitable opportunities to produce. In order to earn profits, entrepreneurs need to keep their costs under control. Entrepreneurs' perceptions about the likelihood of future profits are formed by the prices they are likely to pay for their inputs and receive for their output. In a society with a monetary economy—where exchanges among the economic agents are indirect and mediated by money—if there is a monopoly of the money supply, the monopolistic money-supplier enjoys wiggle room to manipulate that supply without producing inflation, within the limits set by existing spare capacity and expectations. That is, prices in a monetary economy are neither absolutely inelastic nor absolutely elastic.

A final postulate to keep in mind is that in an open society, there are innumerable "norms" that one individual may follow. He or she might adhere to one of many different religions in that society. He or she might decide to have a family, go to college, move to a different place, or take this or that profession. If a society wants to provide conditions for individuals to pursue their own ends, it needs to limit its normativity, to the extent possible, to meta-norms—that is, to rules that would allow individuals to pursue their own ends. Those meta-norms are generally understood as the "rule of law" in Anglo-Saxon countries—that is, the idea of justice provided by a limited government. It is important to keep in mind that not all ways of life are compatible with this classical liberal conception of the state. For instance, the robber, the Islamic fundamentalist, the violent political activist are embarked on modes of living that are incompatible with the classical liberal regime. The liberal society permits a greater variety of human pursuits than the illiberal society; but, of course, there are some that are not compatible with it. The meta-normative character of the institutions of the open society makes economic growth possible. To the extent that the governmental authorities of the open society pursue some measure of economic regulation, to keep it aligned with the general character of the institutions of a free society, the goal should be fostering economic activity resulting in economic growth, as measured, say, by GDP growth. That growth is the result of individuals each pursuing their chosen activities. The possibility of economic choice is compatible with the ideal of a free society in which allowing for individual human flourishing is the guiding principle of political activity.

EPISTEMOLOGICAL LIMITATIONS

Even if the economic agents of the open society were perfectly free to interact with each other, we would not be able to predict exactly how they would behave in reaction to changing circumstances. The uncertainty that plagues our study of the behavior of economic agents in general, also dims our understanding of the mutations of capital in the economy. When economists grapple with the deficiencies in our knowledge of what capital is, their generalizations themselves can suffer from grave deficiencies.

This can be seen from what economists refer to as the "Cambridge versus Cambridge" debate. As G.C. Harcourt pithily summarized (1969), this refers to important discussions on Capital Theory, starting in the 1950s and lasting for about twenty years, between economists from England's Cambridge University (mostly socialists and Marxists) and economists from the Massachusetts Institute of Technology in Cambridge, Massachusetts (mostly social democrats and neoclassicists).[23] The debate ended with the "victory" of the neoclassical economists. Their ideas about the need to treat capital as homogeneous and quantifiable in order to be applied in economic modeling formulas became, for all practical purposes, the dominant position in mainstream economics.

A major part of the "Cambridge controversies on Capital Theory" was initiated by Joan Robinson of Cambridge University in 1953. It involved how one cannot attribute a single present value to the stock of capital in the economy for use in an equation meant to calculate a society's aggregate production. This is so for many reasons, one of them being that the interest rate theoretically should be determined by the marginal utility of capital. However, such determination is calculated by the very same social production function; therefore, it is a kind of circular reasoning. If one needs to know the "value" of capital to apply the formula, but that value is contingent on the natural rate of interest, and one finds that rate by applying the formula and comparing the return on capital with the remuneration of labor, it is difficult to avoid being caught in the circularity of this proposition.[24]

Such are the problems hampering economists' knowledge of what capital is. In any case, our intention here is to develop a comprehensive and integrated overview of the field in order to understand the state of the art of Capital Theory. That sets the stage for me to offer what I call the Representational Theory of Capital (RTC). After I have done so, the next step will be to present a formal model of the theory. The idea that financial instruments are property titles representing claims over real goods is a commonsensical one if considered at the microeconomic level; however, I argue that with RTC we enhance our understanding at the macroeconomic level as well.

Such a claim, to my knowledge, is a novel one. In any case, the purpose of having a model is to have testable predictions about the hypotheses advanced in theory. For reasons explained elsewhere,[25] I am skeptical that the degree of simplification necessary to design a manageable model will allow the use of the model to make predictions about future events. What I am not skeptical about is the possibility of using the model to test the theory using historical data (something, it is hoped, others will be tempted to do).

This formal statement should not in any way be construed as a final product. It is instead a suggestion for a point of departure for further developments in Capital Theory. It resembles the system of national accounts which most of the data will come from if it is to be tested, naturally; but it is also distinguished from that in many aspects, not least in its narrower purpose.

This is a model that, by my lights, is compatible with Robert Solow's basic model of economic growth (Solow, 1956), though it differs in important respects from Solow's, as will be seen below. As stated by Larry White (Hayek, 2014: xxxii), it was with Solow and others that neoclassical economics found renewed interest in the problems of inter-temporal efficient allocation of resources, after a period in economics dominated by the Keynesian emphasis on consumption. On the other hand, the simplicity of the neoclassicists' models misses some essential aspects of Capital Theory—the heterogeneous nature of capital, just to mention one.

The RTC and its model as presented below do not seem to me incompatible with neoclassical simplified models like those of Harrod and Domar (Boianovsky, 2018), which one can see by revisiting the "Cambridge capital theory controversies" (Harcourt, 1969). Both are in the tradition of Austrian economics as expostulated by Lachmann (1956), Garrison (2016), and Huerta de Soto (2006). They are also connected to recent work done by Horwitz (1996, 2009), Levin (1996), Cachanosky (2014, 2016), Hendrikson and Salter (2015), Lewis (2018), Howden (2011, 2014), Braun et al. (2016, 2017), and Endres (2011, 2014) in that tradition. The RTC also touches on areas addressed by authors interested in economic sociology, such as Smithin (2002, 2018) and others, old (Hahn, 1949, 2015) and new (Bortis, 2016).

JOAN ROBINSON, THE PRODUCTION FUNCTION, AND THE THEORY OF CAPITAL

Professor Robinson, in her 1953 paper entitled "The Production Function and the Theory of Capital," argues that to focus on the "production function" when different combinations of inputs are compared, is to be distracted from the most relevant questions as to what influences the supply of inputs and causes and consequences of changes at the technological level. This is the thesis put forth by Jesus Huerta de Soto, who advocated dynamic efficiency analysis instead of static analysis. Robinson also calls attention to the fact that a production function in the short term may be used, considering that capital is whatever goods may exist and are mixed with labor, but that does not help to explain changes in the ratio of goods and labor, nor does it help us distinguish the effects of an act of God from a human decision (the accumulation of capital). She also calls attention to the fact that C (capital) can only be measured for use in the function if we have an interest rate that is given in order to calculate the present value of capital. But that is precisely what we are supposed to learn from the application of the function for a given technological level, the wages of capital (interest) and the wages of labor. . .

With all of these caveats, Robinson acknowledges that the problem the production function aims to solve (the ideal proportion of capital and labor in a given circumstance) is a real one. The example she gives is of three countries (Alpha, Beta, and Gamma) building a road of the same length and quality, the first with tens of workers and bulldozers, the second with hundreds of workers and picks and ox-carts, while in Gamma they build with thousands of men equipped with wooden shovels and little baskets. The problem of the "most efficient" allocation of capital in each circumstance is a real one (Robinson, 1953: 82).

Robinson defines capital (paraphrasing her) as "all existing goods with economic value" (p. 83). Albeit emphasizing that capital goods are highly specific (a new furnace is different from an old one of the same model) and their value subjective (the same overcoat may be differently appreciated by two ladies), she argues that, in equilibrium, capital may be assessed as a homogeneous quantity by the application of an interest rate that makes the output of similar value to the present value of the inputs used in their production. And that such valuation will equate the three different forms in which the value of capital may be assessed: (1) by its real cost of production; (2) in some unit of purchasing power, or (3) according to its productivity.

When some unexpected event happens, the equilibrium bringing the three forms of capital valuation into sync is disrupted. Robinson calls attention to the fact that, while we usually think of capital and interest (profits) as sums of money, capital is only a sum of money before it is invested in some productive activity. Profits become a sum of money once the goods produced are sold and the expenses actually incurred to produce them are paid (p. 84). At the time the profit is actually received, the value of the productive goods (of the "plant") may have diverged in all sorts of ways from the sum of money used to build it. Above all, she points out that the time gap between the moment capital is invested and profits are realized explains the difficulty of assessing the value of any quantity of capital. Abstracting away this difficulty is *the* methodological mistake of neoclassical economics concerning the value of capital.

Next, Robinson asks why the rate of interest and the "cost of waiting" (time preference) should be the same and positive (p. 87). She remarks that the rate of interest depends on the supply of, and demand for, loans—and therefore on the propensity for savings in the economy. That may lead to "negative" interest rates, but the cost of waiting will always be positive. Interestingly enough, she says that, as long as there are private property and profit opportunities, the demand for loans will ever exist and therefore the interest rate will never be negative in a capitalist society; interest rates are positive because profits are positive. She says that she will not discuss the equilibrium in which profits are negative because by then the scarcity of capital has disappeared and the society in question has ceased to be capitalist.

Robinson's treatment of the technique of production is interesting, as well. "Other things equal," she writes, "a technique involving a longer production period (from clipping the sheep to selling the overcoat) requires a larger run-out of man hours embodied in work-in-progress. This is treated as part of the stock of capital goods required by this technique" (Robinson, 1953: 90). She also says in a note that it is easier to see the inputs as part of the capital required than to consider the capital goods as a "length of time." I agree with her. Furthermore, there is representation in the monetary/financial side of the economy of the property of those inputs that may be represented by tradable financial claims.[26]

Still in regard to production techniques, she continues, "given the hierarchy of techniques, the higher is the wage rate the more mechanized is the technique which is chosen." This she encapsulates in a principle, that of "the substitution of capital for labor" (p. 92). For Robinson, "the relation of capital to labor, in an equilibrium position, can be regarded as the resultant of the interaction of three distinct influences: the wage rate, the rate of interest, and the degree of mechanization" (Robinson, 1953: 95). Considering that, the "Wicksell effect" explains "the influence of the wage rate upon the value in terms of product of a given physical capital." In other words, if capital is considered accumulated savings, and savings are considered refrained consumption, then, at first, the higher the wages, the less savings are made and the less physical capital is produced. In a second moment, less employment and fewer final products would result than under other arrangements in which wages were lower.

The interest rate may "outweigh" the Wicksell effect, Robinson contends, in the sense that higher interest rates may generate lower production even with lower wages if the interest rates are sufficiently high (p. 96). The change in the ratio of factors in equilibrium given a higher wage rate is what Hayek meant by the "Ricardo effect" (Hayek, 1942). She judges that a stretch, though, and suggests that calling it the "Ricardesque effect" might be more accurate. "The more the capitalists have been able to take advantage of the Ricardesque effect," she writes, "the less the workers have benefited from the Wicksell effect." Because it is extremely difficult to find equilibrium when the ratio of factors is changing all the time (both wages and profits are being constantly adjusted to the rates of wages and interests), using the production function to try to solve real-life problems becomes rather quixotic, in Robinson's view (Robinson, 1953: 100).

To improve the usefulness of the production function, she suggests that it be designed in such a way as to incorporate changes in the technique of production by "invention," which can be done if it is defined to be a constant rate of inventions, and if that rate is "neutral" and keeps the ratio between labor and capital constant with increased accumulation of capital similar to the increase in the supply of labor (Robinson, 1953: 103). Still, if that is the extent of the improvement, the economic agent will not gain much assistance in making decisions in the real world.

MORE CAMBRIDGE CONTROVERSIES IN THE THEORY OF CAPITAL

It must be said, in light of the "Cambridge versus Cambridge" debate, that the criticisms of the neoclassicists posed by their socialist critics—the former's unrealistic assumptions about homogeneity, the methodological mistake of using circular reasoning to determine the rate of interest, and the arrogance of using a tool that perhaps, in a limited way, could help to explain the past as an instrument to predict the future—were never adequately answered. As others have observed, the questions raised during those debates would be echoed later in debates between neoclassical and Austrian economists about the same issues.

It seems fair to say that the neoclassical models for the production function, even with all their limitations, help us better understand the way the world works. We simply need to take sufficient account of context when assessing their results. In the end, the most substantive thought to come out of these discussions was that the entrepreneur has a need for capital calculation to make decisions at the level of the firm, but what remains a puzzle is how to move that calculation from the level of daily life to the social level.

Many other interesting insights arose from that discussion. I think, for example, of the neoclassical economists' rhetorical use of mathematics to give an aura of scientific support to their favorite policies. Also, to what degree—on both sides of the debate—did economists' conceptions of the social system influence their modeling? Their ideological preferences were behind their supposedly neutral research. That is not to say that there were not genuine scientific problems to be solved, but it is impossible to believe that the economists involved in the debate took leave of their ideological assumptions when staking out their positions. The debate ended after twenty years without a result, and it was a revisit of previous and later debates. At stake was an understanding of the most intractable problem in economic thought: the role of capital in growth and in the distribution of income.

At bottom, this is a challenge to the marginal utility of labor—since labor is not any more homogeneous than is capital. The importance of the "re-switching" (changes determined by entrepreneurial decisions) in the structure of production was not perceived at the beginning. Samuelson tried to solve that with the multiple production function, but he later acknowledged he was wrong. The more conscious neoclassicals agreed that aggregation (that is, treating capital as homogeneous and quantifiable) should be avoided, although it continues to be widely used.[27]

A final substantive insight, beyond the problem of the abuse of mathematics, was the lack of a synthesis of the different theories of capital. To be sure, current mainstream economics has evolved in the direction of enriching its theoretical "tool kit" with insights from Austrian, law-economics, institutional, and public choice theorists. All the same, the friction between these continues to put roadblocks in the way of our understanding. Considering why that is the case, Tyler Cowen may be quoted as saying that neoclassical theory explains the world in a fairly adequate way for most purposes for which it is required, but that this "good enough" tool has discouraged the development of a more realistic theoretical tool to explain capital as a feature of economic life.

As already mentioned, Joan Robinson first complained, back in 1953, about the "fuzzy nature" of the capital variable in the aggregate production function because in that function, the possible combinations of capital and labor are assumed to be known, and this assumption diverts us from the key questions (in her opinion) of the different technologies possible to apply to have production, and of how they are chosen. She questions whether a unit for this variable could be found that would not be distorted by changes in relative prices.

As explained by Harcourt, because defining the value of capital in monetary terms is contingent on the interest rate, Robinson argues that that cannot be done; as a solution, she proposes to measure the amount of capital in terms of wages (Harcourt, 1969: 371). I think that cannot be done, either, for different structures of production will result in different wage averages, and the present value of that will also be contingent on the interest rate. Robinson's solution is to assume the rate of profits as stable and thus to apply that rate. Well, if that is the solution, you can do the same with the amount of capital measured in monetary terms—no need to calculate them in terms of wage averages, or so it would seem to me.

Trevor Swan, in his model, deems capital to be composed of fungible, interchangeable parts that may be combined in different ways; that is, capital, considered as a whole, is for him homogeneous. Capital both across the economy and over time, writes Swan, is "infinitely durable and instantaneously adaptable" . . . "the clearest statement of the malleability assumption" of neoclassical economists about capital for Harcourt (1969: 373).

W.E.G. Salter was one of the first to state the heterogeneous nature of capital, according to Harcourt (1969: 376). Gradually, though (again according to Harcourt), the neoclassical economists abandoned the hypothesis of perfect malleability. The production function started to be accepted as relevant only ex ante, that is, to inform decisions about which investments to make, not as an instrument to analyze the structure of production ex post the investments in capital were made.

Once the "embodied" view assumed by the discussion of "re-switching" is accepted, capital is seen as composed of different layers, each one with the efficiency allowed by the technological level at the time it is established. Then, "capital augmenting techniques" are necessary to consider heterogeneous capital as one figure, according to Harcourt (1969: 378). The question that follows is: If by utilizing some technology, it is assumed that it is possible to increase the amount of capital in order to "equalize" the return of capital (up to a point), would that make it possible to have a single quantitative measure of capital? Perhaps so, perhaps not, but in any case, that would not solve the problem that capital is heterogeneous and therefore, there are limits to its malleability.

There are two main critiques of the idea of malleability. The first comes from Sraffa's 1960 book and has a perspective like that of the classical economists. The second is associated with Kaldor and has to do with rejecting the usefulness of the ideas of perfect competition and knowledge.

According to Harcourt (1969: 380), Solow finds Capital Theory's controversies to be rooted in two things. One is ideological: the social (production) function gives justification for profits, against Marx. The other is simply that theorizing in this vein is technically difficult. According to Harcourt (1969: 381), Solow thinks that the core concept is return on capital—that is, Capital Theory should be about interest rates, not capital.

At this juncture, we may realize that both sides of the controversy have considered heterogeneity of capital; neo-Keynesians, led by Sraffa, attack marginal-utility thinking as a goal, while the neoclassicists use the same considerations to justify such reasoning. Here, we may note, Harcourt distinguishes between the neoclassical and neo-Keynesian camps (1969: 386). So obviously, he is describing something that happened before the New Neoclassical Synthesis, which came only in the late 1980s.

It is the heterogeneity of the capital stock that makes the double switching possible, according to Harcourt (1969: 394). Once heterogeneity is introduced, it cannot be said that "capital is paid a marginal r," and therefore simple correlations between lower rates of interest and higher profits with capital investment do not apply any longer. Capital in its role as aid to human labor, and capital as representing property in the sense of investable funds, are two separate things. If the rate of profits is different from the money rate of interest and, therefore, the remuneration of capital does not explain the distribution of income in society, recourse to relations other than economic relations is necessary to explain such distribution. The neo-Keynesians acknowledge that marginal return of capital, in a world of heterogeneous capital, does not explain the distribution. They have therefore advanced alternatives explanations (Harcourt, 1969: 395).

FICTITIOUS CAPITAL AND PROPERTY IN MARX

As with other authors in this review of the literature, obviously, the intent is not to survey his entire discussion of capital but to highlight what in it relates to the subject of this work.

Karl Marx's discussion of the capitalist society was, like Henry Dunning MacLeod's, heavily influenced by how capitalism operated in Victorian Great Britain. His treatment of credit and what he styled "fictitious capital" may be understood against the backdrop of a banking system that would issue banknotes or open credit in the checking accounts of its customers redeemable in gold coins—that is, upon resumption of this redeemability in 1821 after a long suspension during the Napoleonic Wars. The BoE strengthened its position as a central bank, moreover, after Peel's 1844 Act. The BoE's leverage of bank credit over the existing amount of gold coins and bullion in the bank's vaults was strengthened even further with the increased trust in the financial system so well depicted by Bagehot in *Lombard Street* (1873).

The puzzle for nineteenth century observers, and something that many today find it hard to grasp, is how the products that owners save from immediate consumption in the real economy are allocated, by the banking system, to entrepreneurs who would invest those resources in productive endeavors, thus increasing production in the future.

First, let us try to understand how it works. Even people not familiar with the operations of the banking system may find this example helpful: A farmer borrows some amount of grain from a grain dealer, both for his sustenance and to use as seeds,[28] and he also leases a tract of land for plowing. After the harvest, if things go according to plan, he will be able to pay back the borrowed grain plus the stipulated interest, pay the landowner his share in the crop, and still make something for himself.

What people unfamiliar with the operations of the commercial banks might not grasp is that savings in the real economy, represented by money deposited in a bank, can in an analogous way be "multiplied" by the banks through their credit operations.[29] Marx drew an erroneous conclusion: that supposedly "capital" (credit) not represented by coins was not backed by previous savings, and therefore, should be deemed "fictitious."[30]

Again, the operation of a bank, like that of any other business, is limited by its marginal costs and the opportunities it finds to make a profit—in this case, profitable lending. Furthermore, the precious metals from which coins are made are expensive, their acquisition requiring real resources invested in mining, for one thing. Hence the incentive for banks to "economize" in gold—a process, incidentally, well understood by Marx. If, instead of using coins as a medium of exchange, you could pay for your acquisitions through the use of credit instruments, it would make economic sense to use credit. That is, to the extent that a borrower is found to be creditworthy.

In other words, to the extent that the opportunity cost of your own capital is higher than the interest payments you would incur by borrowing capital from others, there is an economic incentive for you to go ahead and take out the loan. If a bank is able to pay you with the banknotes of its own issuance instead of coins, it has an economic incentive to do so, and to issue as many banknotes as the prudent management of its cash reserves will allow.

Under normal circumstances, banks compete in a free market to gain deposits and to lend money. In such circumstances, base money is commodity money; it cannot be created by government fiat. In this case, the cost of attracting deposits and the risk of lending money would limit the amount of bank credit that is created to what is profitable. Capital in the form of bank credit, in other words, is limited to the available stock of real resources that may be mobilized for the production of future goods. In this sense, what is called "fictitious" is not fictitious at all—a point that even today is the object of much confusion.

Such confusion is justified when the "normal circumstances" described above are not clear but have been blurred by the fiscal needs of the state, which may infringe on the free operations of financial markets in order to raise funds, either by manipulating the money supply or by financial repression. For Marx, the underwriting of government bonds results in the creation of "illusory and fictitious" capital, under the assumption that the state will not have those resources invested in production (Meacci, 1998: 7), a fine point.

Marx's separating productive from fictitious capital may also perceived—as is the case in *Capital*, volume 3—when the issuance of bills of exchange is not used "to make a profit" in the productive process but "to get one's hands on other people's capital." The latter puts us in mind of a "flight to liquidity" driven by uncertainty in the bust phase of a business cycle, as Professor Meacci points out (Meacci, 1998: 6).

Meacci also mentions Marx's example of the price of a waterfall (Marx, 1993: 787) as an example of "capitalized rent," and in another passage (Marx, 1993: 597), that "the formation of fictitious capital" is a form of capitalization, a variation in the price of an asset that should be estimated by its present value, not by its labor value as is done with any other commodity (Meacci, 1998: 8). The second sense in which Marx uses the term "fictitious capital" may be understood as capital gains, in current terminology.

It is interesting to note that "fictitious" in the first sense employed by Marx is related to the fact that it does not exist in reality. A public bond, say, is not a claim against the state that represents actual income-generating goods. Or, to take another example, a merchant might issue a bill of exchange in times of crisis to increase his cash reserves and not to advance credit to his customers. "Fictitious" in the second sense denotes the fact that it is derived from a property title to something that has "market value" but has no labor embodied in it—for example, the right to use a waterfall to produce energy.

As pointed out by Professor Meacci, for Marx, the two senses are not in contradiction. His "Fictitious Capital Theory of Crisis," identified by Meacci, is a sophisticated insight based on a good understanding of money as a store of value in a monetary economy (Meacci, 1998: 11). It is the excessive growth of fictitious capital that may create the conditions that can lead to financial (monetary) crises (Meacci, 1998: 9), a topic directly related to our subject matter.

NOTES

1. Respectively, when there is no loss to anybody, when there is a loss to somebody, and when both cases are present.

2. I understand the risks of bundling together market economies with the likes of the former Soviet Union, the Democratic People's Republic of North Korea, and

Chavista Venezuela. To meet this difficulty, I like the idea of plotting points along a continuum of economic institutions to differentiate market from socialist economies. Lacking a better marker, the existence of a stock exchange—that is, secondary markets for capital instruments—could be considered a practical divider between the two. However, to the extent that a society uses money, I argue that the dialectic approach of considering a real and an abstract side is useful for studying a given economy, if only to show how inefficient that society's institutional arrangements may be.

3. In chapter 2 of his most recent book (Cowen, 2018: 27–48), Cowen argues for the centrality of economic growth to the moral evaluation of a society committed to human progress. In a recent review of that book, Pierre Lemieux (Lemieux, 2019) seconds Cowen's defense of economic growth, arguing that the annual U.S. income per capita is about 50,000 USD; if this were capitalized at a rate of 3 percent per year for a period of 500 years, it would amount to 130 billion USD per year. Wouldn't one think, says Lemieux, that any environmental, health, or other social problem for which economic resources are nowadays a constraint could be ameliorated if the annual income per capita of all Americans ran in the billions of dollars?

4. John Maynard Keynes, *Essays in Persuasion* (New York, New York: W.W. Norton & Co., 1963), pp. 358–373.

5. For more on individualistic perfectionism see chapter 6 of *Norms of Liberty* (Rasmussen and Den Uyl, 2005: 111).

6. See "We Work Less, Have More Leisure Time and Earn More" (Tupy, 2016).

7. This section is based on my review of *Money and Government*, also titled "The Baleful Consequences of Robert Skidelsky's Keynesianism," in *Law & Liberty*, March 12, 2019. https://www.lawliberty.org/2019/03/12/the-baleful-consequences-of-robert-skidelskys-keynesianism/

8. This is not the place for us to discuss de Soto's thesis about capital formation in its entirety. Suffice it to say that there is a crucial difference, for a prospective borrower, between only having collateral, and having that plus a demonstrable capacity to generate a stream of revenue sufficient to repay the lender (or an investor, for that matter). Furthermore, in early modern times, sureties commonly performed, to some extent, the role de Soto sees for formal property as collateral (see Waddilove, 2018). Sureties have the potential of reducing in the same proportion, the need for prospective borrowers to have good collateral. (These comments should not be interpreted as dismissing de Soto's argument, but as a claim that his analysis requires further elaboration, something for which a more robust concept of representation is required.)

9. Evidently de Soto is just one among many authors in the field of institutional economics who discusses the relationship between law and economics. See for instance Cooter and Shäfer, who claim: "Economic freedom consists in the legal framework for markets and the absence of unnecessary regulatory burdens. The first cause of economic growth is legalizing economic freedom—that is, creating effective property, contract, and corporate law, and repealing unnecessary regulations" (Cooter and Shäfer, 2012: 223).

10. This section is based on my report to a Liberty Fund colloquium on "Liberty, Equality, and Meritocracy," directed by Professor James R. Stoner, Jr., Santa Fe, New Mexico, October 22–25, 2015.

11. In Average Is Over (2013), Cowen describes the kinds of occupations and skills that will likely be in higher demand, and lower, respectively, in the near future and therefore will likely command commensurately higher or lower wages.

12. The reliability of Piketty's estimation of income distribution as derived from IRS data has also been questioned. For that, see Geloso and Magness (2020).

13. In The Federalist Number 10 (2001: 42), "Publius" argues that the purpose of government is to protect the exercise of the faculties of men, assuming those to be diverse and the source of the rights to property.

14. A version of this section was previously published online as part of a Law & Liberty Symposium on the Future of Debt.

15. See Edwards 2010, 2018, and specially 2019. In the opening chapter of Left Behind (2010: 1), he presents the links between certain institutional arrangements and economic growth and contrasts those arrangements with the populist policies that have been a constant in Latin-American countries. In the concluding chapter of American Default (2018: 201), Professor Edwards explains the difference in circumstances between the abrogation of the gold clauses by the Roosevelt administration in the middle of the Great Depression and the problems of fiscal imbalance nowadays in the United States and the likelihood of a similarly extreme solution of a default. In a working paper entitled "Modern Monetary Theory: Cautionary Tales from Latin America" (2019), he develops his argument about the relevance of failed populist policies in Latin America for the understanding of real-world consequences of MMT policy prescriptions.

16. Abba P. Lerner, "Functional Finance and the Federal Debt," Social Research, Vol. 10, No. 1, February 1943. Lerner here posits that fiscal and monetary policy should be assessed by their results in the economy, not by theoretical assumptions about what results those policies may produce.

17. See Wray (2015). For instance, in section 4.3, pages 120–126, the author does not recognize the availability of real resources saved from consumption as a condition for new investments or expenditures.

18. The comments below are based on the editorial review I wrote for Smithin's book (Smithin, 2018).

19. See my discussion on the "Fiscal Proviso" (Zelmanovitz, 2013).

20. See Zelmanovitz (2015).

21. The insight that different monetary systems provoke peculiar forms of disequilibria is also found in a recent essay by Ivo Sarjanovic (2020: 162).

22. In discussing the essential elements of the concept of capital, Strigl argues that "Once one recognizes that the introduction of roundabout production methods has as its prerequisite the setting aside of a subsistence fund and that the productive power of the subsistence fund limits the possibility of lengthening the roundabout production process, then everything else follows without difficulty" (Strigl, 2000: 161). That is, the fact that some production processes are enhanced by the application to them of previously saved goods is what gave us the concept of capital in the real side of the economy. Granted, we are getting ahead of ourselves here, but Strigl continues his discussion of the representation of capital in the abstract side of the economy as follows: "If one starts with free capital in the sense of a subsistence fund, then this

does not become capital because of its material quality, but only because it is used as capital by its owner. The same is true of monetary capital. Owned money is never of itself capital, but through a particular use by its owner it becomes monetary capital. Thus, the supply of capital is always determined by a factor which lies outside pure economic ratiocination" (Strigl, 2000: 164). Monetary capital is an approximation of those saved goods, and if we keep that in mind, as Strigl said, "everything else follows without difficulty."

23. Joan Robinson in particular was known to be an apologist for Maoist China (see Osborn, 2020).

24. A similar problem is pointed out by Mathieu: "No puedo hacer depender el valor del conjunto de las libras esterlinas en circulación del valor de conjunto de las cosas en venta, puesto que el segundo conjunto depende a su vez del primero. . ." (Mathieu, 1990: 128).

25. See section 5.2 in Zelmanovitz (2016: 142).

26. This concept of "tradable financial claims" may perhaps be equated with "negotiable property claims," in order to define "property claims" negotiable in financial markets.

27. For more on the problems posed by "re-switching" the neoclassical theory of capital, see Fernández-Méndez (2019).

28. "Merchant credit," in Marxist terminology.

29. "Bank credit," for Marx (*Capital*, volume 3).

30. This understanding was not exclusive to Marx. See, for example, a passage written by an important New York merchant: "The demand for money advances with the same pace, until all the actual capital of the community is employed. Business still increases and calls into action the use of fictitious capital, or credit; this is of an elastic nature, and is extended in proportion to the wants of trade" (Cambreleng, 1821: 192).

Chapter 2

Austrian Capital Theory, Legal Rights, and Capital Representation

That Austrian economics and the neoclassical synthesis differ in their approach to Capital Theory is noticeable when we look to the very foundations of these schools: their respective heuristics, epistemology, and ontology. Concerning, for instance, the problem of measuring capital, Garrison (2016) calls attention to the fact that capital is radically heterogeneous. Labor and land at least have a dimension (worker-hours and acres), but capital's units are undefined, echoing here Robinson's critique.

Pinpointing the main difference between the Milton Friedman-Frank Knight conception of capital and that of F.A. Hayek, Garrison argues that the former deals with a "capital stock" in which a stock of capital goods yields a flow of consumption goods, while the latter deals with a "capital structure" according to which, there is a temporal pattern of heterogeneous capital goods (Garrison, 2016).

Using the example of a forest in which each year new trees are planted to replace the ones felled to produce wood, Garrison describes how for John Bates Clark or Frank Knight, once a steady stage is reached, the time of production becomes irrelevant. Garrison calls attention to the fact that George Stigler defends Clark against Böhm-Bawerk by saying that production and consumption in this case are simultaneous and therefore the time of production is "irrelevant." But that only holds water under the dramatic assumption of a steady state.

Garrison says that Jerry O'Driscoll called his attention to the fact that in the "Clark/Knight" model, capital stock is "permanent" and the flow of consumption goods produced is "permanent" (once you consider the maintenance as a "technical detail") "so to speak." If for Knight maintenance is a detail, capital is permanent, capital is only one factor (homogeneous), and time is "irrelevant," then it follows that, for Knight, capital is about "stocks" and "flows."

For Hayek, on the other hand, as highlighted by Garrison, maintenance is a matter of choice; capital depreciates, but reinvestment may lead to an expanding, static, or contracting economy; capital is heterogeneous; and time is essential to production. So, for Hayek, the way to understand capital is as a structure of production operating as a dynamic market process (Garrison, 2016).

I would go further. In the example raised by Garrison, you need to know the time of production in order to achieve this "steady state": If the rows of trees mature every fifteen years, you can only aim for a steady state if you cut down the trees in 1/15 of the forest per year—that is, paying attention to the time of production. Of course, this is already implicit in his reasoning; that is how, in designing a Hayekian triangle with time of production in the horizontal axis and output in the vertical axis, Garrison has "solved" the problem of time in the sequence of stages of production leading to higher output.

In regard to how entrepreneurs are able to access the present value of capital goods, we may recur once more to Garrison (2016), who states "Menger's Law" as the following: "The value of higher order goods derives from the anticipated value of the respective consumer goods."

In discussing the nature of capital in the Austrian tradition, Anthony Endres and David Harper refer to three controversies in Capital Theory over the last 120 years: the discussion between marginalists and anti-marginalists from 1880 to 1910, with Böhm-Bawerk and Clark as main exponents; the Knight-Hayek-Kaldor debate of the 1930s; and the Cambridge controversies from the 1960s and 1970s (Endres and Harper, 2011: 358). For the authors, the question those debates attempted to answer was what the meaning of capital is for the analysis of an industrial capitalist society. For them, the debates were inconclusive because the economists involved held radically different ontological conceptions of capital. They observe that Menger is the one who began to think about capital as hierarchically organized according to a structure of production, and for them, following Erich Streissler (Streissler, 1969: 250), what is common to all Austrian followers of Menger is this "structural mode of thinking."

For Endres and Harper, such speculation by Menger on the nature of capital invites economists to think about the "modes of existence of capital" and, according to them, that means: "Whether capital exists independently of human mind, whether it produces consequences outside the mind of the economic agents, whether it surges spontaneously, whether it has properties independently of capital theories and representations, and whether it can be reduce to a more basic element."

They say Menger has three levels of cognition to address those questions: first, we identify concrete realities; second, we relate those realities to abstract concepts; and third, we develop purely abstract "types." This third level is essential if we are to develop a full account of the nature of capital. Nevertheless, Endres and Harper say that Menger has essentially a realist approach to capital; he aspires to integrate his understanding of capital with other concepts of the real economy. In their view, for Menger, grasping the nature of capital requires more than common sense; it requires a theoretical apparatus yet to be developed in the economics field. Capital is a "genus" that cannot exist separately from the "tokens" in the real world that the concept is supposed to represent (Endres and Harper, 2011: 360).

For Menger, capital is not mind-independent; it is not a substance in nature. "For its existence, a capital good depends upon the existence of a use-plan and a judging mind," they write, linking the very concept of capital to the capacity of economic agents to become aware of and to act upon entrepreneurial opportunities (Endres and Harper, 2011: 362). What the authors describe here is what the structure of production is for Menger. The capital "genus" is a combination of goods used in production according to what was mentally selected by an entrepreneur. The money value, in which capital is accounted for, considered in daily life does not reflect completely what capital is, for it misses its productive side (Endres and Harper, 2014: 104).

Most relevant for the project at hand, the authors claim that Menger has solved the problem of the dual nature of capital by considering it as existing on two levels: the level of production, composed of heterogeneous goods; and their *representation* at the level of investment, composed of money or financial instruments. For the authors,

> Menger would not have appreciated major tensions among economists in the three capital controversies that turned on the problem of the "dual" nature of capital: on the one hand, capital as a collection of heterogeneous goods combined in a specific manner in production; and, on the other hand, capital as a fund of value distinct from capital goods themselves that moves more or less freely between alternative uses according to its market-determinate rate of return. (Endres and Harper, 2011: 363)[1]

At this juncture, it seems appropriate to add a table from Endres and Harper's article that illustrates some of the fault lines within the Austrian camp regarding the treatment of capital.

Quoting Hicks, the authors say that Böhm-Bawerk developed an economy of time in which time is just a technical variable, once he proposed to measure the average time of production by using the concept of "roundabout methods of production." For Endres and Harper, contrary to Menger, there is no real uncertainty in Böhm-Bawerk, thus his analysis suits a stationary state. I reserve judgment about that, however. They also claim that this homogeneous concept of capital became known as the Austrian view at the time of the debates between Knight, Hayek, and Kandor in the 1930s (Endres and Harper, 2011: 364).

As we can see from table 2.1, Hayek did not want to abandon Menger's ontology of capital; for Hayek, capital was heterogeneous and had a two-level analysis, but his concern was with the second, since he was interested in macroeconomic ways to explain the business cycle. One also notices in Endres and Harper a reference to Mises's idea that capital is always embodied in something physical aimed at production, or in an instrument aimed at financing something, and it is always associated with a productive plan by somebody. Mises admits that capital may be composed either of money or of sums of money in accounting books, but that it is sufficiently "real" to be taken into consideration in the production plans formed by someone in a market economy. The authors (p. 368) say that for Mises, there is nothing particularly productive about capital since (paraphrasing him) capital goods are merely an unutilized store of nature, past labor, and time (Mises, 2007: 493).

Mises is very much concerned with technology's being able to determine the possible combinations of heterogeneous stores of nature, past labor, and time in order to create capital goods. For Endres and Harper, Lachmann's version of Capital Theory follows Menger's in every detail. Also, for Lachmann, capital is created by an entrepreneurial act of "planned complementarity," and any good may qualify as capital as long as it is used in the plan, the defining subjectivist claim by that author (Endres and Harper, 2011: 369).

To conclude regarding Endres and Harper, they see all Austrians as following Menger, in considering capital to be an "order of goods" in actual production. Following Menger's realist position, his Austrian followers often adhere to the following propositions: Capital has a structure. Capital combinations require entrepreneurial judgment. Capital has real causes. It results from forward-looking entrepreneurial decisions aimed at what it can produce. Capital is not a passive factor of production but requires maintenance. Capital has specificity. And capital results in real economic consequences. The appeal to macroeconomic reasoning—equating capital with savings and investment—somewhat diverted attention from Menger's micro focus on a structure of goods in a non-stationary economy with specificities (Endres and Harper, 2011: 381).

CARL MENGER ON CAPITAL THEORY

In his introduction to the edition of Hayek's *The Pure Theory of Capital* that he edited (Hayek, 2014: xxi), Larry White of George Mason University credits Menger with having inverted the "real cost" doctrine: "Austrian capital theory began with a chapter of Menger's 1871 *Principles of Economics*."

Table 2.1   Austrian Treatments of Capital from Menger to Lachmann

Selected Texts	Real Production/ Monetary Investment Distinction	Existence of Original or Permanent Factors of Production	Aggregate Quantum: Stock/Fund	Entrepreneur's Appraisal Role Elaborated	Capital Specificity	Time Concept	Analytical Domain	
							Stationary State or Comparative Equilibrium	Macro-level/ Business Cycles
Menger (1871, 1888)	Y	N	N	Y	Y	Unidirectional	N	N
Wieser (1889)	N	Y	Y	N	N	Technical parameter	Y	N
Wieser (1914)	N	Y	Y	Y	Y	Unidirectional	N	N
Böhm-Bawerk (1889)	N	Y	Y	N	N	Technical parameter	Y	N
Schumpeter (1912)	Y	Y	Y	Y	Y	Technical parameter and unidirectional	Y	N
Schumpeter (1934)	Y	y	Y	N	Y	Unidirectional	N	Y
Strigl (1934)	Y	Y	Y	N	N	Technical parameter	Y	Partly
Mises (1931, 1949)	Y	Y	N	Y	Y	Unidirectional	N	N
Hayek (1941)	Y	Y	N	N	Y	Unidirectional	Y	Y
Lachmann (1947, 1956)	Y	N	N	Y	Y	Unidirectional	N	N

Menger emphasized that the market prices of "higher order" goods (land, labor, and capital goods) derive from their prospective contributions to the production of valued consumer goods (goods of "lower order").

The first issue to address here is the extent to which a subjectivist theory of capital such as Menger's could adequately capture reality. Basically, if we accept that anything put into productive use by an entrepreneur should be considered capital, its definition obviously becomes subjective.[2] Still, Menger applied a subjective perspective to his understanding of how economic agents assess the value of capital in time, and not only in regard to the opportunity-cost of putting them to a different use.

Menger sees confusion in the welter of terminology used by economists to denote the concept of "capital"; to eliminate this confusion (which, for Menger, began with Adam Smith), he suggests returning to the common ("real") usage of the term (2007: 178). The layperson and the lawyer consider capital only money, and not even all of the money a person has, but just the portion invested to earn an income, be it money loaned on interest, money invested in the shares of a company, or money used to buy an income-generating property. This usage does not confuse money and capital (Menger, 2007: 215). In contrast, there are three different concepts of capital in economic theory: (1) the assets an individual uses to generate income, in contrast to the assets he puts to his personal use; (2) the means of production, in contrast with consumer goods; and (3) goods to be used in the production of other goods, in contrast with natural goods or labor (Menger, 2007: 180).

It is noteworthy that Menger criticizes the first concept, "capital" as both income-generating goods and goods for personal use (such as the land used for agriculture or the furniture of a rented apartment). Although he agrees with the second concept's distinction between consumer goods (first-order goods) and productive goods (higher-order goods), he says it does not explain everything. For instance, some free goods are necessary for production, but are not part of the assets of an individual, while final goods (consumer goods) may be part of the goods necessary for the production of other goods (Menger, 2007: 185). Regarding these first two conceptions of capital, Menger is basically saying that what distinguishes a capital good from other categories of goods is not something intrinsic in the good, but what use it is put to. Basically, any good put to productive use would be capital, regardless of its common use or nature.

Of course, it is difficult to imagine a steel mill being used for leisure. But theoretically, it might be used, for example, for educational purposes, and not for the generation of other goods. Even in this case, however, the "final" good would allegedly be "education," not "steel."

In any case, for Menger, it is a mistake to use the technical sense in which a good may be a production good as a criterion to define what capital is or is not (2007: 187). He describes how capital in the technical sense (goods such as inventories, machinery, or buildings, used for the production of other goods) has an accounting representation as a value of money invested in the generation of income. Regardless of their real nature, goods only become capital when their monetary value becomes relevant for our economic calculus (Menger, 2007: 217). If we stipulate that inventories of inputs are not part of "entrepreneurial capital"—that only the "monetary value" of those inventories of inputs qualifies (Menger, 2007: 222)—my interpretation is that goods in the real world are represented by their monetary value in the accounting books of a business, and this representation is what matters for practical purposes.

Coming now to the third concept of capital—products allocated to the production of future goods—this avoids the problems of the first two. For Menger (2007: 189), capital is the portion of the initial equity that an individual allocated to increase his or her equity; and according to him, Adam Smith would agree. The problem is that Smith would qualify as capital (whose remuneration is "profits") only human-made production goods, not natural endowments (to be compensated by "rents") or labor (to be compensated by "wages"). Therefore, the "income-generating" equity of someone may include "capital" (in this limited sense of production goods) and natural resources (which will be remunerated by "rents").

For Menger, it is an anomaly of Smith's theory that land can only be considered capital to the extent that labor is invested in it—that is, marble may be capital in its totality, but in a marble quarry, only the portion of marble already quarried, that is, which had labor invested in it would be considered capital (2007: 193). I think that Menger is reading too much into Smith's classification of factors of production (land, labor, and capital), a classification he proposed for limited analytical purposes. To be sure, the classification is deficient (there is no room in it for, among other things, entrepreneurial activity and remuneration) but its limitations are no impediment to future advances in Capital Theory. I prefer to think of advances that came later as having been built upon Smithian foundations, not as requiring their destruction.

Much of this discussion has to do with the evolution of the theory of interest rates. Economists have tried to figure out to what degree interest rates are determined by the time-preference of individual agents, and to what degree an interest rate "on money" is different from a time-preference rate for (different) goods. They have also sought to know whether there is a single rate of interest or many, and whether the remuneration of resources advanced to productive efforts pays for just the abstinence of their use or also for the risks of the bearer.

It is important to note that Menger viewed interest rates from the perspective of a businessman, even if his ultimate goal was to develop a theory. He pursued the adequate rate of discount to bring investments in land to present value, and how to sum up the cost of investments while taking into consideration that some of them may have been non-productive. Knowing the original cost is useful, he concluded, but essentially the value of the property is given by its expected future cash flow (2007: 203). For Menger the marginal utility of the new investment is the key information for the investor to have (2007: 203).

As for the all-important comparison between capital and interest on capital in economics, versus in real life, Menger's conclusions are the following: (1) Only the monetary representations of real goods put to production are considered capital for the practical man (not even money itself), while for economists, all goods put to production are so considered. (2) Both in our daily lives and for economists, money lent on interest is capital. (3) In daily life, any claims on future revenue are considered capital in themselves, but not for economics; and (4) Both in economics and in real life, the income generated by loaned money is considered interest on capital (Menger, 2007: 223–224). Furthermore, no practical businessman would consider his fixed assets as part of his "capital" since they are not part of "financial markets" (Menger, 2007: 225). In regard to this passage, I think it may be understood as Menger claiming simply that not all representations of property are part of that special section of the abstract side of the economy that is the financial market.

In a similar vein, Menger reminds us that "capital" for the individual means one thing, but for society, it means another (2007: 207). For instance, a transference or subsidy from the government to an individual may be a source of income for that individual, but there is no value added to society. Here Menger is echoing Smith's distinction between dwelling houses and profitable buildings mentioned in this book's first footnote (p. 11). For Menger, "capital," as understood in political economy (macroeconomics), means the goods that, by their technical nature, are means for producing other goods; while for actual people, goods that are part of their equity (be they jewelry, art, furniture) are also classified as "capital" in that context.

What remains important is "the recognition and understanding of 'capital' as a phenomenon in the real world, and its peculiar social form in economics." For Menger, the economy is not a single entity with the purpose of supplying society with economic goods. It would be better understood as an organism composed of multiple individual economies (families and firms) whose purpose is to allow those entities to fulfill their own purposes through processes that render them interdependent (p. 209). To me this points to the need to clarify what capital means in the context of microeconomics, as compared to what it means in the context of macroeconomics; and to the extent that economics uses models, there is also a need to address the possibly different meanings of capital in the practical world of business and in economic theory in order to find ways to make them intelligible.

For Menger, the inventory of consumer goods and all of what is required for their distribution, in the hands of the producers and merchants, is part of the "capital" of individual economies; without them, society could not be supplied (2007: 212). Here, it is appropriate to ask ourselves how the representation of these goods occurs in the abstract side of the economy. We look to an "abstract" side, of which monetary and financial instruments are just one part, with all other forms of representation of property claims completing the whole.

Perhaps the most substantive issue in regard to Menger's theory has to do with how prices are formed in a market economy. While a mere subjectivist perspective on the decisions made by individual agents may well explain their motivations, it cannot account for prices in the market for goods in general, much less the price of capital. It's also true that prices are not objectively determined, either (contrary to Marx and his followers). So, without rejecting the subjective nature of the evaluations of individual agents making their individual decisions, prices should be understood as resulting from "intersubjective" evaluations.

Some may argue that such an understanding should not imply that there is just one interest rate. After all, there are many different "markets" with differing degrees of liquidity. Different contractual agreements between economic agents may share the risks of the common venture among them in different ways. Different borrowers have different credit ratings. Different banks have different reputations, and therefore different costs to raise funds. Finally, the managers of different lending entities have different individual preferences. The upshot is that, in any particular transaction, a different rate may be agreed upon between the contracting parties, and this does not contradict the idea that prices are formed in the market by the "sum" of individual evaluations.

This treatment of Menger's Capital Theory as it relates to the Representational Theory of Capital (RTC) may be concluded with his statement that income from property is not the same thing as interest on capital, since he seems to reserve the concept of interest for that income which is generated by financial instruments. This can be seen in the fact that he differentiates "productive equity" from capital. A theory of interest on capital, therefore, is deficient to the extent that it is limited to explaining phenomena in financial markets. Menger argues that interest paid on capital is not the "primary phenomenon" but a consequence of the income generated by the goods applied to production itself. In order to develop a complete theory of "earnings from equity," it is necessary to take into account all the lucrative equity, not only its monetary representations in the abstract side of the economy. In order to offer that comprehensive theory, economics needs to go beyond a mere theory to explain interest on capital (Menger, 2007: 226–228). Of course, I agree.

BÖHM-BAWERK ON LEGAL RIGHTS, RELATIONSHIPS, AND ECONOMIC GOODS

While researching what would become his magnum opus, the three-volume book *Capital and Interest*, first published in 1894, Eugen von Böhm-Bawerk wrote an essay in 1881 called, "Whether Legal Rights and Relationships Are Economic Goods." Its goal was to answer "the question of the true economic nature of those 'rights and contractual relationships' which have come to occupy so anomalous a position beside the other constituents of that group of phenomena we call economic goods and which differ so markedly from those remaining members of that group to which they seek to gain entrance" (Böhm-Bawerk, 1962: 30). The marked difference of which Böhm-Bawerk speaks "consists preeminently in the incorporeity which sets them apart from those members, namely, from concrete and objective material goods and from personal renditions of service."

Just as Menger sought to remedy the economists' lack of precision about "capital," Böhm-Bawerk wanted to pin down more precisely the constitutive elements of "economic goods" as a category—particularly whether intangible goods are or should be included. With this essay, he is not claiming to have created a new theory; on the contrary, he presents himself as "a mere interpreter of well-known views" rather than as "the originator of a new doctrine," if that helps to "convince" readers of what he is saying (Böhm-Bawerk, 1962: 31). I can only hope for the same result from my research on Capital Theory.

To begin his interpretation, Böhm-Bawerk puts the following questions:

> Are legal rights and contractual relationships in sober fact genuine economic goods—that is to say, are they goods in the sense in which the science of economics uses and must use that term? Can they, by their nature, be such goods? And what, indeed, is that nature? And what is the economic significance of these abstract and nonmaterial things which play so important a part in economic life? (Böhm-Bawerk, 1962: 32)

Böhm-Bawerk came to realize the importance of properly describing concepts such as goods, rights, and relationships—and of not automatically assuming that others' take on these things is correct (p. 33). It should give us pause to think that this was his intent in 1881 and the problem is still with us. The inspiration to strive for a proper "doctrine of goods" came to Böhm-Bawerk as an effort to replace an erroneous doctrine, and "the erroneous doctrine that I have specifically in mind right now is the view, well known and widely held, that credit not only *conveys* goods but actually *creates* them; and the theorist's contribution to the theory of goods which is adduced in support of that view is the idea that a legal right to make a demand constitutes an independent or an 'intangible' good." Böhm-Bawerk attributes to Henry Dunning MacLeod the doctrine of the power of credit to create goods: "Credit, says MacLeod, creates debts and thereby creates a number of 'intangible' goods. It is therefore not merely a means for the conveyance of exiting product but also for the *'creation of wealth'*" (p. 34, italics in the original).

MacLeod, in *Elements of Political Economy* (MacLeod, 1858), states his thesis that the proper object of economics is not "production, distribution, and consumption of wealth," but exchange. He even attributes to Archbishop Whately the suggestion of changing the name of the scientific discipline of "political economy" to "catallactics" (p. 12) to underline that exchange is its object. I do not consider Böhm-Bawerk guilty of caricaturing MacLeod; but it is important to acknowledge that the latter's thinking is a bit more subtle than Böhm-Bawerk gives credit for. The way I understand MacLeod's claims, he positions himself between a strict *metallism* and the *nominalism* of John Law concerning the nature of money. His work was mainly devoted to explaining the role of bank credit as advanced by commercial banks in the economy of Great Britain in his day. The fact that MacLeod had not distanced himself sufficiently from Law's ideas explains, for Böhm-Bawerk, why MacLeod would claim that credits create new wealth on top of existing wealth, but in any case "the basic principle of that view is in error." He demonstrates MacLeod's reasoning as the syllogistic conclusion of the following premises:

(a) when *A* lends *B* a dollar, then *B* possesses in that dollar a corporeal thing having the value of a dollar; (b) in his claim to the repayment of the dollar *A* possesses and intangible or nonmaterial good possessing a present value approximating one dollar which is not identical with the corporeal dollar itself. (p. 35)

The false premise, claims Böhm-Bawerk, is the second one, because you cannot have a negative good in order to cancel the credit (p. 36). Why is this not clear to economists? he asks—because they think intangibles are "goods" to the extent that they are "useful." Granted, for the individual owning a credit, it is useful, and therefore it is a good. But for society as a whole—since, in the aggregate, the credits and debits are canceled—the debts do not create anything. These different perspectives are simultaneously in favor of and against MacLeod's claim; only a better understanding of the nature of goods could resolve the case. Böhm-Bawerk wants (p. 38) "to show how the whole

MacLeod fallacy patently owes its origin to an obfuscated understanding of the economic nature of rights."

It seems to me that in Böhm-Bawerk's time, the first premise could be accepted as true because the "money" allegedly had an "intrinsic" (metallic) value; nowadays it does not; therefore, his reasoning needs to be restated. It is noteworthy that nowhere in Böhm-Bawerk's exposition is there discussion of the price elasticity that, in a monetary economy, allows for the creation of some goods due to the "inflationary" creation of credits.

This is not the proper place to discuss in detail the operations of banking credit in England under Peel's Act of 1844. Suffice it to say that for MacLeod in *Elements of Political Economy*, (MacLeod, 1858: 265), bank credit could be used not only to transfer existing wealth but to create new products and services. From reading his book, one gets the impression that he recognizes the constraints on credit-creation in a monetary economy in which there is a banking sector. Even so, there are opportunities to put the spare capacity of the economy to productive use through the operation of commercial credit. Böhm-Bawerk stresses this, finding MacLeod unclear in this regard.

In exploring this point, Böhm-Bawerk departs from the traditional concept of economic goods, "those things which *serve human beings as the means or tools for the attainment of their personal well-being*" (p. 39, italics in the original). Here we see that he adheres to the concept of goods as Menger understands it in *Principles of Economics* (Menger, 1994: 55). Economic goods must simultaneously have the following attributes: They must satisfy a human need and be objectively adapted to doing so. Man must be aware of this adaptability and have the power to utilize it. And finally, the thing must be available (Böhm-Bawerk, 1962: 41). These attributes, it is easy to perceive (p. 42), are less inherent in the things and more in relation to the economic agent. That highlights the difference between the individual agent's and the community's points of view of what an economic good is. For the individual, it is what satisfies his needs. For the community, it is the sum of the evaluations of all the individual agents—a fiction, really, since the community in that sense does not exist. What exists, under this hard conception of realism, is only the sum of evaluations of the economic agents (p. 43).

The classification of economic goods used by Böhm-Bawerk is tripartite: material goods, immaterial goods, and legal rights. He acknowledges (pp. 52–3) that his framework is not free of controversy. The way I see the problem, legal rights are representations of goods, which is to say claim instruments on goods, be they material or immaterial. That legal rights happen to be immaterial does not jeopardize their inclusion. After offering the caveat that rights may be analyzed from a juridical, ethical, political, or economic point of view, Böhm-Bawerk asks, "What, in other words, does it mean, *economically speaking*, to possess a legal right?" (italics in the original). To which he answers: "having 'power of disposal' over the good in question" (p. 55).

What follows is a discussion of the correspondent actual existence of the goods represented by rights, and the extent to which these rights are respected (enforced) in a given society.

Böhm-Bawerk claims that "the accomplishment of man's economic purposes demands possession of his goods" (p. 56) Here "legal possession" means legally sanctioned possession, although, as legal theory teaches us, possession is a fact. Böhm-Bawerk explains that because men live in a politically organized society, physical possession is not enough to ensure the economic use of goods. Furthermore, he argues that "a legal claim is regarded as quite null and valueness [*sic*] if it is unaccompanied by physical possession and if there is no prospect that it will furnish the avenue to attainment of physical possession." In that case, the rights would be "false rights" in the terminology of Jacques Rueff, applicable to things beyond the reach of the rightful owner (say, having been stolen), things that no longer exist (say, destroyed by a fire) or things that were never in existence (as will be discussed later in this work). Böhm-Bawerk says that for any good to have economic value, factual possession should be present and that it is "the state's physical powers of enforcement that lends to all law whatever cogency it may possess."

It is not until legal control over goods is combined with physical control that they become "genuine *goods*" (p. 59, italics in the original). Legal possession becomes a good to the extent that it assures the economic use of a physical good; therefore, it is not an "independent" good but part of the reason we consider a physical good to be a good in the first place (p. 61). So "it is by no manner of means an independent good existent outside of and in addition to the good that is possessed" (p. 62).[3] Böhm-Bawerk writes, "The only reason at all *why men desire corporeal goods lies in the prospect they afford of renditions of service*" (p. 73, italics in the original). But even such independent rendition of service does not justify the conclusion that "*property rights* are in no sense genuine goods" (Böhm-Bawerk, 1962: 81).

In order to clarify that distinction, he proposes the concept of *Darlehensforderung*, which was translated by George D. Huncke in the English edition of the work I am referring to as "payment-claim" to express the idea of a "promise to pay," as he argues that the only goods in these transactions involving such promises are the "objects themselves which constitute the matter of the debt" (p. 84). "The right to demand payment is claimed to be merely the condition precedent of *a future* goods-quality" (p. 85, italics in the original). With that, Böhm-Bawerk points to the derivative nature of claims.

Next, after defining wealth as "nothing more nor less than the totality of the economic goods that stand at the disposal of an economizing subject" (p.

86), Böhm-Bawerk computes future income "as part of our *present wealth*" (p. 88, italics in the original). His discussion of future goods ends with a mention of "certain circumstances which lead to future income to be part of . . . the anomalous phenomenon of *wealth without goods*" (p. 89, italics in the original). Here Böhm-Bawerk has in mind promises to deliver goods that do not exist or that the debtor does not possess, and promises that may or may not be honored—in this sense, some of those promises may be beyond the capacity of the existing capital structure to fulfill, which gets us to the "false rights" elucidated by Rueff (to be taken up later in this work).

Böhm-Bawerk's treatment of the dialectical nature of capital goods and their representation begins with this idea: "We must distinguish between the *materials of wealth* and *the forms of wealth*" (p. 97, italics in the original). While he aims to distinguish between real goods and the claims over them (the forms in which rights to their possession are represented in society), he so far does not expressly mention "representation." Thus far he speaks only of "interpretation" and "imagination," writing that "the forms of wealth [are] mere creatures of our subjective interpretation" (Böhm-Bawerk, 1962: 97). He continues by listing goods and then forms in which goods are represented, the latter being termed by him "computation-forms" (p. 98). As I said, it is not yet a developed theory of representation; to the extent it is, we will need to wait for his final chapter.

A first step in that direction comes when Böhm-Bawerk lays out the absolutely distinct nature of goods as opposed to rights, and the derivative nature of rights: A "right can be only a variant of a *computation form*; it can never be the name of an independent *material of wealth*" (p. 112). He offers as an example five different forms of rights over the same material goods. Then he declares that "rights are never goods in and of themselves, *but only conditions of the subjective goods-quality of the things to which they pertain*" (p. 116). Here is the first time that he talks about rights "representing other goods," even if the purpose of such representation is mainly for the "computation of wealth."

The next important step in the development of the idea of representation in Böhm-Bawerk is when the author calls our attention to how mistaken is the traditional distinction between tangible and intangible goods. The correct line to draw is between goods (which may be immaterial) and rights (p. 115). Following this, he makes plain that "relationships" cannot be real goods (p. 117). The meaning here is that, although "good will" (for instance the granting of preferred patronage to some businesses) cannot be considered a real good, that does not imply that it cannot be an economic good, such as when, anticipating Gary Becker, Böhm-Bawerk argues that love and friendship are indeed economic goods or *"useful renditions of service"* (p. 113).

Finally, Böhm-Bawerk argues that, useful as it is to (temporarily, for the sake of his argument) have "disencumbered" the concept of economic goods of "pseudo-goods" such as rights and relationships, the essay's real benefit is to show the importance of conceptual precision. He would have his readers, under that standard of precision, reject the wrong conceptions of MacLeod and Law concerning "credit" (p. 134-6). He claims that the cause of the imprecision is that the economic concept of credit over goods is used simultaneously as the basis for the creation of rights (as in a promise to pay) and for the computation of wealth (as in an equity title over an existing good). The problem is that in regard to the computation of wealth, a fiction is created that the good available now (say, the credit against the issuer of a banknote) and the good that will be available in the future (the repayment of a discounted commercial paper) are both counted as available now (page 137). Böhm-Bawerk blames this for much confusion among economists ("that fiction which turned out to be a trap for many a writer who has written on the subject of credit").

He also urges that his brand of "compulsion" or zeal for the precise use of concepts be employed with capital and interest. The temporal aspect will, I think, turn out to be where we can trace the source of many a mistake in the theory of credit. Böhm-Bawerk's essay is insightful there. Nonetheless, it offers no discussion of the "wiggle room" that a monetary economy permits, nor of representation in any direct sense. This essay by Böhm-Bawerk may be understood as a first attempt to go in the direction in which I would like to go—a valuable, if incomplete one.

HAYEK AND THE PURE THEORY OF CAPITAL

The contributions of Friedrich Hayek to Capital Theory are many. They consumed many years of his academic career, culminating with the publication in 1941 of *The Pure Theory of Capital*. One of Hayek's biggest contributions was to advance our knowledge of the equilibrating role of interest rates in the economy and its fluctuations. As Professor White points out in his introduction to the 2014 edition (Hayek, 2014: xxv), Hayek, contrary to Irving Fisher and other neoclassicals, used the interest rate to explain the intertemporal structure of production, and not the reverse. In this sense, Hayek's work may be understood as an integration of, and a continuation of, the works of William Jevons, Knut Wicksell, and Eugen Böhm-Bawerk.

Professor White quotes a summary of the book that Hayek offered in a 1970 interview: "To put it briefly, I think that while Bohm-Bawerk was fundamentally right, his exposition in terms of an average period of production was so over-simplified as to mislead in the application. In addition, if we want to think the Bohm-Bawerk idea through, we have to introduce much more complex assumptions. Once you do this, the things become so damned complicated it's almost impossible to follow it" (Hayek, 2014: xxiii). The important insight to be gleaned here is that you do not need to explain capitalist production in every detail to make it understandable. Relying on some degree of simplification, while it makes the theory inapplicable to concrete cases, may still serve as a heuristic device to explain how production happens. That is all that is needed from a concept in Capital Theory; we may leave the rest for the study of industrial processes.

Professor White mentions that Hayek acknowledges the importance to his *Pure Theory of Capital* of the work done by Wicksell (a Swedish economist who lived from 1851 to 1936) on capital and interest. There are four key concepts in Hayek's book that White points out were already present in Wicksell (Hayek, 2014: xxiv):

(1) "The essential role of capital arises from the time-consuming nature of production."
(2) Two features distinguish capital from other inputs: "Capital goods (a) are non-permanent (get used up) and (b) can be used up faster or slower."
(3) It is possible to slice the capital structure of the economy either at a given moment (which allows the economist to compare the use of capital with other inputs) or over time (which allows the economist to see capital as semi-finished goods along the process of production of a given final good).
(4) "Net capital formation requires a diversion of input services that could otherwise go to the immediate production of consumer goods." In addition, Larry mentions that Hayek's perspective on capital is "forward-looking" while Wicksell's is "backward-looking."

As we can see, Hayek's research agenda in Capital Theory is highly specific and largely unconnected to our investigations here, except for two topics.

The first is that, in his final statement about Capital Theory in the book, Hayek developed a framework that assumes that capital is scarce. This contrasts with Keynesian assumptions, both in the mainstream (in which stores of unemployed labor and idle natural resources are assumed to exist) and in the more radical perspective of a "secular stagnation" (which assumes that profitable opportunities for investment become increasingly harder to find).

The second is a difference that I perceive between Hayek's methodology in *The Pure Theory of Capital* and the Keynesian methodology prevailing in 1941. For Hayek, disposable income at any given time is determined by the productive capacity of the existing capital structure—that is, by investment decisions taken in previous periods—while for Keynes and his followers, income is determined in the present by the current aggregated demand.

It is my contention that one of the things that has misled some economists into insisting that capital may not be scarce is the failure to clearly differentiate between the real sector and the abstract sector of the economy. This is a topic that will be taken up later in more detail.

The issue of "secular stagnation" requires further elaboration. As mentioned earlier, regulations and taxes may impose costs on business and marginally make them unprofitable. It is reasonable to assume that profitable opportunities are harder and harder to come by the more that regulations and taxes proliferate. If securing an environmental license to build anything minimally complex in any Western society nowadays comes to take over ten years, it is no surprise that the capital costs of such a project will be much higher than if the licenses could be obtained in a year. Some projects may die aborning as the costs become prohibitive. The freedom of action allowed to owners by virtue of their private property rights diminishes accordingly.

The result of this narrowing of the scope of property rights is a less efficient allocation of capital. If a government creates so much red tape that profitable allocations of existing capital are stymied, economic actors may, for a time, have the impression that capital is abundant, and the inefficient allocations still possible may make a low growth environment a self-fulfilling prophecy.[4]

Professor White reminds us that *The Pure Theory of Capital*, with its concerns about the efficient allocation of capital, was published at the peak of Keynesian economics, when capital and labor were not scarce factors, and that Hayek's ideas were at the time dismissed as outdated. White writes that Keynesian theory

> depicted current income as proximately determined by current expenditure (Y=C+I+G) rather than by prior production. The "circular flow" supplanted capital theory in macroeconomics. Current-period analysis displaced intertemporal analysis. The interest rate no longer played an equilibrating role. Left to its own devices, the economy could readily get stuck at a level of expenditure too small to achieve full employment.

He goes on to say, "Though it never became mainstream doctrine, some Keynesians nearly overthrew the idea that capital is scarce, and needs to be carefully allocated, in favor of the 'secular stagnation' thesis that remunerative uses of capital are or soon will be hard to come by" (Hayek, 2014: xxxi). It does seem to me that finding "remunerative uses of capital" really is a problem for us today. The reason is the distortion created by the above-mentioned false impression that there is more capital around than what actually exists, due to (1) the large amounts of capital being invested in government securities that have not been discredited yet; (2) there being so many claims against governments that the governments cannot possibly repay in full. On top of these is a third factor: that undue regulation has rendered production so expensive that it is more difficult than in the past to produce things that can repay the investment with profit. All that is not to say, *a la* the "radical" Keynesians of whom White speaks, that capital is no longer scarce. Quite the opposite, in fact. It is actually much more scarce than people realize in the real world. But financial markets have not yet acknowledged this. They have not priced the ravaging of capital by sovereign debtors in the last decades.

Finally, the methodological difference mentioned above is one more example, I argue, of the confusion that comes of not differentiating between economic resources and the stocks of claims on them that exist at any given time. While most of the economics profession was derailed by this error, and a flawed theoretical apparatus built upon it, Hayek was not. Professor White shows how he was able to hew to a better course.

"Pervading the book," he writes, "is Hayek's rejection of the Knightian propositions that (1) capital may be regarded as a homogeneous fund; (2) the permanent maintenance of capital is to be taken for granted; (3) there is no economically meaningful distinction to be made between 'original factors' (land and labor) and capital; (4) input and output are synchronous, so production is essentially instantaneous, and concepts of time-duration in production (the period of production or the investment period) are useless; and (5) production and consumption are simultaneous, so it is pointless to speak of 'waiting'" (Hayek, 2014: xxix).

LACHMANN AND THE CAPITAL STRUCTURE

As mentioned earlier, for another of the Austrian economists, Ludwig Lachmann, capital is created by an entrepreneurial act of "planned complementarity"; goods qualify as capital as long as they are used in the entrepreneur's plan. Lachmann, who wrote *Capital and Its Structure* (1956), has been neglected as a thinker who can guide us to a better understanding of a free and open society. Furthermore, he believed that there was a general neglect of Capital Theory among economists. Lachmann offers three reasons for that neglect: (1) Most economists do not think a fully explained capital framework is necessary for understanding economic phenomena; (2) Capital is difficult to quantify; and (3) The relation between capital and knowledge is a problem because static analysis does not capture changes in knowledge that affect the use of capital. Walter Grinder, in his introduction to Lachmann's *Capital, Expectations, and the Market Process* (1977), writes that "most mainstream economists find no comfort in [Lachmann's] work because as a member of the Austrian School he opposes the direction taken by modern economic analysis" (Lachmann, 1977: 3). Yet his contributions to Capital Theory have resisted the test of time; while not as influential as one would expect, they have not been challenged, either.

The intent with this section on Lachmann is to understand better his discoveries about what capital is, and from that, to draw out the implications for a society of free and responsible individuals. From Lachmann's perspective, what aspect of the real side of the economy is the concept of capital in the monetary side of the economy supposed to represent? Why is it important to the good functioning of a market economy for that representation to be accurate? What may hinder that adequate representation?

Was Ludwig Ludwig Lachmann a Historicist?

We may begin by looking at a commentary on the Austrian thinker by Hans L. Eicholz. To Eicholz's penetrating essay, "Ludwig M. Lachmann: Last Member of the German Historical School" (2017), my first response is, it depends on what you understand by the German Historical School. Classical economics—or "Anglo-Saxon Economics" in Eicholz's phrase—developed its models of human behavior as applied to economic activity and came up with the model, *"Homo economicus."* From this it derived prescriptions for political economy that its adherents saw as universally applicable. They conceived of human behavior as constant in regard to economic activity, and their prescriptions are often summarized as laissez-faire domestically and free trade with other nations.

Votaries of the German Historical School, which first arose in the nineteenth century, questioned whether the classical economists' ideas really had universal value, since the former thought that they were not applicable to Germany. Regardless of how much they accepted the idea that there are universal laws of human conduct (see the *Schemata* Eicholz mentions on page 234), the bottom line for such thinkers as Wilhelm Roscher, Gustav von Schmoller, and Werner Sombart was that those laws were not strong enough to trump the particular historical circumstances of Germany in order to justify adoption of laissez-faire and free trade. (It is not a coincidence that the German Historical School advocates became known as "Socialists of the Chair.")

Analyzing where, and to what degree, Lachmann's thinking partakes of both camps is important. Eicholz pegs Lachmann as someone who does not eschew abstract theories about human behavior, making him more theoretically minded than the German Historical School but also, and crucially, more willing to qualify his axiomatic thinking than were economists of the Austrian School. What Eicholz contends is that Lachmann was not as firmly in the Austrian camp as he himself thought he was.

For my part, I do not think Lachmann would say that laissez-faire or free trade are not good prescriptions of political economy for Germany, during his time (1906–1990) or ours. Nor do I think that Eicholz would say that Lachmann would say such a thing. The upshot, for me, is that in all this discussion about how much the theories explaining human behavior in general are "ideal types" or "categories of thought" (as Eicholz mentions on page 230), what is most important is that the degree to which those theories explain human behavior for Lachmann separates him significantly from the German Historical School. Enough, in my estimation, to leave Eicholz's hypothesis unsustained.

Keep in mind, when it comes to comparing the methods of the Austrian economists with those of the German Historical School, that for both, economics is formed by theory + history. However, for the Austrians, the historical details do not invalidate the constancies of human behavior; they just give the context in which those constancies will manifest themselves. For the German Historicists, the historical context has such importance that theory has little explanatory value. That is why Mises observed that, if they intended to avoid inconsistencies, they should limit themselves to doing history and not economics.

For Lachmann, each business cycle may manifest its history of how the interest rate deviated from the natural rate. I doubt, though, that he would say that Wicksell's theory is unable to explain what happened in any particular business cycle, which would be the position of the German Historicists.

By the same token (as Eicholz quotes Lachmann on page 251), theory or "the logic of choice," cannot explain "by itself" "every concrete transaction." True. We should not infer from that that "history" would be sufficient—and I do not think that Lachmann, Mises, the German Historicists, or Eicholz would say it was.

On the Order of Capital and Expectations

As Lachmann observed (in line with many others we have been cited in this discussion), "The word 'capital,' as used by the economists, has no clear and unambiguous meaning." He went on to say that "Sometimes the word denotes the material resources of production, sometimes their money value. Sometimes it means money sums available for loan or the purchase of assets" (Lachmann, 2007: 1). What are, for Lachmann, the implications in positing that the generic concept of capital has no measurable counterpart among material objects? Does capital reflect only the entrepreneurial appraisal of such objects? Because capital resources are heterogeneous, shall we speak of a multiple specificity of capital goods?

The answers to these questions come from *Capital and Its Structure*, Chapters I and II.

One substantive idea that arises at this point is how to accurately characterize the entrepreneur. For Frank Knight, it was said, the role of the entrepreneur is to manage uncertainty. Israel Kirzner focuses on the cognitive aspect of entrepreneurial activity. For Joseph Schumpeter, the distinctive contribution of the entrepreneur is to promote the process of creative destruction by which economic efficiency is achieved and enhanced. Finally, for Ludwig Lachmann, the key element is the ability of the entrepreneur not only to become aware of the opportunities for arbitrage but also to be able to make a decision to act upon such information. Lachmann, therefore, has added a fourth definitional element to the entrepreneur's role.

Kirzner, for his part, distinguishes between capital goods in the real world, be they material or immaterial, and capital as an abstraction, which may be an object of economic evaluation. Although we may acknowledge the problem of how to treat human capital—faced by Lachmann in particular, and Austrian economists in general—we may agree that capital goods are goods with an economic function that are evaluated by the entrepreneur as he interprets information provided by the price system. That is, the same physical resources may be evaluated differently by different people. Capital is the evaluation of the resources, and when those resources are represented by liquid financial instruments, such as the ones traded in stock exchanges, their intersubjective value is revealed by the market.

We can see that in Lachmann, who writes: "The function of the capital market is to allocate scarce capital resources among a number of alternative uses. This is simple where these uses are known, not so simple where they are not known. . . . 'Market,' in the true economic sense, means a process of exchange and allocation reflecting the transmission of knowledge" (Lachmann, 2007: 28).

Commonsensical as this observation is, it has important implications for understanding the economic process; for capital goods are in the world, whereas the value of capital is in the mind. Lachmann and Mises hold that the value of capital is not "praxeological"; that is, not a result of any human action. The value of capital is "catallactic"; that is, defined in the market. That may be the case in our market society while it may not be the case in a more primitive, autarkical one; in any event, it is an import insight about how value is perceived and informs entrepreneurial decisions.

It is noteworthy that Lachmann worked on *Capital and Its Structure* during the 1940s, when he was working with Hayek at the London School of Economics. Lachmann wanted to deal with Keynes on expectations—to show that Keynes was wrong, for example, about the diminishing marginal returns on capital, when, thanks to complementarity, adding new capital to some productive processes may result in increasing marginal returns.

Lachmann also rejected the homogeneity of the capital structure as seen by Keynes. Heterogeneity requires thinking. Prices are not an objective guide to action in a world of change. To come up with an interpretation, an instrument of interpretation (a mind) is required. As that is done, new information is created and made accessible to others. That is a radical interpretation of the market process; for Lachmann, it is a process whose dynamic component is its endogeneity. There is, of course, a political dimension to how Lachmann came up with these ideas: Businesspersons and politicians were reading Keynes, and Lachmann was against interventionism; therefore, in order to have an impact in the public debate, it is no wonder he made Keynes's core assumptions his main targets in the book.

Process Analysis, Capital Theory, and the Meaning of Capital Structure

Next we should tackle what a capital structure is. Why are capital goods used in the way they are? What does "free capital" mean for Lachmann? How does one take malinvestment into consideration in assessing "economic progress"? On these questions one can turn to *Capital and Its Structure*, Chapters III and IV.

We may begin by exploring the implications of the existence of a stock exchange for the overall market order. I understand Lachmann as saying that a stock exchange is not only an essential aid to entrepreneurs as they try to evaluate capital investments but also, as Mises said, *the* defining feature of capitalism. Among the institutions that the price system needs so as to fulfill its coordinating function, says Lachmann (p. 68), are futures markets and a stock market. His understanding of the stock market differs from Keynes's to the extent that, for the latter, "when the capital development of a country becomes a by-product of the activities of a casino, the job is likely to be ill-done" (quoted on page 69, from Keynes's *General Theory*, page 159). For Lachmann, the stock market, coupled with the futures market, gives a better indication of expected asset prices. Lachmann finds Keynes oblivious to the knowledge-transmission function performed by the stock market in general, and to intertemporal transmission in particular (p. 71).

The profound philosophical implications of the way in which value is formed and understood in society were well perceived by Lachmann and, it would seem to me, totally ignored by Keynes.

More than that, in the mid-twentieth-century academic debates, the entrepreneur was nowhere to be seen. In this sense, Lachmann's book was revolutionary. His understanding of the relation between the individual and the social structure went against the accepted wisdom of his time, not only in economics but in the social sciences in general.

Lachmann's point about an entrepreneur's individual agency is well highlighted by his rejection of a static definition of capital structure, such as Hicks's. He also calls "structural maladjustment" the inconsistent changes in capital in which the coincidence of expectations fails to happen thanks to personal factors, such as stubbornness, or institutional factors, such as "certain forms of Patent Law" (Lachmann, 2007: 61). Meanwhile, first among the forces bringing consistency to expectations is the price system. But since prices only indirectly "translate" supply and demand, "the transmission is often delayed and sometimes faulty" (p. 62), which is why we often end up with those "structural maladjustments."

The book is not only against Keynes, though. Lachmann sees the individual not as a passive pawn in the structure, but as taking the initiative (changing the plan). In this sense, the book was truly revolutionary vis-à-vis all of the social sciences. It was a project launched not only against Keynes but against neo-Marxians, Comteans, and Durkheim; it was against negations of individual autonomy in psychology and philosophy, to name two disciplines.

A basic Lachmannian correction of mainstream economics is his attack on the mainstream thinkers' assumption of equilibrium and homogeneity—their assumption that all individuals' plans are coordinated.

At the same time, not much attention was paid by the mainstream economists of that time to the reality of the individuals' interactions or to the institutional framework under which they interacted, which, for Lachmann, are considered natural requirements of any description of economic reality. On page 41, for instance, he argues that classical economists assume, without explicitly acknowledging, an institutional safeguard to assure interpersonal consistency: the bankruptcy court, through which economic agents who are unable to conciliate costs and prices are expelled from the market.

The immensely important ontological contributions of Austrian economists, Lachmann foremost among them, center around their emphasis on the structure of capital, which is composed of heterogeneous goods that can only operate in complementarity with one another, and on how that complementarity is perceived at both subjective and intersubjective levels.

On that point, we may highlight that Lachmann differentiates a "financing stage" in which homogeneous capital in some monetary form is raised, from the production-plan stage, which implies the allocation of capital in a heterogeneous form (Lachmann, 2007: 36). One instance in which the "financing stage" represents the soundness of a capital plan may be seen, says Lachmann, in the reserves of capital that firms keep for contingencies. He argues that the supplementary character of those reserves, their quantitative feature, allows a third party to assess the success of the firm just by looking at the level of such reserves (p. 42). Each capital plan requires some different amount of working capital and the soundness of the plan is reflected in its financial statements.

Furthermore, Lachmann defines "money capital" as not part of capital in order to avoid double counting. By "money capital" he means the monetary resources needed to pay for the regular operation of the plant. However, the "cash reserves" should be considered as any other reserve, as part of the firm's capital (p. 43).

Another instance in which Lachmann implicitly assumes that the capital plan of a firm is represented in its financial "stage" may be found in his discussion of investment portfolios, such as when he writes: "Where action has to be taken in such a way as to safeguard the future control of productive resources without as yet making detailed plans for the future, there arises the complementarity of the Investment Portfolio which refers not to the productive resources as such, but to the titles to their control, not to operating assets but to securities" (p. 55). With that, Lachmann not only explains the relation between securities and "operating assets" (they are titles to their control) but also elucidates that there are many forms of complementarity, since that is a "praxeological category."

If the heterogeneity and complementarity of the capital structure and the indirect way in which capital is evaluated by economic agents go without acknowledgment, an economic theory obfuscates the reality it is trying to explain. Lachmann points out (p. 37), for example, that capital accumulation is not the only factor leading to progress; changes in technology and the division of labor are also important. Anyone who treats capital accumulation as identical to progress is bound to disregard malinvestments. Moreover, the cause of those possible losses are unexpected changes in the most adequate uses of capital goods, which, I argue, are caused by (among other reasons) deficient knowledge, as should be taken into account by a realistic Capital Theory.

Once entrepreneurs became aware that changes in the most adequate uses of capital goods would be warranted, they would move to reset their capital plans. For Lachmann, what he calls "capital regrouping" helps us separate "idle" and "active" money, which distinction is relevant to understand a shortcoming of the Keynesian theory of money (p. 50). For Lachmann, if a firm takes out a loan or uses its capital reserves to buy a new capital good, either one makes the money "active." If the firm buys an existing piece of equipment, that money has not generated new production and, in this sense, remains "idle." Because Keynesian money theory is a theory of equilibrium and considers capital as homogeneous, it does not perceive this distinction.

Furthermore, a firm's cash balance is determined by its "cash preference," according to Keynes, while the need for regrouping its capital may be the determinant of those changes. In this particular instance, however, I understand that there is a difference between ordering a new piece of equipment and buying an existing one. But I do not see that as explaining the difference between "idle" and "active" money. After all, the "existing" equipment is now put back in production, whereas it was risking becoming scrap.

Also the "cash balance" is, of course, influenced by the operational needs of the firm. If it needs to sell or buy a new piece of equipment to remain competitive, this will affect its cash balance; but one cannot say that the reasons for keeping cash balances are not there anymore only because some of the reasons happened, and part of the cash balance has already been used. It could be that the distinction between "idle" and "active" money could best be explained by the use to which a certain amount of capital, in the form of money, is devoted in the plan.[5]

In the end, the call for realism in Capital Theory is the recognition, ignored by mainstream economics, of a world full of incompatible plans—a world in which capital combinations have to be recomposed every day because the capital structure is continuously being composed and broken. By using process analysis, Lachmann says (p. 41), we are able to perceive the dynamic process by which firms allocate their capital resources.

A concrete example of how such process analysis would help us develop a more realistic understanding of the economic process in general, and capital allocation in particular, we may find in his statement that "idle capacity" is the amount of unused capital goods that, becoming idle under a firm's restructuring, the owners still do not want to sell as scrap (which is what the "worst scenario" strategy would recommend, p. 49). The question for Lachmann, then, is not only why those pieces of capital were not put to their originally intended use but why another alternative use was not found for them. According to Lachmann, one possible explanation is that the cost of complementary capital became momentarily more expensive (p. 50).

One topic that we will not discuss in this section but will discuss later in this work is the extent to which capital allocation has become increasingly dictated by political influence in the United States—not only by the political agendas pursued by, for example, pension fund managers and investment managers, but also directly by the government. Such *dirigisme* may be seen both at the national level, with the Federal Reserve acting as a "central planner," and at the state level. Such experiments in "financial repression" (the political allocation of credit) brought an enormous waste of resources in Latin America, and it is sad to see it becoming conspicuous in the United States. A proper understanding of why capital investments directed by political considerations usually end badly is greatly helped by Lachmann's concept of capital structure, for he helps us make great strides in accounting for "consistent capital change and therefore economic progress" (p. 71).

Capital Structure, Asset Structure, and the Meaning of Economic Progress

Chapters V and VI of *Capital and Its Structure* can tell us about changes in the capital structure when the economy expands. Lachmann provides insight on the ramifications of viewing capital as the entrepreneur does, on what happens to the capital structure when capital is accumulated, and the role of a stock market in promoting "consistent capital change."

We must note at the outset that, for Lachmann, the accumulation of capital does not happen through replicating the same capital goods, but through the adding of new capital goods, which will result in a different composition of goods in the capital structure—one that is supposed to be more productive. More than that, new capital makes some of the old capital unproductive; capital may lose value without being physically destroyed.

Lachmann infers from this that it is wrong to say that new capital investments will lower the "marginal efficiency of capital" when in reality it will destroy the value of some less productive forms of existing capital (p. 80). Highlighting one of the main insights of Austrian economics, we may mention that the pressure of diminishing returns can only be resisted by changing the composition of capital, by learning better ways to produce things. In that sense, we can acknowledge that, while the accumulation of capital always destroys some capital, such destruction is merely a by-product of economic growth—a process that may be better understood as one of increased knowledge.

Another related insight from Austrian economics, one that is often misunderstood, is the relation between time and productivity. It may be said that there are three dimensions of capital: quantity, value, and time. However, time is not productive by itself; and labor is not necessarily productive just because it takes more time.

We only consider longer production processes if they are more productive, or as Böhm-Bawerk always qualifies, if we make "wisely chosen" investments; so sometimes it pays to engage in a lengthier production process, but not always. Lachmann considers Böhm-Bawerk on what the typical changes to the capital structure would be once capital accumulation is going on: "that the 'period of production' increases and causes an increase in output per man-hour." This, Lachmann deems an oversimplification. He does not accept Böhm-Bawerk here and challenges the thesis of higher productivity of "roundabout production" (p. 73). For Lachmann, Böhm-Bawerk's answer is deficient because his framework is neither completely static nor dynamic. For

Böhm-Bawerk, "roundaboutness is not a form of technical progress"; still, progress happens in a predictable way by capital accumulation, in a process similar Smith's division of labor (in which capital became more specialized and complex). In other words, Smith and Böhm-Bawerk may share a conception of the economy as an "evenly rotating economy." Lachmann explains that Böhm-Bawerk's theory is only valid when it is possible to invest capital and avoid diminishing returns; therefore, "higher roundabout productivity" will occur only when "a higher degree of division of capital" is permitted (p. 82). The "stages of maturity" in Böhm-Bawerk's thesis is one more element of compatibility with his own theory according to Ludwig Lachmann.

Note that it was with this idea (of considering longer production processes only when they are more productive) in mind that Irving Fisher first suggested the idea of assessing capital as the present value of the productive process in which it is applied. That leads us to the relevance of time for production. Lachmann tries to figure out whether interest rates are "real" or "monetary," and his answer is an attempt to make compatible a "neo-Wicksellian" theory of interest with chapter 17 of Keynes's *General Theory* (pp. 222–224, "The essential properties of interest and money") by beginning from a barter economy, in which "the rate of interest is the overall rate of exchange of present for future goods. It is thus an intertemporal exchange rate . . . [that] Wicksell had in mind when he spoke of 'the natural rate of interest.'" (Lachmann, 2007: 75)

That is why, incidentally, Lachmann considers it unreasonable to expect negative commodity interest rates to occur (p. 77-8). Once we move away from barter, "The money rate of interest will have to adjust itself to the overall commodity rate of intertemporal exchange" (page 76). Lachmann says that the Cambridge economist Piero Sraffa understood that, for Wicksell, the "natural rate" was an average of "actual" rates, while "in Keynes' system, by contrast, an over-all commodity rate does exist: the marginal efficiency of capital" (p. 77). A related insight worth mentioning is that for Lachmann, "the distribution of money holdings cannot be adequately explained by the 'liquidity preference,'" (p. 89), which seems fine as far as it goes. You cannot fully explain money holdings without it, either.

The questions Lachmann asked regarding the relation between capital structure and asset structure were whether there are other complementarities besides those arising from the heterogeneous nature of physical capital goods; and if there are, how might they correlate with the complementary nature of capital goods in the physical world. That is, Lachmann questions whether there is "an asset structure of which the forms of [physical] capital" comprise some of but not all of its elements (p. 87).

In such a structure, money deserves special attention. He already said that variations in cash balance are a good measure of economic success, but that does not explain the difference. For Lachmann, money "is not a capital good like other elements of a production plan." I would argue that it is a fallacy to say that to avoid double counting, money should not be counted as a capital good because it pays for the goods used in production. Lachmann, it seems, does not take into consideration his own qualification that you need a certain margin to deal with changes and, even more important, you need a certain amount to pay for the flow of goods, for advances made to labor, rents, and inputs. That quotient of circulating capital is also capital. In the end, he accounts for that fact by calling money a "proxy" for actual goods and services (p. 88), that is, whatever amount of cash balance the entrepreneur deems necessary to have is also part of the plan.

Lachmann's proposal is to develop a "theory of business finance" based on his knowledge of how entrepreneurs react to change (p. 89). He first distinguishes between operating assets and securities (p. 90). Among operating assets, there are first-line assets (fixed capital), second-line assets (revolving capital), and reserve assets (supplementary capital to be used in case of unexpected needs). The securities category he divides into debt and equity (p. 91). That is necessary to understand the "control structure" and explain how ownership and control are related.

Next, as a continuation of what we said earlier about the centrality of liquid secondary markets to capital instruments—that is, stock markets as a defining feature of an open society—let us highlight the last resort that shareholders have against managers when the latter do not perform as expected: The former sell their shares. That mechanism, a market for corporate control, is a feature of capital markets that leads to a "closer" representation of capital goods in the capital asset structure. However, it can only work this way under a given institutional framework of economic liberty—that is, a framework that allows for entrepreneurial freedom. Free markets, in this context, operate as a selection mechanism of productive processes and entrepreneurs. We may compare it to guests at a hotel: there are always some, but they not always the same.

We are able now to see how Lachmann integrates the two threads discussed so far (the relation between new and old capital goods, and the differences between the capital structure and the asset structure). He elaborates three kinds of structure: the "plan structure," which is "based on technical complementarity," the "control structure," which is "based on high and low gear of the company's capital," and the "portfolio structure," which is "based on people's asset preference" (p. 91). The core idea here is that the feasibility of any physical plan of production depends on the willingness of investors to acquire the securities that represent that plan.

Lachmann says that the three structures are integrated into an "over-all asset structure" and that such integration becomes possible only through the transmission of knowledge; money payments or the expectation of such payments are an important part of such transmission of knowledge (p. 92).

Lachmann explains further by saying that capital gains and losses are representations of the success or failure of given production plans (p. 94).

He warns us that securities do not represent only operating assets; there is a more complex network of interwoven relations, and even a pyramid of assets (p. 96) (a topic we will have an opportunity to delve into in Part V, with the presentation of the RTC model). With the three levels of plans, Lachmann calls our attention to the notion that, in the modern corporation, control and ownership are separate. He says this notion represents a "praxeological misconception" (p. 97), and clarifies by saying that the stockowners, even if they do not bother to confront the managers they oppose, still constrain the managers' actions by selling their stocks (p. 98). As already mentioned, the liquidity that secondary markets offer is essential to balance the power of shareholders and managers, which nowadays is so tilted in favor of managers.

An interesting insight from Lachmann is that a capital structure's becoming more and more complex may lead to its increased fragility, in some respects. For me, the more complex economic relations are, the more dependent on sophisticated institutional arrangements they are. More complexity may lead to more specificity of some capital goods, and that is the source of the greater fragility.

For Lachmann, there is no progress without the pressure for change. A corollary is that without the role of the entrepreneur in bringing about coordination, there is no civilized society. Opponents of a free market reject the normativity of the voluntary arrangements as justifying the outcomes of the spontaneous order. They say that the outcomes—for instance, inequality, environmental degradation, injustice—are bad, and therefore we cannot leave individuals to act without regard to consequences and must override the open society. It is only the realization that without free markets, civilization is at risk—as I hope I have demonstrated with these discussions on capital—that can challenge the prevailing moral judgments informing interventionist political decisions.

As a conclusion, Lachmann tells us something that to me sounds like common sense: that more sophisticated economies are more dependent on the sophisticated arrangements allowed by sensible institutions. Among these we can think of the good money of the early Roman Empire, which led to a degree of economic sophistication that the less adequate monies of the late Empire did not allow.

Capital in the Trade Cycle

Finally, what did Lachmann understand the "business cycle" to be? How does his definition play into the discussion at hand? Are investments equally relevant to explaining all forms of business cycles?

To answer these questions, we look to *Capital and Its Structure*, Chapter VII. An important insight to be found in this last chapter of the book is that, for Austrian economists such as Lachmann, there is no direct application of Say's Law of Markets (that production creates its own demand) as it is commonly understood. In a monetary economy, there is some wiggle room for the remuneration of factors that do not quite match the supply of available goods in the market without some friction.

So in a monetary economy, production and consumption are not directly related. This creates the conditions for monetary disequilibrium and business cycles, with the part of cycle theory that Lachmann is most interested in—maladjustments in the structure of production (p. 101)—of particular import. He underlined its significance by writing, regarding Hicks's Cycle Theory, that "a theory of investment without a theory of capital . . . is very much like Hamlet without the Prince" (p. 102). While for Keynes, the trade cycle is basically a fluctuation in the utilization of existing resources that Keynes deems homogeneous (p. 111), the Austrian Business Cycle Theory (says Lachmann) takes into consideration not only maladjustments between savings and investments but also the very structure of production (p. 114).

This contrast takes on added importance when we realize that Lachmann and Schumpeter are very close in their ideas about "creative destruction," or the tearing up and redoing of capital plans that, again, cannot work without some friction. Unexpected change is part of the system. Every day the plan is torn up and devised anew. Our task is to go into the mind of the entrepreneur and see how he deals with this constant change. For Lachmann, the entrepreneur is an epistemological agent, and the Austrian theory of expectations is a theory of the entrepreneur. To produce the best results possible, this epistemological process requires free markets, since "where prices, wages and rates of interest are inflexible, investment decisions, to a large extent have to be made in the dark" (p. 116).

Lachmann here underlines one particular price as the most important for economic coordination: interest rates (p. 124), to which I would add (in an open economy with a foreign sector) exchange rates. However close Lachmann's and Schumpeter's ideas, they are not identical. The former's idea of capital structure is similar to Schumpeter's in that it is in disequilibrium, but a disequilibrium does not, for Lachmann, disrupt any previously existing equilibrium. The structure of production is the sum of all the different individual plans of production, which are not necessarily compatible, and although there is no mechanism in the market to prevent incompatibility, the market does continuously eliminate inconsistencies over time (Lewin, 1996: 120).

That is not to say that Austrian economists like Lachmann reject Say's Law; only that, for them, the market may have endogenous forces that operate in large swings, and monetary "disequilibrium" is in part responsible for that, which is why Lachmann wants to have a discussion about monetary policy. He writes that "any sudden and unexpected change in the 'real situation' will probably affect the demand and the velocity of circulation of money" (p. 119). Furthermore, considering that for Lachmann, when plans need to be changed, what guides the changes is changes in the profitability of alternative uses (that is, a matter of relative not absolute scarcity [p. 120]), a "severe" or less accommodative monetary policy would help that adjustment to happen.

According to Mises, other reasons that frictions exist are that, while Say's Law applies to the market as a whole, specialization requires us to learn what other people want. From there comes not only a structure of production in which most investment plans are made compatible but also civilization and shared values.

Another relevant point in the final chapter of *Capital and Its Structure* is that one of the main reasons to study Capital Theory is to better understand how business cycles occur. They do not repeat themselves, for if all business cycles had the same cause or causes, economic agents would have learned what they were, and henceforth we would not have business cycles. The fact is that each business cycle is different from previous ones. To the extent that economic theory does not recognize the heterogeneity and complementarity of the capital structure, and treats capital as a homogeneous quantity, any policy designed merely to restore macroeconomic aggregate magnitudes will fail if it does not also aim to reshuffle the capital structure. Lachmann concludes that although public deficits would help in a crisis, it is only the acknowledgment by the owner that he has more profitable uses for his capital that can put the economy back on a path of growth; public policies should help that happen (p. 126).

In the end, trying to assess the main theme of the book, we may conclude that it is an anti-Keynesian story, and that it is about entrepreneurship—and that these two stories are not incompatible.

The Compositive School and the Classical School

Let us now pull back to situate Lachmann in the history of economic thought about capital, and then in the Austrian tradition, with the assistance of Peter Lewin. In describing the course on capital that Lachmann taught undergraduates in South Africa, Lewin argues that, for Lachmann, Smith was the precursor of the "compositive" school while Ricardo was the first in the "classical" school. Although Böhm-Bawerk was a disciple of Menger's, he diverged from him. Smith, Hayek, and Lachmann were from the "composite" school while Böhm-Bawerk, and later Joan Robinson, were from the Ricardian, classical school (Lewin, 1996: 110).

A difference between Lachmann and the neoclassical synthesis derives from this composite approach. Substitution and complementarity are, under Lachmann's dynamic analysis, unlike substitution and complementarity in static neoclassical equilibrium. For Lachmann, capital goods are complementary when they are all part of a successful production plan. The concept of substitution enters the picture once the production plan fails, in total or in part, and some goods need to be excluded from, added to, or replaced in the plan of production. In addition, the capital goods that can be regrouped without losing value are the ones retaining the attribute of "multiple specificity" (Lewin, 1996: 118).

To grasp the meaning of such a distinction, it may be useful to follow Lewin's transcription of Professor Lachmann's "Short Course in Capital Theory" (Lewin, 1996: 124). The course was centered around the idea that, although the border between financial and non-financial capital is clear-cut, that between capital accumulation and economic development (growth) is not.

Lachmann delineated for his students two schools of thought in regard to capital. The classical one, associated with Ricardo as I said, is mostly concerned with how returns on capital are distributed. The classicals pay little attention to the composition of capital, but a lot to capital stock; not much to capital per se, but a lot to the rate of profits (rate of interest) and rate of return. The votaries of the compositive school, aside from their interest in the stock of capital and its total return, are primarily focused on why capital, perceived as a heterogeneous collection of goods, is grouped the way it is in each of the individual plans of production.

The "measuring of capital" comes next. Lachmann believed it could be measured if it were in equilibrium, but since that condition does not exist, it cannot be measured. It cannot be measured because its evaluation is subjective; it is heterogeneous; and its future rate of return is unknown. Lachmann says that Hicks accepts that capital is heterogeneous but, like the GDP, it can be measured in price terms. Lachmann dissents from this. For me, as I have said, the purpose of having an aggregate for capital or for national accounts may be satisfied with a number that is "good enough"—or at least with a number to which mutations can be compared. I am not saying that it is a perfect representation of reality, but it may be a good enough representation of reality (realism without precision).

In historical terms, Lachmann writes that the composite school is older, since the mercantilists would prefer industry to agriculture—that is, would prefer one composition of the stock of capital more than others. The development of Capital Theory starts with Adam Smith, with capital's being described as homogeneous, static, and existing in an agrarian and poor society in which the capital is only "corn"; it is basically a "subsistence fund theory."

Next, Lachmann describes Ricardo's theory as developed in an industrial context. Ricardo thought that with his "labor theory of value" he had managed to make compatible and commensurable all heterogeneous forms of capital, as Smith had done in the simpler, agrarian context. Ricardo's answer to the problem of allocation of capital versus labor is to define a homogenous "rate of profits" measured, as is anything else, in hours of labor (Lachmann, 2007: 133). Contemplating these two schools serves our purposes, allowing us as it does to ponder why the idea of representation is so important. The heterogeneous capital goods once represented in financial instruments can more easily be measured in monetary terms, although the financial instruments are also heterogeneous.

According to Lewin, the most important Austrian capital theorist was the author of the magisterial (a three-volume work from the 1880s) *Capital and Interest*, Eugen von Böhm-Bawerk. Hayek's 1941 *Pure Theory of Capital*, which was an attempt to complete Böhm-Bawerk's project, addressed intertemporal production issues in conditions of equilibrium. Hayek intended to produce a second volume to address capital in dynamic conditions of disequilibrium but never wrote it. Lachmann, Hayek's student and colleague at the London School of Economics, came out with *Capital and Its Structure* in 1956, and in its 1978 edition declared that almost no advances had been made since 1941—with the exception of Kirzner's 1966 "An Essay on Capital" (Lewin, 1996: 107). In the tradition of Austrian economics, the retreat from Böhm-Bawerk's classical objectivism in regard to capital started, according to Lachmann, with Hayek's reply to Knight in 1936 (Lewin, 1996: 107).

Let us now address how Lachmann describes Böhm-Bawerk's contribution to Capital Theory. The latter distinguishes manmade capital from original factors. That is why he asks why rents and wages do not comprise what he calls interests (which we should understand as "profits"). Under Böhm-Bawerk's assumptions, there are three reasons for that. The first two deal with the scarcity of capital and the third with the price that borrowers are willing to pay. Different expectations about the availability of goods in the future as compared to the present determine an adjustment of those expectations at the margin, through the introduction of an interest rate. However, Böhm-Bawerk is dealing with a static economy, and in that context, Lachmann cannot see how a future stream of income could be higher than at the beginning of the series, even if people are accumulating capital.

Here, an interesting question arises: Methodologically, a static equilibrium means that all other factors are constant; therefore an increase in capital will not increase the return on capital, it will only generate diminishing marginal returns. On the other hand, in reality, even absent technological leaps, the sheer accumulation of capital makes society more productive and increases the income derived from capital.

Lachmann's critique of Böhm-Bawerk runs as follows:

(1) "There is a temporal division of wants." Some people will save more and some people will save less than they need for the future; therefore, a positive interest rate should not emerge under those static conditions.

(2) Böhm-Bawerk argues that there is a psychological law that makes people save less than they need to. He was criticized for assuming that most people are not rational. Lachmann was among those critics; for him, again, there is no reason to assume a positive rate of interest under those conditions.

(3) "On the whole, capital is productive." Because better instruments can increase human productivity applied to the original factors, it makes sense to pay people to produce those instruments; however, they need to survive while producing both the means to produce consumer goods and while producing the consumer goods properly, which is the ultimate goal of economic activity.

That is again a "subsistence fund" kind of theory, for Lachmann. He says that Böhm-Bawerk tries to measure capital in terms of time: If you have an output of 2 units after using 10 units of labor, you have produced goods valuing 5 units of labor each in the average time of production of your cycle; therefore the capital stock is the capacity to support the 10 labor units for the average period of production, and any increase in the average period of production would need an increase in the capital stock (Lewin, 1996: 135).

Lewin recalls no reference to Menger in Professor Lachmann's course. It would nonetheless be important for us in this assessment of the Austrian theory of capital to take into consideration Menger's contributions to the idea of capital in disequilibrium. It is clear from *Capital and Its Structure* that Lachmann does not deem Menger to be part of the compositive school initiated by Smith with the Smithian insight about the division of labor. On the other hand, Lachmann finds Menger insufficiently clear in rejecting the Ricardian/classical school that intends to explain capital in terms of its size; this despite that Menger pioneered the study of capital in terms of a time structure of capital goods, and, in this sense, provided a good departure point for the study of capital (Lewin, 1996: 111).

Menger surely is a good departing point, if for no other reason than his subjectivism. Lewin quotes Menger (1871: 150) as saying that the value of capital goods is derived from the price fetched in the market for the low-order goods you can produce with them. If those prices fall, the value of the capital goods will fall to their next-best marginal use (Skousen, 1990: 19).

For Lewin, this is Menger anticipating Lachmann's "multiple specificity" notion, suggesting a strong link between the structure of production and the structure of consumption, and the source of what would later become known as Lachmann's radical subjectivism (Lewin, 1996: 113).

Lachmann's subjectivism is also seen when he points out the need to view investment decisions in light of the whole life of the investment—that is, the need to consider both profits and depreciation. Hours of labor invested in the equipment are not relevant to depreciation; only the subjective evaluations of what the investment can earn matter; and that is the weakness of Ricardo's theory. Ricardo tried and failed to apply the short-term (one-year) approach that Smith used with an agrarian economy to the industrial context. Expectations about the future were important, and missing from Ricardian theory; however, in differentiating (as a matter of degree) fixed from working capital, Ricardo was, according to Lachmann/Lewin, the first to pay attention to time in regard to production (Lewin, 1996: 134).

Another departure that Lachmann and his disciples took from Böhm-Bawerk we may find precisely there, in the treatment of time. For Lewin, the "average time of production" with which Böhm-Bawerk hoped to transform a collection of different capital goods into a single "stock" is a failed attempt because the time that matters is the one in the mind of each entrepreneur. My understanding here is that both measurements make sense in their different contexts. It is one thing for Böhm-Bawerk to say that there is an "average time of production," and changes in that time may indicate important changes in the structure of production. It is another thing to say that what matters for each entrepreneur in the making of a business decision is the time he thinks it will take to produce final goods with the piece of capital he is considering.

Lewin sides with Lachmann against Böhm-Bawerk: To come up with an "average time of production," it would be necessary to have a static economy and more knowledge than it would be possible to get about each entrepreneur. I tend to agree, if what you want is a precise number; but I think that for the purposes of identifying changes in the structure of production, approximation would be good enough, and a valuable tool for understanding where the economy is going (Lewin, 1996: 115).

To illustrate the problems with Böhm-Bawerk's conception of time of production, Lewin brings in the example I touched on before, of a forest in which each year new trees are planted to replace the ones felled to produce wood. According to Clark's critique of Böhm-Bawerk (Clark, 1893: 313), that would represent an "average time of production of zero" and add nothing to our understanding of capital or the decision to grow the forests in the first place.

I disagree with this analysis. The average time of production in this example is tremendously important not only to evaluate the return generated by the investment in the forest but also to weigh prospective investments in forests in the future. If this forest had, for example, 800 hectares and the average time of production (the time needed for a tree to grow to its optimum cutting size) were twenty years, then the amount of wood produced each year would be the wood produced in 40 hectares. On the other hand, if the average time of production were twenty-five years, then the amount of wood produced would be the wood produced from 32 hectares per year. This difference, of either a 5 percent or a 4 percent return per year, would make a huge difference in assessing the present value of this particular forest and the value of investing in any similar forest (Lewin, 1996: 116).

As we can see from this example, the entrepreneur assures complementarity of resources inside each production plan, while the market takes care of complementarity of the structure of production (Lewin, 1996: 121). Since the plans most compatible with other entrepreneurs' plans are the ones likely to survive, the entrepreneur has a say about the plan he puts together. Keeping that in mind, he is also responsible for the complementarity of his plan with the overall market—although he may be wrong in that regard, since he does not have complete information and is not immune to error. In any case, "The capital structure changes by capital gains and losses," as we have already mentioned, and here reiterate that, for Lachmann, capital gains and losses are the main direct cause of changes in the capital structure (Lewin, 1996: 121).

Lachmann and Lewin comment on Böhm-Bawerk's concept of time by quoting Clark and Knight. For them, the Böhm-Bawerk's model has either infinite or zero period of production, and the entire idea of the period of production is a mistake because production and consumption occur simultaneously; and lastly, the increases in productivity have nothing to do with the passage of time. In principle, I disagree with these criticisms. It seems to me that for analytical purposes, it makes sense to think in terms of a period of production. Nor does it seem accurate to say that, for Böhm-Bawerk, the period of production is either infinite or zero. That is not what he describes. (The mathematical model could be interpreted that way, but if that is the case, the problem is with the mathematical model, not with Böhm-Bawerk's theory.) Finally, Böhm-Bawerk's conception of time of production seems a good approximation of the impact of capital accumulation in terms of gains of productivity. It is not perfect, perhaps it is not complete, but it is useful to understanding the operations of capital in the economy (Lewin, 1996: 140).

Lachmann and Lewin use Knight's criticism to restate the essence of Böhm-Bawerk's theory. They reject the relevance of Knight's criticism but say that we should stop talking about period of production as Böhm-Bawerk's does, and start talking about investment period (Lewin, 1996: 141). To salvage Böhm-Bawerk's theory, since he thinks that it is an oversimplification to express variations in capital using only time, Lachmann proposes that, instead of using "period of production," we should consider changes in the stock of capital to be changes in the "degree of complexity." Capital accumulation does not lead to the extension of the period of production, but to an increase in the degree of its complexity.

Lachmann (2007: 79) says that, as for Smith, the division of labor is the source of greater productivity, so we could apply the same reasoning to increases in capital. Capital should specialize in order to result in greater productivity. Böhm-Bawerk (and Menger) uses the concept of "stages of production," which better reflects the added complexity of more roundabout forms of production. However, there is a caveat in Lachmann about increased complexity: It makes the economy more vulnerable. I agree that the greater the complexity, the greater the vulnerability of social arrangements, the more sensitive they are to changes. For Lewin, capital becomes more complex in the sense that it requires and applies more knowledge (Lewin, 1996: 151).

In any case, the most important implication of Lachmann's disequilibrium approach is that any capital accumulation implies a changing capital structure. Capital accumulation is not simply more capital doing the same things. The addition of capital is associated with new technologies. I would note that, to some extent (not always), new capital may be "simply" doing more of the same. A concrete example of that is new construction, new homes, and new apartment buildings. Lachmann's views on capital, Kirzner's views on entrepreneurship, and Hayek's views on information blend "nicely" and yield important insights for assessing "investment policy," Lewin rightly says (Lewin, 1996: 123).

There is much here to ponder in the way that Lachmann correlates capital accumulation and technological change, and the way he links economic development and capital specialization. I do not dispute that there is a correlation in general between capital accumulation and more complex forms of production, or that economic progress is accompanied by capital accumulation. But neither do I reject the possibility of having simply more of the same—in other words, that you can have progress just by adding new capital in the way you have been combining capital without technological leaps, as already noted.

Lachmann also links the increased vulnerability of more complex structures of production to the time necessary for the complementarity to happen (Lewin, 1996: 155). An example of that is the "Just in time" forms of logistical arrangements, wherein supply lines are inflexible and there is little wiggle room for disruptions in them. The calculation here is that disruptions will be rare, and so what you economize in inventories will cover the risks of them happening. In that regard, Lachmann and Lewin also raise the question of whether more complexity always implies more vulnerability; they answer that it depends on the case. I think that, in principle, more complex structures of production are more vulnerable to disruptions in the sense that second-best combinations of factors cannot match the higher level of productivity. On the other hand, those second-best combinations may be more available and with recourse to them, total a breakdown of production is less likely. So while "deeper" reservoirs of capital would make the society and the economy more resilient and able to absorb strong shocks, the complexity of the arrangements in place would mean that small changes in the environment would more likely disrupt the existing level of higher productivity.

As this review of the literature draws to a close, let us review the topics it has sought to address: What aspect of the real side of the economy is the concept of capital in the monetary side of the economy supposed to represent? Why is it important to the good functioning of a market economy for that representation to be accurate? What may hinder that adequate representation?

It goes without saying that one does not need to agree with Lachmann to benefit from his insights. For instance, Lachmann, Lewin, and Schackle seem to believe that it is not possible, except in war, for a complex society to destroy capital (Lewin, 1996: 156). I strongly disagree. What we see nowadays in Europe and the United States is exactly that; and the ways in which the destruction of capital takes place today is reflected in financial markets—a key application of the ideas proposed in the present work.

This lengthy analysis of Lachmann's contribution to our understanding of capital structure will help us in exploring Capital Theory, its social relevance due to its relation to economic development, its scientific relevance (given its power to explain the workings of a market economy), and finally, the rhetorical uses that such knowledge allows in defending the ideal of a free society.

NOTES

1. Such view is a more sophisticated one than the one that sees Austrian Capital Theory as divided between two groups, a majority that sees capital "in a physical way," and a minority (Menger and Mises) who sees capital "partly or totally" as "financial capital"; a vision for which there is no discussion of the concept of representation (see, for instance, Braun et al., 2016: 2).

2. Menger considers an antonomasia the classification as "product" or "capital" of anything in nature in which labor has been invested, that is, just the use of archetypes (2007: 193). For Menger, contra Adam Smith's tripartite framework, an economic good of any kind may become capital (2007: 197). We will not elaborate here on disagreements between Menger and Smith about what is properly deemed capital. Suffice it to say here that Menger did not believe Smith to be mistaken, exactly, but that after all, Smith's only goal was to add a third factor (capital) to those existing in his time (production of land and labor), not to lay out an entire theory of capital (2007: 201).

3. An interesting aspect of *Böhm-Bawerk on property rights is that he calls* ownership a "full and present power of control over tangible goods" to be distinguished from partial rights, and the latter he splits in two: (1) those that, although they are rights to present use, offer "rights to partial utilization," such as emphyteusis and servitudes, and (2) those that "apply to the future proceeds to be derived from goods," such as a mutuum (p. 65). It will be assumed later in this work, when I take up the RTC in detail, that the bundle of different rights in which property consists is essentially the same in all circumstances. I am using this simplifying assumption for the sake of presentation to readers, but they should always keep in mind that the reality is more complex, as we can observe here with this discussion about partial rights.

4. Yet consider, for example, that the economy of China today seems not to have been bogged down in the same quagmire, and the accumulated results of different growth rates will become evident as the years go by, if this trend continuous. The reasons for that are worth exploring, and I would argue that property rights over there offer broader freedom of action to its owners than in most Western societies nowadays and offer "good enough" protection to create the proper incentives to enterprise. However, an exploration of this hypothesis goes well beyond the scope of this work.

5. While this seems to me a key distinction to make, the present work is not the place to flesh this out, although I am certain that Lachmann's distinction is not satisfactory.

Part II

Chapter 3

The Reification of Capital, the Representational Theory of Capital and Its Model

The goal of this book is to present my ideas about representing, on the abstract side of the economy, capital as it exists on the real side, and to offer a model of what this "Representational Theory of Capital" (RTC) consists in. As I have said, that financial instruments are property titles representing claims over real goods is an uncontroversial statement at the microeconomic level. What I would convince readers of is that such a concept of representation helps our understanding at a macroeconomic level, as well.

An interesting insight about money in society is that it is just a veil covering the actual economy—in other words, that there are actual goods and services in the real world, and there is a monetary side that in one way or another represents, in an abstract form, some of the things that exist on the real side of the economy. We can discuss the reasons why such representation is never perfect; but we should also recognize that some forms of representation are better than others.

When I say "better" or "more accurate," in what sense? Well, better representations of what actually exists, and a representation that better serves the function those financial and monetary instruments perform for society. We may also think that some monetary institutions are not particularly designed to represent the economic realities of society, nor to fulfill the purpose for which money and financial instruments were first developed, but to serve the interests of whoever has the political power to impose such arrangements on others. Be that as it may, the fact remains that various monetary and banking arrangements will represent more accurately or less accurately stocks and flows of goods and services on the real side of the economy, and such representation has consequences in terms of the allocation of resources in the economy.

These are concerns that have already been expressed by King Juan Carlos University economist Jesús Huerta de Soto, for whom it is important to "examine in detail both the theory of capital and the productive structure of a real economy, since a clear grasp of both is essential to understanding the processes triggered in the market by bank's concessions of loans not derived from a previous increased in voluntary savings" (Huerta de Soto, 2006: 265). The dialectic nature of capital is nothing new; what we learn from Huerta de Soto is how very seldom this relation is made explicit.

After describing what human action consists in, Huerta de Soto states:

> The plan is a mental picture, conjured up by the actor, of the different future stages, elements and circumstances his action may involve. The plan is the actor's personal evaluation of the practical information he possesses and gradually discovers within the context of each action. . . . All human action is directed towards the attainment of an end, or consumer good, which can be defined as a good that directly and subjectively satisfies the needs of the human actor. (Huerta de Soto, 2006: 266)

For this author, first-order goods are the ultimate end of human action, and intermediary goods are instruments to their achievement by their application in the different stages of production, which takes time as subjectively perceived by the individual actor.

Huerta de Soto also calls attention to the importance of time: "What separates the actor from the achievement of his goal is the period of time required by the series of successive stages that compose his action process" (Huerta de Soto, 2006: 268). It seems to me that there is a link between liquidity and the time needed to mature the return of capital investments. That link may well pass through the level of certainty about the return of the investment. A capital investment that requires many stages of production yet to be completed in order to generate a consumer good as a product (a first-order good in Menger's terminology), that then needs to be sold and the sale's proceeds received, is subject to many uncertainties not only given the time required for the investment to mature but also given its possible complexity. It is only at the end of the process that the result of the investment, whether it paid off as expected, is known.

The upshot for instruments representative of property rights over the processes of production is that claims over the lengthier and more uncertain processes tend to be "close end" forms of investments, like stocks, that you cannot cash out but only resell. Also, they tend to have the feature of a "last claimant" investment—that is, once everyone else is paid, what remains of the proceeds belongs to the owner of those titles. On the other hand, shorter and less uncertain processes may well be represented by instruments which entitle their holders to cash out their investment after a certain period of time and, in many cases, at a certain rate of return, such as with fixed-income investments like corporate bonds.

In describing economic agents' purposes when they decide to engage in projects with longer maturities, Huerta de Soto states: "If the actor did not attach greater value to the results of longer actions, he would never undertake them and would opt for shorter actions instead" (Huerta de Soto, 2006: 270). Here, he highlights the subjective evaluation (as manifested by time preference) of the greater value of the result of lengthier processes of production being what leads the economic agent to choose them over shorter processes. He also notes that such greater value might be thanks to the quantity or quality of the first-order goods expected to be produced by the lengthier and/or more complex process. The "law" of time preference, says Huerta de Soto, may well date to Saint Thomas Aquinas; he quotes Aquinas' disciple Giles Lessines to support this contention (Huerta de Soto, 2006: 271, footnote 8).[1]

Next, Huerta de Soto emphasizes the teleological character of capital goods (quoting Israel Kirzner in support [2006: 272, footnote 10]). "Capital goods," he writes, "should always be placed in a teleological context, in which the essential defining elements are the aim pursued and the actor's subjective view or the stages necessary to fulfill it." For Huerta de Soto, "the economic nature of a capital good does not depend on its physical properties, but on the opinion of an actor, who believes the goodwill enable him to reach or complete a stage in his action process." His view of capital goods as part of the intermediary stages aiming toward a certain final good implies considering capital only something that is already "applied" to a given production process.

Here Huerta de Soto points to the heterogeneity and specificity of capital goods. I would not say that he is mistaken, since each production process is composed of specific capital goods, but I would argue that goods with the potential to be part of intermediary stages of production may also be capital goods, if its owner's "opinion" is that such a good may be incorporated in a production process. If a bakery has a stock of flour from which its workers may bake cakes or bread, it is difficult to say that such stock is not part of the baker's capital. If a construction company has a number of trucks that may be used to carry construction material or to tow other pieces of equipment, again, it is difficult to say that those trucks are not part of the company's capital. Things get more complicated when we think of a car in a dealership, which is part of the inventory of final goods for sale, in the mind of the dealer, but may become a capital investment to a Uber driver—or to the aforementioned bakery or construction company, if that car is used in either of those businesses.

Another example of this we can find in Smith's *Wealth of Nations*, where he distinguishes between productive and unproductive labor. It may be understood, also as paraphrased by Mathieu (1990: 167), that the same job of serving a banquet may be a consumption item for a host entertaining his guests, and a productive activity for a restaurant.

So, in the sense that anything may become a capital good once an economic agent decides to use it as part of a process to produce other goods, Huerta de Soto is right to emphasize its heterogeneity and specificity; to the extent that only goods "applied" to specific processes may be deemed capital goods, I disagree. One of the main characteristics of some forms of capital goods is this "stored" potential to produce many different things and, generally speaking, inventories of almost anything may have multiple uses, not only as instruments to produce many different final goods but even as final goods themselves, and still be part of the capital stock of a given individual or society.

How little the ontology of capital is taken into account in most treatments of capital may be seen in a recent book entitled *The Dao of Capital: Austrian Investing in a Distorted World*, in which the author Mark Spitznagel writes: "At the outset, we must think of capital in a new way, as a verb, not a noun. Rather than an inanimate asset or piece of property, it constitutes an action, a means to an end—to build, to advance, to deploy the tools and instruments of a progressing economy. Indeed, capital is a process, or a method or path—what the ancient Chinese called the Dao" (Spitznagel, 2013: xxiii). I really do not have any idea whether that is the meaning of *Dao* in ancient Chinese, but it is useful for understanding the concept to think of capital as a verb and not as a noun.

AN EXERCISE IN ABSTRACTION

Starting with Aristotle, and continuing through Smith, Mill, and countless others, the idea that money was introduced in society by convention in order to facilitate the exchange of useful goods has been a cornerstone of economic thinking. From this basic insight evolved the conceptualization of the economy as having a real and a financial side (called, in this work, the abstract side).

This dialectic understanding of the economy may be further developed so as to encompass in the abstract side all forms of property claims, not only financial instruments (or even more narrowly, just money). It is in this fully developed sense that the concept of an abstract side is understood in this work. As we will soon see, it is assumed in this work that everything that exists in the real side of the economy belongs either to someone or to no one. This statement is common knowledge for the law student, but it reveals for the student of economics the entire scope of the abstract side of the economy, and it the reason why, in this work, we are not using the "financial side," a somewhat narrow category that economists often favor.

At the highest level of generality, when it is said that everything that exists has a counterpart in the abstract side that is either represented by some property title or else included in the category of *res nullius* (the things that belong to no one), the claim seems to be that there is a direct relation between the things that exist and the property titles representing them.

That, however, only holds water at that highest level of generalization; once we move to lower levels of generalization, we encounter cases in which such relation is not a direct one.

We will have an opportunity to discuss in this work a number of cases in which the process of representation that we are positing is not a precise one. In this section, the reasons for the imprecision are introduced.

St. Thomas Aquinas in the first objection to question 85 of the *Summa Theologica* (Aquinas, 1981: 431, Volume I) argues that we may create our abstractions from our observation of concrete things or from ideal types.

So, there is one mode of abstraction—"abstraction with precision," which is generated by our observations of concrete things—and another that Rasmussen calls "abstraction without precision," generated from ideal types. This distinction is summarized by Rasmussen as follows:

> When one abstracts the form or character of something *without* precision, one does not explicitly express or specify the differentiating traits of the abstracted form or character; and the individual differences are treated as implicit, which allows them to be clearly different in each instance when they are made explicit (Rasmussen, forthcoming, page 15).

The existence of different modes of abstraction, each fulfilling a different function, gives rise to a "moderate realism," or "mild realism," as I call it in the next section, which acknowledges abstractions as a tool for cognition (Den Uyl and Rasmussen, 2016: 72).

Which kind of abstraction we are talking about in this work? Well, when we are talking about the representation of a particular, determinate piece of equipment, or a plot of land, in their respective titles, we are being extremely precise about the characteristics of the thing so represented. Meanwhile, when we are talking about the representation of claims over all the assets and liabilities of a corporation in their shares, there is a sort of indeterminacy, and we are being less precise. To speak, as I did earlier, of the representation of all things that exist in property titles, is to be very imprecise, with no determinacy other than this general claim that they are so represented. And yet, such representation does not cease to occur due to its indeterminacy. Such representation can still help us understand and act upon one aspect of the reality.

The existence of these different levels of precision, of determinacy, in our abstractions, helps explain why I will observe later in this work that the market is not a phenomenon open to Cartesian analysis (page 130).

FROM WHAT STARTING POINT?

John Searle, in his 1995 book *The Construction of Social Reality*, differentiates "brute facts," such as the atomic composition of hydrogen, "which are facts totally independent of any human opinions," from "institutional facts" that are "dependent on human agreement," which "require human institutions for their existence." However, the inquiry into "how institutional facts are possible, and what exactly is the structure of such facts" is based on the assumption that there is an objective reality independent of our minds and that true statements are those that correspond to the facts (Searle, 1995: 2).

This distinction between brute and institutional facts, between the physical and chemical reality and social reality, gives context to the understanding of capital proposed in the present work.

Other, rather complementary, frameworks also deserve consideration.[2] There are, for example, the "Three Worlds" offered by Karl Popper (Popper, 1978). For Popper, the first world would be the physical world; the second would be that of our mental processes; and the third, the world of abstract "products of the human mind." Popper's main insight is that the three worlds have "real" existence to the extent that they exercise causality over one another (p. 164). The physical world has been greatly transformed by the products of human mind, such as language or scientific theories—products that came about as a consequence of human mental processes. I think that Popper's framework is compatible with Searle's, but Popper misses Searle's insight about "social facts," which would have helped him to solidify the case for the existence of "World 3" things.

What capital goods are (part of a productive process to create more goods and services) and what financial instruments are (property claims with special features that enable them to be more easily tradable than other property claims) become easier to understand if we take a longer look at Searle. As already noticed by Austrian school economist Steven Horwitz, Searle's work can help elaborate the idea of the representation of reality, especially in relation to capital.

In *The Construction of Social Reality*, Searle asks how it is possible to have an "objective world" of money, property, and other social constructs in a world "that consists entirely of physical particles in fields of force, and in which some of those particles are organized into systems that are conscious biological beast, such as ourselves" (Searle, 1995: xi). The author argues that such fundamental questions of the social sciences were not answered by the great sociologists such as Weber, Simmel, or Durkheim because they did not have the necessary tools—namely, a "theory of speech acts, of performatives, of intentionality, of collective intentionality, of rule-governed behavior, etc." (Searle, 1995: xii). For Searle, "there are portions of the real world, objective facts in the world, that are only facts by human agreement. In a sense, there are things that exist only because we believe them to exist. I am thinking of things like money, property, governments, and marriages. Yet many facts regarding these things are 'objective' facts in the sense that they are not a matter of your or my preferences, evaluations, or moral attitudes" (Searle, 1995: 1).

One need not, as Horwitz does not (Horwitz, 2009), agree with Searle's arguments as a whole or even particularly in regard to money to use his work to better understand social reality. For instance, Horwitz states that "the problem with Searle's formulation, to a Hayekian, is that institutional reality is not the direct result of anyone's intentions" (Horwitz, 2009: 80). Here, Horowitz forgets that some institutions, such as a written constitution, are the result of human design; although others, such as an unwritten constitution, fit his model of the unintended consequences of spontaneous institutional evolution as a consequence of individuals' choices.

Horowitz uses the distinction between a mere "medium of exchange" and a "generally accepted medium of exchange" to explain the distinction between intentions in Hayek and intentions in Searle. For Hayek (as for Menger) individuals simply wanted to use something as a medium of exchange in their dealings and, by the sum of their actions, that thing became a generally accepted medium of exchange, which was not part of anyone's intentions.

Further, calling attention to the limitations of Searle's requirement of "collective intentionality" for the creation of institutional facts such as money, Horowitz states: "It is not the performative that creates the reality; rather it is the process by which that practice has been accepted that creates the institutional reality. The sort of explicit performatives that Searle uses in his money example are neither necessary nor sufficient to create the institutional fact of money, and this claim holds true for institutional facts in general" (Horowitz, 2009: 81). Horowitz's acknowledgement that Searle in the example of the wall (Horwitz, 2009: 82) may be understood as accepting that "collective intentionality" may not be explicit, which solves part of the problem. But Horowitz is right to emphasize "Hayekian intentions"—that is, the consequences that are not part of anyone's conscious intentions, such as the creation of a GAMOE from the intention by each agent to have a MOE for his transactions. On the other hand, Horwitz seems to forget that there are consciously created institutional facts in open societies, such as a legal system; not all institutions are spontaneous.

Searle argues that in order to explain the ontology of social facts, we need to explain "how the existence of social facts relates to other things that exist" (Searle, 1995: 5). For that, a strong statement of "how the world is in fact" is necessary, because Searle's project is to fit his ontology of social facts into a broader general ontology. Searle argues that as much as we have doubts about the nature of the world, atomic theory and evolutionary theory are beyond dispute.

His definition of "intentionality" as "the capacity of the mind to represent objects and states of affairs in the world other than itself" is very interesting. Once the organism (living system) is conscious of the natural world, it can attribute (intentionally) the capacity of representing something else to some aspect of the natural world. Therefore, "money, property, governments and marriages" are created. Searle continues, "here, then, are the bare bones of our ontology: We live in a world made up entirely of physical particles in fields of force. Some of these are organized into systems. Some of these systems are living systems and some of these living systems have evolved consciousness. With consciousness comes intentionality, the capacity of the organism to represent objects and states of affairs in the world to itself. Now the question is, how can we account for the existence of social facts within that ontology?" (Searle, 1995: 7).

Horwitz answers that question by saying that "social facts are facts because people believe they are facts" (Horwitz, 2009: 76). For my part, I neither adopt a strict realism—which would say that "there were no Roman legions, only Roman legionnaires"—nor would I assign attributes such as feelings or thoughts to social constructs like a "Roman legion." My approach to social realities, similar to that of Horwitz, Searle, and Böhm-Bawerk, is one of mild realism in which I acknowledge the existence of social facts. Yet social realities do not exist aside from the physical world, but are part of it.[3]

A "PROPERTY RIGHTS" THEORY OF CAPITAL

As a definition, it may be stated that the RTC is a claim that bundles of goods and processes put to productive use in the real world are represented by different forms of property rights, among them financial instruments. It is, therefore, a "property rights" theory of capital, and it is based on common-sensical legal assumptions like, for instance, the ones used by Jacques Rueff to explain monetary inflation in his 1964 book *Social Order*. (However, Rueff used the concept without explicitly defining it, as in many other references in the literature.)

Clearly a notion of property rights is essential to the theory here proposed. Therefore, a brief exploration of the nature of property rights becomes a necessary step. Specifically, about the two main categories in which we may place capital—capital goods and financial instruments—it seems a good point of departure to consider whether financial instruments are an independent feature of economic life and not related to the things on the real side of the economy used to produce more goods.

After all, the idea of an interdependent analysis of a real side of the economy and a financial one in itself may be questioned. It is conceivable to see financial instruments simply as the present value of streams of revenue, without regard to the source of the revenue. Furthermore, it may be argued that, if there is a relation, information about what this relation consists of does not exist.

I tentatively disagree with that and will demonstrate my disagreement by recurring to a simple historical example. Still, considering the possibility that financial instruments are independent entities from real goods and services in the economic life of human society seems important to our understanding of Capital Theory.

In nature, all living beings have as their ultimate goal to survive and pro-create. In order to fulfill their *telos*,[4] they interact with both the animate and the inanimate world. Living beings' interactions with the inanimate world that do not concern other living beings, do not concern us here.[5] Interactions that do concern other living beings may be adversarial or cooperative according to the particular way in which each species has evolved, and the circumstances in which each individual finds himself or herself. Be that as it may, there is a moment in each interaction between a living being and the world when the individual takes possession of something required for his or her survival or procreation. Such possession may be of no consequence to other animate beings (as when an animal breathes); or it may be not only consequential but also adversarial (as when a plant grows in front of another to get better sunlight), or it can be of consequence but cooperative (as in any symbiotic relationship).

If not for the fact that resources are to different degrees finite or scarce, possession would not imply exclusion of others in most cases. Usually, when an animal breathes in an open space or drinks from a water hole, there is enough air and enough water for its use of those resources not to require the exclusion of others. When a monkey plucks a fruit from a tree or a wildcat kills its prey, that is a different story. Ripe fruits at hand and fresh carcasses (or cleared fields, for that matter) are scarce in nature, and the enjoyment of them is necessarily exclusionary. The rationale by which first possession becomes the source of a legitimate claim on something cannot be understood if scarcity is not taken into consideration.[6]

I do not intend to argue that there is a moral sentiment among irrational beings, or that the fact that a lion has killed its prey grants it some "right" in the minds of surrounding hyenas; but the fact that the lion will be willing to fight for the carcass of its prey is part of the same natural order that evolved in a way that most birds make their own nests instead of cuckooing, and most carnivores do their own hunting, or scavenging, instead of stealing.

Whatever other values human beings may hold, they will not be held for long if those human beings do not survive and procreate like any other living being. For that, human beings, like irrational beings, need to interact with the world.

THE INHERITANCE FROM ROMAN LAW

Because human beings live in particular forms of societies, in political societies (unlike the social organization of insects, for instance), an important part of the rules governing their interactions is social constructs. These rules have evolved by trial and error in human societies as a consequence of the interactions themselves. In the particular form of human societies, for the individuals to cooperate with one another, in the absence of "hardwired" instincts, and given the limitations of what may be achieved by coercion, a particular set of rules that have evolved and proved to efficiently foster cooperation among individuals (by assuring the most reasonable distribution of the rewards of their interactions) has been the institution of private property rights.

Because of the foresight that their rational faculties allow, once human beings were able to produce and accumulate goods necessary for the fulfilling of their values—among them, goods necessary to facilitate the production of more goods—they envisaged a way to secure their possessions so as to minimize aggressive interactions with other human beings.[7] We will, like Hume (1987), call this security of possession property rights.[8]

If human interactions existed in a Walrasian universe of perfect competition, clearly defined entitlements, and zero transaction costs, a complex system of property rights would not be necessary. However, transaction costs are positive, and because of that, to solve some of the problems inherent in the allocation of resources, other methods are necessary—among them, the institution of private property rights (Barzel, 1997: 11).

Private property rights are claims, not on nature, but on the behavior you expect from other human beings. Humans were able to build extended societies because they were able to develop institutional arrangements like private property. It is because animals do not have property rights that the lion and the hyena need to fight and kill and maul each other over every carcass, while humans are able to toil in neighboring fields without killing each other, once good fences are installed and have gained social recognition. Private property rights are social arrangements establishing the conditions under which social recognition would be granted to individual claims, and not any unilateral claim will pass muster. That is, moral criteria inform what the majority of the members of a given society perceive as fair, and a definition of what is just is then accepted by the community and enforced by the community against transgressors.

Once those rules have been developed and acknowledged by a given society, they will create the conditions for wealth to be produced and stored through voluntary cooperation among the members of society and their mutual respect for the fruits of the labor of their neighbors. However, if there are no rules developed for the just acquisition of private property that gain the support of the majority, civil strife may be expected, as it has been the norm in those human societies which have proved themselves unable to develop to this day.

Discussions of the origin and nature of private property rights are as ancient as political thought, and an extended review of that topic goes well beyond the scope of this work.[9] What will be discussed next are the minimum postulates required to make sense of the concept of private property rights as they are applied here. For our purposes, private property rights are considered social relations sanctioned by the legal institutions of each sovereign state. Whether the moral justification for the establishment of a sphere of autonomy for the individual members of society to act and dispose of certain things pre-existed the politically organized society, we do not need to discuss here. The fact is that such a sphere for individual autonomous action and freedom to dispose of the goods over which the individual has ownership is made effective by the recognition of its existence by the state and the other individual members of society. In this sense, private property rights are part of the positive law and by the positive law they are regulated.

The traditional conception of which bundles of rights comprise private property rights is one we inherited from Roman law, under which one has the right "to use and abuse" one's property.[10] In the case of rights claimed over land, this was summarized in the statement that "Whoever owns the surface, owns the underground all the way to hell and aboveground all the way the heavens."[11]

However, this conception was not literally true, although the scope of the proprietor to use his property was very ample for significant part of Roman history. Not only were private property rights gradually encroached upon and made less secure, but even at the peak of their acknowledgement, they were never absolute. Proprietors were not compensated for the state's "takings" to build a road or an aqueduct, for instance. Horse carts were not allowed inside the city of Rome during the day. Building regulations were established already at the time of the Roman Republic.

The way that an absolutist conception of property was transmitted to us by the civil codes inspired by the 1804 Napoleonic Civil Code was that private property was limited by "local ordinances" in matters of health and security. These, too, were hardly absolute, yet they connoted very ample discretionary powers. Again, we do not need to delve into all the details of the nineteenth-century common law and the Continental system of law that define this ample scope, or the ways in which private property rights could be acquired, held, or transmitted as they became enshrined in the different national constitutions beginning with the U.S. Constitution of 1787. Suffice it to say that that conception proved to be exceedingly efficient for the mobilization of resources for productive use in the societies in which it was adopted.[12]

Nowadays, in general, in most of the Western and Westernized societies, our conception of private property rights grants much fewer discretionary powers to ownership. Consequently, the scope of action allowed by law is much narrower than before. The number of uses that were clearly and objectively taken away from owners were greatly expanded. So, there is an unknown number of uses and exchanges that are not happening because they are illegal. Furthermore, the positive law of most Western countries, in the words of Larry Summers (2014), "promiscuously" distributes "veto" powers to governmental entities, to neighborhood associations, to public prosecutors, to administrative agencies, and to interest groups. That is, there are many uses that are not clearly and objectively excluded from what the proprietors may do, but they are subject to the discretionary will of all those stakeholders.

The latter prohibitions, it should be pointed out, are as bad as straightforward ones. Take, for example, a stricture against building a multi-family building in an area zoned as single-family. If, in this example, acquiring a license to build a multi-family building in an area zoned for single families depends on buying off some stakeholders, such as bureaucrats in the city hall, environmentalists, or the leadership of the homeowner association, these activities may be time-consuming, expensive, and may end in nothing. The key aspect to consider here is that, in granting "veto" powers to all of those constituencies, the legislators created immense opportunities for "rent-seeking," and for the consequences that inevitably follow. Rents, when they are open to be captured, result in a competition for their capture that results in their being wasted in the process. That is why, for example, the first line of the subway in New York City began in 1900 was built in less than five years, with twenty-three stations, at a cost of about one billion 2019 USD, whereas the most recent expansion (in the year 2000) took seventeen years, had just three stations, and was done at a cost of 4.5 billion USD.[13]

THE MODEL

The basic notion of property rights on planet Earth, where there is only one species of rational beings, is that everything that exists in the world (*Wt*) is either the property of someone human (*Pr*)[14] or a *res nullius*, that is, a property of no one (*Rn*). We may enunciate this basic notion as follows:

$$Wt = Pr + Rn$$

It is from this basic enunciation, after some elaboration, that I intend to derive a model of a RTC.

TWO SIMPLE EXAMPLES

The link between the rent of a property and a financial instrument such as an annuity is easier to see if we look back to the beginning of capital markets.[15] When the right to the income of a property is sold through a transferable instrument, actual property becomes linked to actual income, with that financial instrument representing a claim over that property equivalent to its income (Kohn, 99, p. 6).

A good example of an equity investment prior to the seventeenth century is that of a single ship voyage *commenda* (partnership). In this type of partnership, the passive investor receives a share of the proceeds of the enterprise if and when the ship comes back. Here, the real side of wealth creation (a percentage of the amount of resources invested in the sea voyage, plus the profits generated once the merchandise is sold) connects with the abstract claim representing it—that is, the share representing the passive investment in the partnership (Kohn, 99, p. 17).

Not as clear as an example, yet worth mentioning, would be war bonds. Around the year 1260, "The towns of Douai and Calais were the first to sell *rentes*" (Kohn, 99: 8) and war was the main reason they did. The income pledged to pay these *rentes* (annuities) was usually generated by an excise tax or custom revenues. These revenues were usually collected by tax farmers, a feature that facilitated their mobilization. The relevance of this Medieval issuance of war bonds and creation of instruments to back the repayment of these obligations is that it demonstrates, albeit indirectly, the link between the actual creation of wealth (the trade subject to the excise or custom duties) and the likeliness of the obligations' being repaid. To be sure, in this case, the authorities issuing the *rentes* could arguably have used their taxing prerogatives to tax existing wealth, not only to create new wealth to pay their creditors back, if they perceived it to be in their interest to do so.[16]

Another reason to mention early forms of public debt is that the market for government debt was a direct competitor with the market for shares in equity ventures (Kohn, 99: 19). This competition is clear evidence that the money interest rate is related to the profitability of capitalist enterprises. If the money rate of interest is lower than the possible profit opportunities, there will be funds to finance long-term borrowing and enterprises. The moment that the government demand for funds increases, and it starts to pay higher interest rates on money, these operations crowd private takers out of the capital markets, and the situation starts to become unsustainable (or to put it differently, incompatible with a growing economy).

The relationship between monetary instruments and capital markets is shown by examples provided by Dartmouth economic historian Meir G. Kohn. Professor Kohn states: "The principal driving force in the development of the financial system of preindustrial Europe was not lending per se, but payments" (Kohn, 2001: 2). For Kohn, the bank deposit and the bill of exchange were first developed to foster transactions among strangers, not as lending instruments. The economic incentive to economize in specie was the force driving most innovations.

It is possible to reduce the need for cash by, for instance, netting credit transactions (Kohn, 2001: 4). Netting may be bilateral or multilateral; it may be centralized (in a stock exchange or clearing house) or decentralized (by assigning third-party debt). "To flourish . . . , wholesale commerce had to be conducted on the basis of credit," writes Kohn. "These problems of wholesale commerce among strangers . . . stimulated the development of the two principal financial innovations of the period—the deposit bank and the market for bills of exchange" (Kohn, 2001: 7). By the fourteenth century, "in all the centers of international trade and finance, whether they were fairs or commercial cities, payment in bank predominated" (Kohn, 2001: 9). Finally, Professor Kohn describes how "the discounting of bills provided the basis for the reinvention of private banking in England, where it played an important role in financing the expansion of trade and the Industrial Revolution" (Kohn, 2001: 22), which takes us up to the beginning of our history of modern finance with the creation of the Bank of England.

WHAT DO STOCKS AND FLOWS OF FINANCIAL INSTRUMENTS ACTUALLY REPRESENT?

Financial instruments may take many shapes. If we accept that, a question that necessarily follows is whether there is a relation between certain goods and certain instruments; and it seems that there is a link between the different levels of liquidity of financial instruments and the time necessary to mature the return of capital investments they represent. That may well have to do with the level of certainty about the return of the investment. If we were to state it in formal terms, we might express it as: *liquidity: (f) maturity, certainty.*

Such a formula must not be understood as denying that maturity mismatches may happen. The link between the maturity of financial assets and the income-generating life of physical assets, be they goods or processes, may be understood as a tendency. Of course we will not, in all circumstances and all cases, reach the limit of that tendency. In other words, there would not always be a perfect correlation between the maturity of financial instruments and streams of revenue that they are meant to represent. For that matter, there are mismatches not only related to maturity. These we will discuss later in this work, for at the core of what I hope to accomplish is elucidating that not all forms by which claims on actual wealth are represented in property claims are good representations. Mismatches may happen even in the best arrangements, an issue already raised when we discussed whether financial instruments are an independent feature of economic life (see page 106). It would be apt to consider, as Adam Smith does in *The Wealth of Nations*, Book II, chapter iii (Smith, 1981), instances of private or public "prodigality" and "misconduct," by which capital is invested in unproductive purposes or in projects that turn out to be unprofitable, with the consequent destruction of the capital invested.

As we will discuss in the next section, one particular case in which financial instruments are not well matched to the things on the real side of the economy used to produce more goods is that of mismanagement of the supply of money.

MONETARY DISEQUILIBRIUM AND CAPITAL THEORY

For the "price of money" to remain stable—that is, for the purchasing power of money in relation to all the goods money can buy to remain stable—by definition, a point should be reached that is as close to equilibrium as possible, between the supply of money and the supply of all other goods. Such "price equilibrium" should exist as mediated by changes in the demand for money as a liquid store of value. So money, and less liquid financial instruments, have an immediate quantitative relationship to goods in the economy that are readily available for multiple uses. These goods include inventories, and perhaps even fixed assets in the structure of production.

Money and less liquid financial instruments may also have a qualitative relation to those goods, in the sense that the amount of very liquid financial instruments should ideally represent the sum of the most readily disposable goods, while the amount of less liquid financial instruments should be related to the availability of not-so-readily disposable ones. Yet it seems worth exploring whether the stock of money and other financial instruments with monetary properties also has a mediate quantitative relation to all the goods transacted in society, not only capital goods, in a given period of time, under "existing" circumstances of demand.

What do I mean by that? At any given moment, there is a constant "aggregate demand" in the economy and a demand for cash balances, as well. That "aggregate demand" is not only for capital goods but it is for goods in general. Actually, the most important component of the demand for economic goods is the demand for consumer goods, whose production is the end goal of all economic activity (Huerta de Soto, 2006: 267). Economic agents need a certain amount of money not only to clear the transactions they are engaged in in the process of production, but also to maintain their level of consumption. Money is required to pay for purchases—from the flour used daily by bakers, to the turbines used to produce electricity—as well as to pay for the groceries they consume at home. Since the frequency with which homes and electric turbines change hands is not the same as the frequency with which flour or groceries are traded, the stocks of monetary and less liquid financial instruments should vary accordingly.

The demand for cash balances, to the extent that a substantial portion of the stock of money is endogenously produced, may be defined by the opportunity cost of holding interest-generating financial instruments (bonds) instead of money substitutes that generate less income or no income whatsoever. If changes happen in the aggregate demand—with economic agents revealing a preference for holding cash balances not only by moving from income-generating financial instruments to monetary ones but also by refraining from buying goods—the result is that, since the stock of money proper exogenously supplied is constant in the short run, the demand for endogenously supplied money substitutes will increase. That movement will be counterbalanced by both a reduction in the price level of goods and an increase in the interest rate in financial markets in order to slow the movement from income-generating financial instruments to quasi-money ones.

Hence the price level, or the purchasing power of money, being the relationship between the stock of money and all goods in the economy that money can buy, is related to (1) the relation between the stock of money and capital goods in the real economy; (2) the relation between the stock of money and other financial instruments; (3) the rate of interest;[17] (4) the speed with which exogenous money can be supplied; and (5) the transaction costs for the supply of endogenous money. According to Hansjörg Klausinger of the Vienna University of Economics and Business Administration, Hayek explains equilibrium by recurring to the concepts of relative prices and the interest rate of equilibrium (Hayek, 1999: 28). Since the point of departure of Hayek's theory of the business cycle is a hypothetical condition of equilibrium, in such condition, there is an existing structure of production and a set of relative prices that allow the continuation of the production of consumer goods and the use of funds that indefinitely maintain existing capital goods.

This hypothetical equilibrium is brought about thanks to the fact that those relative prices signal to economic agents that they can earn the rate of profits of equilibrium (which is the same as the rate of interest in equilibrium, that is, the natural rate and the rate of interest on money) by continuing to do what they have been doing. So, the spontaneous coordination among economic agents to stay in equilibrium happens as a response by each of them to the relative prices of the goods and services in the economy and the profit opportunities that such prices allow.

We may add more realistic assumptions, such as envisioning an economy always trending toward equilibrium without ever reaching it, with relative prices changing in response to changing circumstances. But the fact remains that profit opportunities in the economy (with new entrants in particular industries, and some agents exiting those industries in response to current relative prices) in general tend to harmonize the rate of profits in the economy, and with it the allocation of capital to producing the goods and services demanded at any given time.

Given that not all goods and services are directly represented in the stocks and flows of monetary and financial instruments, an interesting question would be: What, after all, do those stocks and flows actually represent? My tentative answer is that money and other financial instruments represent a portion of the existing goods and services in the economy that (1) are being saved to make current purchases (liquidity on demand); (2) are being saved for purchases that we might need to make (short, medium and long-term liquidity); (3) are being stored for or are in the middle of the process of production as intermediate goods and services (working capital); or (4) are assigned to the production and distribution of final goods and services (fixed capital).

The financial instruments representing these goods may take many forms. For instance, they may be (but are not necessarily limited to): money, warehouse receipts of deposits (warrants), bank deposits (both on demand and time deposits), shares of money market mutual funds, publicly traded notes, bonds, stocks, or derivative instruments. If we tentatively accept my list of the goods being represented by financial instruments, and my list of those instruments, a question that necessarily follows is whether there is a relation between certain goods in the former list and certain instruments in the latter.

A THEORY OF CAPITAL AS A PARTICULAR
SORT OF PROPERTY CLAIM

The asset structure of the firm is represented by its financial structure, its debts and equity, and the value attributed to the productive prospects of its assets as reflected in the assessment the market gives to the financial assets of the firm. "Thus, there is a financial structure that is related to the capital structure of the economy," according to Peter Lewin, the student of Ludwig Lachmann whose observations we discussed in chapter 1 (Lewin, 1996: 122). For him, the capital structure is related to the plan (of production) structure—that is, the structure of production. For Lachmann (1956: 68–71), the stock market is the key capitalist institution, the one that differentiates it from a socialist economy and the one that gives it the agility to regroup capital constantly in an ever more efficient way. I would argue that it is in the financial structure that capital gains and losses are "revealed," thus the financial structure performs an essential function in reshaping the capital structure. It does so, I would argue, in the same way that changes in a firm's cash balances would signal the need for changes by that firm.

A caveat on what has been suggested in the previous section is that not all of the goods that potentially could be represented by financial instruments are so represented. Tentatively, as our working definition, let us call financial instruments "property claims negotiable in financial markets." Trying to avoid the circularity of the argument, later we will discuss which features of some "property claims" allow them to be traded in financial markets while other features render a claim not tradable (in organized markets).

For now, keep the concept in mind and consider, on one side, the shares of a limited liability company (LLC) that owns, say, a textile plant and all the inputs necessary for the production of fabrics, and on the other side, a publicly traded company owning a sister plant and all of the same inputs as the LLC. In the first case, the shares of the LLC are property claims on the equipment, inventories, and everything else the LLC owns, but those claims are not tradable in the stock market. In the second case, the shares of the publicly traded company, representing similar assets and liabilities, similar goods, rights, and obligations, are traded in stock markets—are part of the financial markets—and in this sense, its shares are financial instruments. They are easily tradable property claims—they are "property claims negotiable in financial markets" while the shares of the LLC are not—or at least not to the same degree.[18]

It is not that you cannot negotiate LLC shares; you can, but not in an organized market intended to provide the liquidity that a stock exchange provides. However, the difference is not only in the structure of the stock market. If the LLC's shares were allowed to be negotiated in stock markets without fulfilling the requirements of transparency, accountability, and governance required from publicly traded companies, they would not achieve the degree of liquidity that the shares of most publicly traded companies enjoy.[19]

However, if we accept that only some of the "physical capital" is represented by "financial instruments," out of necessity, we accept that not all physical capital is so represented. Some components of the capital structure of society do not have the features required to be classified among the "financial instruments" of that society—although they belong to someone, and therefore are the object of some "property claims." Those claims themselves do not have the features required to be classified as "financial instruments."

Perhaps a better way to describe the relationship between capital on the real side of the economy and on the monetary/financial side is to understand it as part of a bigger picture, in which all the objects of property rights on the "real" side of the economy have a counterpart on the "abstract" side. This abstract side is composed of all property claims and the instruments which embody them, meaning all the property right titles. Financial instruments, monetary instruments included, are just a special part of those titles—ones that, on a continuum of "salableness" or "marketability" (its capacity of being sold), are closer to the higher end.

IS THERE A RELATIONSHIP BETWEEN CERTAIN GOODS AND CERTAIN FINANCIAL INSTRUMENTS?

The example of building a house may help us to find out whether or not there is a relationship between certain goods and certain financial instruments. Home construction is a process in which the potentiality of creating wealth may be actualized with the realization of a profit, the creation of a capital gain. Before the house was built, what existed were a stock of construction material, a vacant lot, equipment, and workers with different skills who, among other possibilities of employment, were available for hire. Once the house was built and sold, the compensation for the use of those pieces of equipment, and the compensation for the work, were transferred to its owners, the construction firm, and the workers in terms of financial instruments, possibly cash or checks, while new wealth (the house) could at that point become part of the assets used as collateral for a mortgage-backed security (MBS). In this sense, I argue, there is representation of existing wealth, and representation of the generation of new wealth, in the real economy. Its representational counterpart on the monetary/financial side is to be found in changes in the stock of financial instruments and their flows.

We might as well ring changes on this example by being more specific. Let us take the resources necessary to build a house in the suburbs of Indianapolis. You need to buy the lot and have sufficient resources to hire the labor, rent the equipment, and buy the materials to build, say, a 2,500-square foot home. You can buy that home, the result of using of all those resources, from a real estate developer for 250,000 USD. All of the resources are owned by someone, likely as working and fixed capital (for the sake of this example, let's add human capital to the mix).

So, a thirty-year mortgage loan contract is signed between the homeowner and the bank simultaneously with the house being purchased from the developer. The bank gives the developer the 250,000 USD. The developer transfers the house to you. You become a debtor to the bank in the same amount. A lien is established on the property as collateral to the bank, in case the stream of revenue you expect to receive (your wages) and devote to the monthly mortgage payments is interrupted.

The bank immediately sells the mortgage contract it has with you to an investment bank, which bundles your loan with thousands of others, creates a kind of bond representative of those thousands of mortgages (let's call it "Carmel MBS"), and sells that bond to an insurance company, which will own the bond until it matures—that is, until the last payment is received.

Regardless of what happens in the future, the creation of this new instrument, which is representative of the 250,000 USD in long-term liquidity (generated by your mortgage), is more or less simultaneous with the transfer of resources to the different owners of the inputs used in the construction of your new home. Alas, it is because they are credited fractions of that total 250,000 USD that they have transferred first to the developer the inputs that, once put together, became the house, and later the developer transferred the property of the house to you. That lien (plus your own obligation to make monthly payments) is now part of the collateral of that new financial instrument, the Carmel MBS.

Let us assume that the added value of the wealth generated by the construction of your new home equaled about half the total price of the house; that is, the remuneration of the labor and effort put into your house by the developer and his suppliers.[20]

To measure production here, let us use the method of Vittorio Mathieu, who posits that money's nature is one of "potential work."[21] This allows us to compare potential work employed with potential work obtained. What we pick up from this, I argue, is that there is representation of existing wealth and of wealth-generation in the real economy in changes to the stock of financial instruments and their flows on the monetary/financial side—and that what is going on on the real side is represented by mutations and permutations on the abstract side of the economy.

IF NOT ALL GOODS ARE REPRESENTED BY FINANCIAL INSTRUMENTS, ARE THERE FINANCIAL INSTRUMENTS THAT REPRESENT NO GOODS?

Consider now a second example. Suppose the government sells Treasury bonds and uses the proceeds to pay current expenditures. Now we have on one side, the government, which has squandered the resources it borrowed, and on the other, the investors, who expect to receive back not only the capital they invested but also interest on that investment. That is, the funding of current expenses is consumption, not capital investment. Wealth that is consumed is destroyed; it will not be there in the future, nor will it generate income for repaying the principal to the investors or for giving them a return on their capital. As stated by Professor Ludwig Hahn "Private debts are ordinarily incurred against transfers of goods from one member of the community to another, whereas . . . government debt is counterbalanced not by real wealth but by its destruction" (Hahn, 49: 12).

A refinement of this second example is as follows: Let us suppose the government raises 500,000.000 USD by selling ten-year Treasury bonds, and that it uses half of the proceeds to pay contractors doing maintenance work for the Bureau of Land Management, and the other half to pay the wages of the bureau's civil servants. The Treasury auctioned the bonds through the dealers. Two buyers appeared, each taking half the issuance: a money market mutual fund (MMMF) and a pension fund.[22] The pension-fund managers plan to keep the bonds to maturity, since they have long-term obligations with their pensioners. The managers of the MMMF simply add the bonds to the assets of the fund, with no idea of how long those bonds will be held for.

To keep the example simple, suppose that both buyers received the resources paid to the Treasury the previous day, one from future pensioners and the other from money market investors.

In regard to what the government did with the money, arguably, the investment in maintaining federal lands could be classified as a capital investment. To the extent that some income is generated in consequence, we may assess what the present value of such "investment" might be.[23] For the sake of the argument, let us suppose zero income will be generated; therefore, the present value of the investment is zero.[24]

In regard to the money raised to pay the bureau's employees, certain it is that no capital was acquired by the government to repay it; the money being used to meet payroll is a current expense.

So, now we have on one side the government, which has squandered the resources borrowed with the issuance of the bonds, and on the other side the investors, who expect to receive back not only their principal (the capital they invested) but also interest. The investors have different time horizons for their investment: The MMMF's investors expect to take the money from the fund at any moment by giving short notice (D+1) to the fund managers. The pensioners expect to receive monthly payments for the next ten years from the proceeds of those bonds and the other investments in the pension fund's portfolio.

Both investors believe they have invested their savings in financial instruments that represent real wealth—that is, real resources they intend to consume in the future. Such representation may be vague, loose, only indirect—but still, the fact remains that the expectations of the investors holding these abstract financial instruments (the ten-year Treasuries) are that their property, the bonds, will entitle them to acquire actual goods and services at a future time (as soon as tomorrow, or as far out as the next ten years in the pensioners' case).

However, unlike the investors who invested their money in the "Carmel MBS" in the previous example, a private bond that would fund the fixed or working capital of some enterprise, the government has simply spent the money it got from the investors with the bond sale. The wealth that was created by the investors and used to purchase the government bonds, in this example, has been destroyed in consumption. It goes without saying that this wealth is now no longer available to facilitate the production of future consumer goods, and with that, to increase the productive capacity of society. Rather the government's action reduced the society's economic growth rate and prospects for future wealth. As pointed out by Mises: "Nothing can inflict more harm upon the masses and frustrate more effectively all attempts to raise their standard of living than capital consumption" (Mises, 2000: 204).

PUTTING THESE ISSUES IN THE CONTEXT
OF MODERN ASSET PRICING

Measuring the capital stock, depending on the purposes and on the circumstances, is commonly done either by accounting for the costs of acquisition or by market value.

Since we are at present talking about liquid instruments such as Treasury bonds, it would be reasonable to recur to instruments of modern asset pricing to get a fix on how those instruments are currently priced in financial markets. The standard asset pricing formula may be summarized in two equations:

$$P_t = E\left(M_{t+1}x_{t+1}\right)$$

and

$$M_{t+1} = f(\text{data, parameters})$$

Where: P_t = asset price, x_{t+1} = asset payoff, m_{t+1} – stochastic discount factor (Cochrane, 2001: xv).

If private firms are riskier than public firms, as we saw in the just-discussed example (the publicly traded versus the privately traded company) that difference in evaluations could be explained as:

$$= \Rightarrow P_t (\text{Privately traded corp.})$$

$$= E(M_{t+1} x_{t+1}), f(\text{private corp. data}) < P_t (\text{public traded corp.})$$

$$= E(M_{t+1} x_{t+1}), f(\text{public corp. data})$$

But this only demonstrates what we already know: that the market price of one is higher than the market price of the other. What this equation does not explain are the elements of the legal arrangements that reduce the risk for investors more in the one case than in the other. These differences in legal arrangements justify the difference in their evaluations. This formula may give comfort to traders and undergraduate business students that they can explain what they are observing, but it sheds little light on the underlying factors shaping the realities depicted in it.[25]

Some literature in mainstream economics aims to explain why the assumption of perfect information known to all agents is not supported by the evidence provided by the prices of different asset categories (see, for instance, Nimark, 2015). That literature (rightly) claims that in the presence of private information, that assumption is not valid. Economic agents, even assuming perfect rationality, will behave differently based on different information they may have. That may explain why the price of sovereign debt is not "priced" to the risk of default that it seems to carry almost everywhere. That is not the claim I am making here, however. I am not talking about private information that some traders may have that others do not. What I am talking about here is the myriad institutional conditions that lead investors to systematically discount the government-issued financial obligations' risk of default in most countries, most of the time, in the last few decades. We can see why that happens in spite of the objective measurements of doubtful fiscal sustainability (government's actual capacity to repay its debts), such as measurements of fiscal imbalances and of the fiscal gap.[26]

If we approached public finances as asset pricing, as most mainstream economists do, we would assume that the government's budgetary constraints would be reflected in the price of public bonds, and we could safely ignore the fact that the resources raised by the issuance of bonds had been used to pay for current expenses or in capital investments yielding low or no returns. Following that line of reasoning, if the government wanted to raise additional money, but the total flow of government surplus was zero, the equilibrium of the budgetary constraints would have been reached and no one would buy the additional bonds.[27]

The implication of such reasoning is that it is not possible for the government to borrow in excess of a budgetary "hard" constraint (otherwise, it would not be a "hard" constraint). That is very true, but the conclusion should not be that therefore the constraint has not been reached yet. It should be that there are almost no "hard" budgetary constraints in the short term, since the government can almost always find ways (again, in the short term) to change the parameters of the equation. Furthermore, such reasoning assumes a state of permanent equilibrium[28] in which prices convey all the information needed by economic agents, an assumption that evidence can easily disprove.[29]

For instance, any mandates forcing financial institutions, insurance companies, or pension funds to buy bonds compulsorily are not taken into account. Whether those particular resources will or will not increase the future total flow of government surplus—that is not computed in the formula, either. At least, not if you intend to keep formal rigor.[30]

The bottom line is that governments often borrow more than their verifiable capacity to repay their debts. Why they get a pass on that is not the focus of this current work, despite being interesting and crucial. We cannot rely on the idea that there are budgetary constraints, and that therefore if the government has succeeded in placing its bonds in the market, it is evidence that it has not yet reached the limits of those constraints since otherwise the "market" would have known and would have stopped buying the bonds.

There are questions of agency involved in the bond market, for instance. The dealers in bonds rarely keep the bonds for themselves; it is not their fiduciary duty to care about whether those bonds will be repaid. The time horizon for most bond fund managers is much shorter than the maturity of the bonds they buy for their customers, which means that they will not likely be there when something "bad" happens.

In most cases of sovereign default in recent decades, a little bit of everything happens—that is, there is some inflation reducing the real value of the obligations, there is an increase in tax revenues from increased tax rates, and the defaults are usually selective, with different classes of creditors being not only disproportionally affected but also affected at different times.

Given all of that, it might seem rational to stay in this economic game of musical chairs while the music is playing—even more so, if you have a reasonable expectation that others will have their taxes increased for your obligation to be repaid, or that you will have time enough to dump the credits you may have on someone else.

My point here is not simply the familiar one, that the government issues uncollateralized bonds. The idea here is not that financial markets are insufficiently developed to have created different classes of bonds, both public and private, with different levels of collateralization. Even if we assume that part of public debt is "secured debt," the point with the example in this chapter is to call attention to the fact that, in the real world, real resources— resources that are ultimately scarce—are transferred to the government when it sells public bonds. The owners of those bonds, the creditors of those obligations, expect to have their claims to real resources repaid. That seems so obvious, to the point of being silly, but a rational measurement of the current capacity of most governments around the world to repay their obligations, both funded and unfunded, secured and general, explicit or implicit, would reveal that they are unable to repay their obligations *given their current levels of revenues*—something that could not be assumed away just by pointing to the fact that bonds are still being sold at a low cost on a daily basis.

NOTES

1. In any case, it is the inescapable reality of our mortality what induces us to utility maximization, and our individual expectations about our longevity mostly is what determines our time preference.

2. Paul Lewis and Jochen Runde define a similar ontological approach as "Transcendental Realist Social Theory" (TRST) by saying that "TRST suggests that the market process, just is the process whereby people draw on (preexisting, historically driven) social structures (such as the legal system) in order to act and, in doing so, subsequently either reproduce or transform those structures." They describe how, in the end, Lachmann's theory about the relation between human behavior and social order may be classified as an example of this approach (Lewis and Runde, 2007). Considering that with the present work I am only trying to make explicit what is implicit in Lachmann and others, such a definition seems applicable to the thesis presented here. The idea of "Transcendental Realism," as first proposed by Roy Bhaskar, has, incidentally, already been applied to economics by Tony Lawson in his efforts to understand the interaction between the physical and the social world in economics (Lawson, 1997: 20).

3. See my earlier discussion of Böhm-Bawerk (page 65) and his concept of wealth ("nothing more nor less than the totality of the economic goods that stand at the disposal of an economizing subject"), and also his statement that men only desire corporeal goods "in the prospect they afford of renditions of service." Even such independent rendition of service does not justify ruling out property rights as constituting "genuine goods" (Böhm-Bawerk, 1962: 81). Property claims as claims on real goods are perceived in civil society, as long as they are likely to be honored, to be equivalent to a physical instrument that would allow the production of future goods, or to a store of physical goods for future consumption. To explain the value

of intermediary goods, Böhm-Bawerk states that "the value of goods first comes into being in terms of the latter unit (means for fulfilling a purpose)" (Böhm-Bawerk, 1962: 76). The value of property claims may be deduced in similar fashion. As an expression of the social "materiality" of property claims, Böhm-Bawerk uses the concept of the "payment-claim," as I explained earlier; it is important here as expressing a "promise to pay." He argues that the only goods in the transactions involving such promises are the "objects themselves which constitute the matter of the debt" (Italics in the original) (Böhm-Bawerk, 1962: 84). The social value of a property claim has to do with the likelihood of its being honored. "The right to demand payment is claimed to be merely the condition precedent of a future goods-quality" (Böhm-Bawerk, 1962: 85). This is Böhm-Bawerk asserting the derivative nature of claims on the credibility that that particular claim would be a sufficient instrument to access goods and services in the physical world.

4. I am following Searle here. The attribution of teleological purposes to natural phenomena (such as the "function" of pumping blood we perceive a heart has) implies the previous acceptance of a value by the observer, in this case, the value of contributing to the organism to remain alive; other than that, there are no "functions" in nature, just causal relations (Searle, 1995: 15).

5. Obviously, Robison Crusoe had an "economic" problem to solve, even before the arrival of the man he met on a Friday, given that resources were already scarce. Even alone, he was required to make choices about which course of action he would take in order to address his needs. Would he invest time and effort in building a fishing net to make his fishing more productive, even if that would entail not having fish to eat for a day or two? Despite using economic reasoning to make up his mind, in the absence of social interaction, one may say that his choices were "moral" or "psychological," and not "economical." In any case, they are beyond the scope of what we are dealing with in this work.

6. For more on possessiveness among animals, see Pipes (2000: 65).

7. Tony Lawson, in discussing the nature of rights, goes so far as to say that "The existence of the rights and obligations seems to presuppose the ability to represent obligations and rights in some at least rudimentary manner" (Lawson, 2012: 364). That is, Lawson sees in the attribute of representation the very essence of rights.

8. Steven Horwitz explains how the special way we organize production, and the development of our understanding of reality, make our lives better: "Following the rules of payment and contract, allows us to manipulate the physical world in ways that enhance our lives. More generally, innovations that have made human life longer and better are the result of the interconnected constitutive rules of the market and science" (Horwitz, 2009: 79).

9. To anyone interested in the matter, a good point of departure, of course, is John Locke who, in the Second Treatise of Government, argued that no person would produce more than what was required for the consumption of his own family if not for the possibility of trade, which he equated with the invention of money: "And thus came in the use of Money, some lasting thing that Men might keep without spoiling, and that by mutual consent Men would take in exchange for the truly useful, but perishable Supports of life" (Locke, 2000: 300).

10. Under Roman law, property encompasses the right to use—or abuse—one's own property within the limits of the law, jus utendi et abutendi re suâ. Usual interpretations of this doctrine read the word "abuse" as taking in an absolute domain.

11. This is usually referred to as the ad coelum doctrine.

12. The perception of the existence of this relation between the institutional setting and economic performance, obviously, is nothing new and yet, to this day, has not been well understood. The separation of disciplines, in this case, between law and economics, in spite of efforts to integrate them in the last decades, still leaves much to be desired. Here is Hayek on that: "The rules of just conduct that the lawyer studies serve a kind of order of a character of which the lawyer is largely ignorant; and that this order is studied chiefly by the economist who in turn is similarly ignorant of the character of the rules of conduct on which the order he studies rests" (Hayek, 1973: 4).

13. COLLISON: It's very clear that our productivity has fallen off a cliff and for reasons that we can be pretty sure are not that it's getting intrinsically harder. And so, for example, when New York decided to build the subway in 1900: 4.7 years later, they opened twenty-three subway stations, and in 2019 dollars, they spent just over a billion dollars doing so. So twenty-three stations, just over a billion dollars. When New York decided to build the Second Avenue subway in the year 2000, seventeen years later they opened three stations and they spent $4.5 billion doing so. And so our productivity in subway construction has, at least in New York, decreased by a factor of 40. Here in the Bay Area, we decide to build the Golden Gate Bridge and the Bay Bridge starting in 1933. Both projects finished within four years, and to celebrate it we decide to build man-made island, and we built that island in eighteen months. And I haven't tried but I would wager that if one tried to build a new island in San Francisco, it would be difficult to do so today in eighteen months. When France decided to build the TGV, its high speed rail, it opened the first line after five years. California started pursuing high speed rail eleven years ago. We forecast being finished in 2033, so we project a twenty-five-year project, but of course that's a projection. It'll probably end up being much longer still. So this is the domain where it's hard to imagine that building infrastructure had gotten intrinsically harder, right? The atoms aren't physically heavier than they used to be, right? And so clearly there's something institutional, sociological going on with infrastructure. Larry Summers talks about the idea of the promiscuous distribution of the veto power and how much harder it is to get things done. Inasmuch as that's true, then there's the question of, well, have other institutions, other progress-generating mechanisms in our society— have they also got less efficient? And if so, what can we do about it?

ZUCKERBERG: So as an aside, if you're watching this, Patrick collects these examples of historical projects that went fast and that you can't imagine how they went that fast. So if you Google his website, he has like a whole list of these that I think is pretty interesting and compelling when you go through all of them." From transcript of a podcast interview with Tyler Cowen, Mark Zuckerberg, and Patrick Collison, from November 27, 2019.

14. We are familiar with jurist Karel Vasak's three-generation theory of rights (Vasak, 1977) and the attempts to create even a fourth "generation," which would

not belong to human beings. To the extent that a river is not a sentient being and a monkey is not a rational being and they do not understand the concept of rights, all rights continue to belong solely to human beings and continue to exclusively involve ways, more or less successful as they may be, to avoid conflict among them.

15. The proliferation of the uses of financial instruments to represent real wealth is usually understood to have begun at the end of the Middle Ages (Boldizzoni, 2008). Not that property claims were not present since prehistoric times, or that formal legal systems, with intense use of financial instruments, were not present at least since Roman times (Andreau, 1999). In any case, it seems adequate for our purposes to stipulate the beginning of capital markets about the time of the Renaissance.

16. It is outside the purpose of this chapter to discuss sovereign obligations backed by tax revenues. But to highlight how soon sovereign debt becomes relevant in the history of financial markets, as shown by many previous authors, I will just mention that by 1550 the juros (annuities) of the Castilian monarchy exceeded 100 percent of ordinary income and became transferable (Kohn, 99: 10) and, at that moment, their bankers became essentially brokers. The relation between representation and public finances can also be seen at this very beginning. In the low lands, first the Burgundians and then the Habsburgs (Burgundian themselves) start to use their parliaments as instruments to get credit in order to enhance their creditworthiness (Kohn, 99: 11), creating the foundation of modern state finance. Professor Kohn even claims that the compera (syndicated loans) by Italian city-states were the first examples of securitization (Kohn, 99: 12). The difference between it and the rentes in northern countries is that the issuer of the compera is the entity tax farming that special tax, not the municipality. As the author suggests, likely the instrument of the compera evolved from tax-farming arrangements—again, emphasizing the importance of creating mechanisms to link the likeliness that those obligations will be repaid with some claim, albeit indirect (such as a tax), on the creation of actual wealth, or, failing that, on the taking of some existing wealth. From these early examples provided by Professor Kohn, we could advance our discussions even further, to touch on the creation of liquid instruments with monetary properties. For instance, on page 13 (Kohn, 99), the author describes how, in Italian cities, they eventually consolidated their debts in Monti, with transferable shares, defined interests and "funded" them with tax revenues. With 11,000 shareholders, the Monti of Genoa and others similar to it were liquid instruments with heavy trade above and below par (Kohn, 99: 14). As noted by Kohn, "The book-entry form of shares in the various Monti made transactions in them especially easy" (Kohn, 00: 14). This is the kind of technology that enhances liquidity and differentiates those claims from illiquid ones. One more element of "modern finances" to which Kohn calls our attention is the liberative power (for tax purposes) of shares in the Monti, which gave them "monetary properties" according to the chartalists (Kohn, 99: 16), and I would add that one does not need to be a chartalist to acknowledge that. A final element relevant for our discussion later in this work is the link between finances and sovereign prerogatives seen by Professor Kohn when he acknowledges the fact that access to capital markets "became a question of life and death" for the sovereigns and a decisive factor in the choice of political regime (Kohn,

99: 24). I have developed this topic elsewhere as part of my discussion of the Fiscal Proviso, and that research was what led me from monetary theory to Capital Theory.

17. At this juncture, let us assume that the natural rate of interest, the one revealing the intersubjective time preference of the economic agents, is the same as a "core" interest rate on money that is the main component of all different interest rates on money practiced in the market.

18. The argument here, as pointed out by Alchian and Demsetz, is that we do not live in a world of zero transaction costs as assumed by the Modigliani-Miller theorem. The relatively lower level of transparency of units in an LLC versus shares in a public traded company, although explained by that (Alchian and Demsetz, 1973: 26), cannot give us new information in order to assess their relative prices without delving into the details of their respective institutional arrangements. Therefore, again, the capital structure of the LLC makes it unsuitable to organized markets.

19. See the discussion below on putting these issues in the context of modern asset pricing (page 122).

20. What we are describing here is not an automatic process, but one which, in this case, resulted in profits as we are reminded by Mathieu: "la producción económica, (que) no aumenta automáticamente cada vez que aumenta la producción física, sino que, al contrario, puede disminuir. Cosa que sucede cada vez que la producción ha sido mal planteada" (Mathieu, 1990: 171).

21. In a sense, it can be accepted as correct; money is an instrument to acquire economic goods and, in this sense, it has the potential of obtaining work; but I am not certain the author is using this concept in that sense or in the sense that money represents future goods not yet produced, for example (Mathieu, 1990: 177). I think that for the author, money represents the process of wealth creation, of the act of production and not of the product bought and sold, as when he states "Para que sirva para producir es preciso que, además del pasado, exista un paso hacia el futuro; y eso no es un hecho (un producto), sino una actividad (un trabajo). De esta actividad real el dinero es el equivalente ideal" (Mathieu, 1990: 179). My understanding is that without this original productive activity, there would be nothing to be bought and sold, but, once the things exist, money can be used to purchase them independently from new acts of creation. That is the main difference between inside and outside money; outside money may be created without a necessary relation to increased production, while inside money can only be consistently created in relation to successful acts of production.

22. A ten-year Treasury bond would only qualify to be purchased by a MMMF if it were coupled with a short-term repurchase agreement; for the sake of the example, let's assume that there is one, say, with a ninety-day maturity, and the reason I am using a money market fund in this example instead of a bond fund (which would dispense with the need for this footnote) is to call attention to the fact of the monetization of public debt going on nowadays through money market funds beyond short-term notes—a subject we will return to later.

23. The "golden rule of public finance" is the budgetary principle according to which it is acceptable for a government to take long-term debt to pay for capital investments under the assumption that they will be able to generate a revenue

sufficient to repay the debt. The example we are discussing here, obviously, is an infringement of such a rule. For a discussion on the impact on capital formation, and consequently, economic growth of infringing that rule, see Minea and Villieu (2009).

24. For the sake of keeping the example simple, I am assuming that if the net income of the asset (NPV) is zero, or even negative, that the present value (PV) of the assets is also zero. This assumption, evidently, disregards the possibility of the assets' being repurposed or having an emotional value to someone who would be willing to pay for it even if that is a money-losing proposition. The point here is not that the American people would be quite willing to keep open most, if not all, of the National Landmark sites, despite the fact that they are only kept open as a loss. The point is that if that is to be done, the money to pay for the deficit they generate must be paid from current tax revenues, and not by borrowing against future tax revenues.

25. In other words, a mathematical formulation like this one may be equated to what the late Professor Aaron Levenstein (1911–1986) said about statistics: "Statistics are like a bikini. What they reveal is suggestive, but what they conceal is vital."

26. Reinhart and Rogoff (2012), for instance, mention a number of cases in which large amounts of public debt are kept outstanding, with one (unsurprising) result being low economic growth—but another, surprising result being low interest rates. Possible explanations for that are discussed below in this section.

27. Of course, not everybody in the mainstream fails to see that "asset-pricing theory shares the positive versus normative tension present in the rest of economics" as stated by John Cochrane, who rhetorically asks, "Does it describe the way the word does work, or the way the word should work?" (Cochrane, 2001: xiii).

28. As, for instance, William Sharpe and other believers in an efficient market do (Whitman, 1999: 43). The position adopted in this work is different from the Efficient Market Hypothesis or EMH. As stated by George Bragues, "the Austrian Markets Hypothesis is that financial market prices are constantly endeavoring, but never actually succeeding, to assimilate all available information" (Bragues, 2016: 76).

29. See, for instance, Graham and Dodd's discussion in chapter 50 of Security Analysis of the discrepancies between price and value (Graham and Dodd, 2009: 669).

30. You can always pretend to be applying a formula rigorously and introduce a subjective parameter into your equation. The result is that you will keep the appearance of objective reasoning when you have already abandoned it in defining your assumptions.

Chapter 4

The Epistemological
Problem of Capital

As I said, stocks and flows on the monetary/financial side of the economy mirror what is happening on the real side of the economy. The mirroring or representation is not exact; it is but an approximation. Why is that? One reason is that we simply do not have the theoretical tools we need to deal with such a complex reality. Even if the information exists (which is far from certain), we do not have a way to find and interpret it.

That observation yields two hypotheses about what it is possible to know about capital. Let us first assume that the information exists, but we simply do not know how to gather it. Capital is heterogeneous in a way that renders mere quantitative measurements inadequate to reflect the phenomena we are trying to understand. That leads to the following question: What proportion of all financial instruments represents actual capital goods?[1]

Another way of asking that is, what is behind the smoke and mirrors of public finance as currently practiced? How will the government repay the borrowed money? Well, the government has the power to tax its subjects. This means that, ultimately, the capacity of the government to repay its debts relies on the capacity of the citizenry to pay taxes.[2] The problem is that the taxpayers more or less take into consideration, in their calculations, the taxes they expect to be required to pay, not the taxes necessary to repay all government's liabilities in full.

Some estimates show that the U.S. economy is an economy in which all private material wealth (net worth) equals something like 90 trillion USD. With human capital added to that, the total private wealth is estimated to be something like 120 trillion USD, and the total of goods and services produced each year (GDP in 2015) around 18 trillion USD.

Economic agents' current expectations are based on the notion that the assets owned by the government at all levels in the United States would be sufficient to cover its funded liabilities—that is, all the bonds it has issued (around 27 trillion USD).[3] The problem is that there are unfunded liabilities, such as obligations to pensioners in publicly funded pension schemes, and other unfunded entitlements such as Social Security, Medicare, Medicaid, and the like, which are not transparently reflected in the government's financial statements.

For the purposes of this exposition, let's assume that all the assets of government in the United States, like those of the Bureau of Land Management in our earlier example, cannot actually produce a positive net flow, and that therefore the present value of those assets is zero. Let us also assume that the acknowledged, yet not counted, obligations at all levels of government in the United States (federal, state, and local) total another 27 trillion USD. So, if it is to meet all of its obligations, on top of obtaining the revenue necessary to cover its current expenses, the government would need to collect, in taxes, an additional amount close to three times the total of what is produced each year in the country.

There are other ways to see this problem. We may think about the total assets and the total liabilities in the country, for instance. There is something like 300 trillion USD in assets and something like 180 trillion in total liabilities, both public and private. But the fact remains that the total goods and services produced each year is only 18 trillion USD, and all payments to service the obligations owed by individuals and the government should derive from that amount. If the average interest on the liabilities were 3 percent per year, that would represent 30 percent of GDP. To service the public obligations, about 30 percent of total liabilities, would represent 9 percent of GDP or about 40 percent of all taxes collected by all spheres of government each year in the United States.[4]

There is yet another way to look at this. The 54 trillion USD in public obligations, with zero present value of assets to back them, are understood by the government's creditors as part of their wealth, as part of their property. So, the pensioners of public pension schemes, the beneficiaries of Social Security and other entitlements, and last but not least, the investors in public bonds issued by all levels of government, expect to consume in the future actual goods and services to be paid with the proceeds of those claims against the government. But the government has spent the money and created no wealth to be used to repay those claims. The fact is that the wealth saved by the claimants was destroyed by the government and no longer exists.

This bleak reality has not been reflected on the abstract side of the economy yet, in that the obligations of all the spheres of government in the United States still command credibility.[5] Because people still think that their claims against the federal, state, and local governments will be honored at face value, the reality that there is no actual wealth from which those obligations may be paid has not become clear to very many of the claimants.

How could all of those obligations be paid? The only way would be to force a fire sale of assets to foreigners by a private sector forced to pay a much higher level of taxation (which would destroy the economy even if politically viable). Otherwise there would be a default in the payment of those obligations, either de facto or de jure. That is, either the payments would (1) be done nominally only with money with lower purchasing power or (2) there would be a legal default, forcing the claimants to accept a "discount" in their credits, be they bond repayments, publicly funded pensions, or Social Security or other benefits.

The bottom line is that the circumstances on the real side of the economy (more claims over goods than the existing goods or the possibility to produce more goods) are reflected on the financial side of the economy (bonds and other obligations which cannot be honored at face value, money which needs to be created "out of thin air" to pay obligations at a nominal value inferior to the current purchasing power of the currency, etc.). The fact that the price of financial instruments does not reflect the present value in real terms of those claims is an important challenge to the theory of financial instruments as representatives of claims on real goods and services.

There are some possible explanations for this incommensurability. First, it is possible that the theory now proposed is mistaken. Second, it is possible that the situation of public finances is not so dire as it seems to me at this moment. Third, there are opportunities for arbitrage since economic agents do not have perfect information. Tentatively, and for now, I will reject the hypothesis that the theory is mistaken and that I have gotten the facts about the state of public finances wrong, and I will stick with two ideas: that there is imperfect information and that there are chances for arbitrage.[6]

THE MARKET IS NOT A PHENOMENON OPEN TO CARTESIAN ANALYSIS

If you think the epistemological problem is big concerning monetary phenomena, take a look at it with regard to capital; it's even bigger there.

Let us assume that the information simply does not exist. In an open society—where coordination of the economic activities of its members is done by the spontaneous order of the market created by the price system—the behavior of economic agents is guided by the information they receive through the price system. The informational function of the price system means that people assess the demand for goods and services by the relative price of those goods and services—that is, by their prices in the market. Market prices, it is worth mentioning, capture not only changes in preferences but other changes as well, such as technological changes and institutional changes, directly affecting the allocation of resources in the economy. Think about Uber or a retrofit of an old building, for instance.

This means we cannot consider the permutations of the stocks and flows on the financial side of the economy as if they were simply a bookkeeping record of what is occurring on the real side of the economy. They aren't because money provides intermediation; it allows for indirect exchanges, thus creating the conditions for those equivalences to be only approximate. Because money and other financial instruments serve not only to clear spot transactions but also to be instruments that serve as a store of value, and because the incentives generated in the market may induce producers to mobilize resources in unpredictable ways, we may say with confidence that market phenomena are not open to Cartesian analysis.

Changes in relative prices alone may induce alternative uses for certain goods and alternative applications of human capital—or to express it differently, of the uses of one's time (Huerta de Soto, 2006: 271). But there are other changes, such as technological changes and institutional changes, directly affecting the allocation of resources in the economy (aside from their indirect effect through changes in relative prices). So, for example, a car that until yesterday was just a consumption good, becomes a capital investment now that its owner has decided to work for Uber. Contrariwise, an old building in the downtown area that was previously used by a small clothing factory that closed long ago has become the residence of its new owner. How is it possible to define what the stock of capital is if things exhibit such fluidity?

If one viewed capital goods as part of the intermediary stages aiming at a certain final good, this would entail considering capital only something that has already been "applied" to a given production process. I would not say that this is a mistake since each production process is composed of specific capital goods; but I would argue that goods with the potential to be part of intermediary stages of production may also be capital goods, if their owner's "opinion" is that such goods may be incorporated in a production process.

In the previous chapter, we mentioned a bakery's stock of flour from which it may bake cakes or bread, and observed that such stock could be considered part of its capital. We also noted a construction company's trucks, in which it might carry construction material or tow other equipment, and there, too, one could well call the trucks part of the company's capital. Things get more complicated when we think of a car in a dealership, which is part of the inventory of final goods for sale in the mind of the dealer, and may become a capital investment for an Uber driver—or, come to that, for the baker or the construction company, if that car is used in the business of the bakery or construction. So, in the sense that anything may become a capital good once an economic agent decides to use it as part of a process to produce other goods, Huerta de Soto and others do well to highlight their heterogeneity, and also their specificity. As I said earlier, to the extent that only goods "applied" to specific processes may be deemed capital goods, I think the concept should be expanded.

One of the main characteristics of some forms of capital goods is this "stored" potential to produce many different things. Generally speaking, inventories of almost anything may have multiple uses, not only as instruments to produce many different final goods, but even as final goods themselves, and still be part of the capital stock of a given individual or society.

There is no disputing that people change their behavior in reaction to the relative price of the goods and services they have to offer, and the relative price of the goods and services they need both for their own consumption and as inputs for what they will offer in the market. On the other hand, changes in the money supply may change the price level, aside from the changes in relative prices that, among other reasons, may occur as a consequence of the way changes in money supply are implemented.

For instance, for Larry White, "When the economy is away from the natural rate of output, it is because agents are making misinformed decisions. The economy is regrettably discoordinated [*sic*] when real income is below, or above, its natural rate" (White, 1999: 216). The fact that the structure of production is composed of a substantial portion of goods that are not narrowly specific to production, and therefore may be added to or subtracted from the productive effort according to changes in the set of incentives, means that evaluating an entire economy's production possibility frontier (PPF) is no simple exercise. Granted, there are many highly specific capital goods whose limited availability in the short term may result in bottlenecks for increasing production, but generally speaking there are inventories of goods and services in the economy that, in existing circumstances, would not be used as capital goods but may be applied to the productive activities if the proper incentives are in place.

Obviously, this wiggle room is not infinite. Different societies in different times have more or less of it; but still, the relevant point to keep in mind is that the PPFs are not rigidly defined in actual economic life.

Economic agents perceive increased demand for the goods and services they produce caused by changes in the money supply exactly the same way they perceive changes in the demand for their products caused by changes in the demand patterns of the public. In the case of increased demand, we may say that as long as it would be possible for production to be increased and profitably sold, there are incentives for the producers to do so.

Because, in the real world, individual agents do not operate along a curve of maximum production possibility in a static economy without changes in the technological level, but instead are always developing new ways to do things (and incorporating in the productive effort resources that were not available before for such purposes), it is possible to say that prices are not absolutely inelastic in the economy. That is, faced with an increased demand for their products, producers will perceive that as an incentive to increase production and not to directly increase prices. Of course, the moment that procurement of the inputs necessary to increase production do force an increase in the price of those inputs, the price of the products the economic agents are selling will go up in order for them to net any profit necessary to keep them producing. That is to say, prices are not perfectly elastic, either; there are real constraints that cannot be ignored.[7]

So, there is no direct and immediate relation between changes in demand and supply for goods and services in the market economy because prices are not all or always "inelastic." That means that we cannot consider the permutations of the stocks and flows on the financial side of the economy as if they directly marked what is going on on the real side.[8] That is the case because the intermediation that money provides in allowing for indirect exchanges creates the conditions for those equivalences to be only approximate. Because money and other financial instruments serve not only to clear spot transactions but are also instruments which serve as a store of value, and because the incentives generated in the market may induce producers to mobilize resources in unpredictable ways, we may again invoke our refrain that the market phenomena are not open to Cartesian analysis.

We could call this a *juris et de jure* premise, one that is not capable of being rebutted by evidence. The fundamental idea is not that we do not know where to get the information, but that the information has not been created yet.

PRICE ELASTICITY'S IMPLICATIONS FOR MONEY AND BANKING ARRANGEMENTS, BAD AND GOOD

The implications of the previous section are that some wiggle room exists and that it can benefit the economy in general and money-suppliers in particular to the extent that the latter can manage the marginal costs of supplying additional amounts of money.

Another implication is that different money and banking arrangements have different levels of elasticity in the money supply. This is important because, to the extent that unused productive capacity in the economy exists, systems with more elastic money supplies can better harness those resources. We can see this when Hayek, for instance, accepts that some elasticity exists, with the caveat that we cannot count on elasticity beyond a limited range above what is believed to be nominal "full employment." As Hayek notes, without previous savings, given that there will not be enough intermediary goods, "the impression that the already existing capital structure would enable us to increase production almost indefinitely is a deception" (Hayek, 1999: 259).

Hayek even goes a step further, concluding that it is the natural actual state of the economy to have (except at the peak of a boom) a certain amount of unused capacity (Hayek, 1999: 260). This point is crucial for understanding that there is some flexibility and elasticity in the economy—the spontaneous order in fact requires it, precisely because there is no one in command. People are guided by the market's price signals to arbitrage the existing differences in the structure of production; when they do, those differences tend to be reduced, but they cannot ever be eliminated.

Thus the limits to what can be achieved by elasticity in the money supply. As I had an opportunity to discuss elsewhere,[9] ideally, the supply of money should be entirely endogenous and provided under a competitive regime, which would allow the monetary system to benefit from the marginal costs of money-production. Its supply would, under these ideal conditions, be limited to that which is necessary to fund profitable employments of capital in the economy.

NOTES

1. Unsatisfactory as the verb "to represent" is for our purposes, the fact is that the economy is in trouble if the claims that financial instruments "represent" cannot be all paid back. Furthermore, we are not talking only about government's obligations, but also about other occasions in which capital was destroyed and about occasions in which financial instruments are representative of other financial instruments. To the extent that there is an underlying asset that is productive, derivatives do not seem to be a problem within certain boundaries, but exploring that is beyond the scope of this discussion.

2. This assumes that those debts would be repaid to the citizens with currency of about the same purchasing power as the one borrowed. Mere repayment in nominal terms, at the disposal of any sovereign entity able to devalue the currency of its own issuance, is considered only implicitly here, since inflation may be considered, in its effects, a form of taxation. To the extent that economic agents weigh the current level of inflation in their calculations, they are considering some of that taxation as part of the context of their decision-making. However, if they factored in the level of inflation necessary to erase the public deficit and balance public revenues and expenditures, inflationary expectations would be much higher than they are today. Following along the lines of the Lucas Critique (Lucas, 1976), the fact that inflationary expectations are not as high as they should be to repay the debt, and that

economic agents are acting as if taxes will not increase in the foreseeable future, implies that there are rational expectations that the debt, or at least, some part of it, will not be repaid. One may speculate as to what will happen, or what the economic agents expect to happen, but that is not the purpose of this work. For present purposes, it is sufficient to recognize that the current fiscal unsustainability results in real world consequences for levels of consumption and investments in the economy. For instance, Benjamin Friedman, in "Implications of Government Deficit for U.S. Capital Formation," argues that a fiscal policy of substantial deficits in conditions of full employment has the effect of crowding out net capital formation (Friedman, 1984: 73). He also suggests that the best way to assess the public deficit's impact on capital formation is to compare flows of net savings and net investments in the economy, and table 5, in the same chapter, charts that phenomenon from 1946 to 1983. The public deficit really crowded capital formation out in the early 1980s (Friedman, 1984: 80). According to Friedman, "If government budgets were always balanced (and if the foreign accounts were balanced too, I would add), the share of the economy's output available for net capital formation would simply be the share set aside as net private saving" (Friedman, 1984: 83).

3. To bring close to home what that means, the burden alone of federally funded debt in the United States was USD 42,500 per person in 2015 (DesJardins, 2016). Given that the U.S. Census Bureau reports that the real median household income was about USD 60,000 ($59,039) in 2016, and the average household has 2.6 (2.58 in 2010), if the federal government could miraculously erase its annual deficit and new taxes were imposed to repay the debt in, say, thirty years, at interest rates of 3 percent per year, that would represent an annual tax liability of an extra USD 5,600 (5,597.23) or 9 percent (9.33 percent) of the median household income for the next thirty years.

4. For the most recent long-term budget outlook, see the projections of the Congressional Budget Office (CBO), June 2018.

5. It seems that it is possible to have an extended lag between what is happening on the real side and how it is represented on the abstract side of the economy.

6. An interesting object for research would be to try to understand what prevents economic agents from acting on the information they have about the dire state of public finances. Perhaps one possibility worth testing would be that all the owners of claims against the government think that the moment the state will be unable to honor their obligations, the coercive powers of the state will be used against others (other claimants or other taxpayers) in order to make their claims whole. A second possibility—and the two are not mutually exclusive—is advanced by Richard Salsman: "The (seeming) paradox is that as public leverage ratios have climbed in recent decades, public bonds yields have plunged, explicable partly by the resumption of the autocratic wartime policy of 'financial repression'" (Salsman, 2017: 3). Government mandates may distort demand and supply for credit as with any other market, and "reveal" a price that would not exist except for the presence of coercive measures.

7. This description—of how firms are first supplied along an elastic demand curve, then they must replace inventories, input prices rise, and the supply curve becomes inelastic—is a classic Alchian problem, as was pointed out to me by Jerry O'Driscoll.

O'Driscoll's treatment may be found in, "Information Costs, Pricing and Resource Unemployment" (Alchian, 2006: 53).

8. That, incidentally, is what "saves" the advocates of Modern Monetary Theory—namely, their acknowledgement that what matters in the end, in regard to how much may be spent, is the economy's capacity to create real goods. In the jargon of mainstream economics, that is a recognition that prices are not perfectly elastic.

9. See Zelmanovitz (2016, chapter 11).

Part III

Chapter 5

The Real Side

In the section above about the model (p. 111), I enunciated a formula to indicate what my Representational Theory of Capital (RTC) would be built upon. I had said that everything that exists in the world (Wt) is either the property of someone human (Pr) or a *res nullius*, that is, a property of no one (Rn), and that this state of affairs could be expressed as $Wt = Pr + Rn$.

In a somewhat analogous fashion, we can say that the things in the world that pertain to human beings may be either part of the material world (Wm) or they may be social constructs, part of the intellectual world (Wi). So, we can say that everything that either has a material existence or exists only in our imagination belongs either to someone (Pr) or to no one (Rn); and we may enunciate that as:

$$Wt = Wm + Wi$$

and

$$Wm + Wi = Pr + Rn$$

Obviously, there are almost infinite categories into which we may divide the things that exist in this world, and since our concern is with the representation of capital, I should move as fast as I can in that direction. The original factors of production were classically classified as land and labor. In a more modern nomenclature, we may classify the factors of production as either natural resources (Nr) or as human capital (Kh).[1]

Human capital is basically knowledge (Khk) and dexterity (Khd), which is to say, respectively, the knowledge of what and how to do, and the actual capacity of doing things.[2]

From the original factors of production (and aside from natural resources [Nr]), during the evolution of human societies some utensils, useful tools, and processes of production were conceived, produced, and stored. I will call these either equipment—that is, technical capital (Kt)—or intellectual capital (Ki).

Although things may change categories as human beings become aware of things they did not know existed or of new uses they did not know were possible, generally speaking we may classify them thusly: things known (Kn) and unknown (Ku) to mankind, things with economic value (Eg), things with no economic value (En), and among the things with economic value, we may sub-categorize things as consumer goods (Cg) and capital goods (Kg).

We now have a multidimensional matrix of things that are known and unknown to man, which have material or immaterial existence, which may or may not have economic value, and among the ones that have economic value, which may serve for human beings to satisfy their final needs as consumer goods or things that may serve human beings as instruments for the production of further goods (that is, capital goods).

An illustration deploying the aforementioned terms may help the reader visualize the many combinations in which factors of production may be classified. An exhaustive listing of the possible permutations would not, of course, serve the purpose of this book. By way of illustration of that purpose, let us postulate the following:

From all things that exist (Wt), there are some we know exist (Kn) and others we do not (Ku). Among the things we know exist, some are consumer goods (Cg), and others are instruments for the production of final goods—that is, capital goods (Kg). Among the capital goods, some have physical existence (Kp) while others are immaterial (Ki). Among the ones that have physical existence, some are natural resources (Nr); others are pieces of equipment, stocks, and inventories of intermediary goods that we have referred to above as technical capital (Kt); still others are that part of human capital that represents the capacity to actually do things, which we have called human dexterity (Khd).

In regard to immaterial/intellectual capital, we may find the knowledge already ingrained in social interactions, in processes; for the lack of a better term, let's call that human social capital (Khs), and what each individual person possesses as part of human capital we will call knowledge (Khk). There is a part of human capital that is in part the capacity to do things; this is in part the skill of becoming aware of the surrounding environment, and in part, the knowledge of particular circumstances which someone becomes aware of. Such entrepreneurial capacity I will also classify as immaterial, as part of human capital, divided respectively between knowledge of particular circumstances (*Khc*) and entrepreneurial skills (*Khe*).

$$Wt - Kn + Ku$$

$$Kn = Cg + Kg$$

$$Kg = Kp + Ki$$

$$Kp = Nr + Kt + Khd$$

$$Ki = Khs + Khk + Khc + Khe$$

A CONTINUUM OF USE

The differentiation between consumer goods (*Cg*) and capital goods (*Kg*) is almost never of an absolute nature. The differentiation I am talking about here speaks to the degree to which some goods are used more as final consumer goods than are other goods.

The cutoff line separating capital goods and consumer goods can be drawn by taking economic agents' subjective evaluation of the profitable prospects of having some goods and not others applied to productive processes.[3]

In saying that it is hard to absolutely distinguish consumer goods from capital goods, I am not referring to the fact that some goods may be a capital good while part of the inventory of a retailer, and then become a consumer good after purchase by a final consumer. That particular difficulty in representing actual goods will be discussed at length in part IV, when we move to the abstract side of the economy.

The differentiation I am talking about here involves the degree to which some goods are more obviously used as final consumer goods than are others, with still others very rarely, if ever, being so used.[4] Menger describes the production process in terms of time: It is a sequential process in which lower-order goods are consumption goods, higher-order goods are capital goods, and first-order goods are produced by the application of second-order goods. Although capital goods vary, they may be classified according to where they fit in the sequence of production (Lewin, 1996: 112). However, what put them in that place in the sequence is their use, not necessarily their inherent nature as given by their position in the spectrum of "capitalness" (although the two are obviously related).

When thinking about the real side of the economy and the actual resources necessary to engage in productive processes, we will see cases in which the availability of "consumer" goods are the essential tools required to engage in those ventures. In that sense, they are part of "capital goods," applied to that project.

Consider, for instance, a road-building project in the middle of a sparsely populated region, and the required trailers, food supplies, toiletries, and the like necessary to be supplied to the construction crew. Would anyone reject the idea that in that case, those goods are part of capital goods applied and/or consumed by the construction of that road?

Departing from the distinction between circulating and fixed capital in Menger's stages of capital, we can see that he acknowledges some instances in which circulating capital gets closer to final consumption. The fact that that author has never implied that consumer goods may be equated to circulating capital in some circumstances does not prevent us, however, from going a step further along the same path and perceiving that anything that may be put to a productive endeavor may be considered a capital good, and that this insight is extremely useful for grasping the nature of capital goods—a nature that has eluded those economists who, different from us, do not allow themselves this leap of imagination.

As Lachmann states, "The theory of capital is thus primarily a theory of the material instruments of production" (Lachmann, 1956: 54). His premise is that any structure has a function, and even homogeneous materials may have a different function as part of the structure, and to understand the role of each capital good in a given structure of production is what helps us to understand whether something is or it is not capital. Only then can we gauge its economic significance, and for that, thinking in terms of a continuum of the attributes of some goods and processes may be useful.

So, there is a continuum of the predominant use (f), at any given moment, in which, for the sake of a static classification of what exists, we are forced to establish a threshold between what we consider a consumer good (Cg) and what we consider a capital good (Kg). And yet, the known goods may serve different purposes. The existence of such continuum may be stated as follows:

$$f:(Cg, Kg)$$

Among the goods with economic value (Eg) (defined above), we may classify them either as capital goods (Kg) or consumer goods (Cg). Even acknowledging the permutations of capital and consumer goods, it is reasonable to show different goods as having different degrees of "capitalness" (see figure 5.1 below), in analogy with the concept of "moneyness" that serves to define money as an "adjective" and not as a "noun." Here, it may be perceived

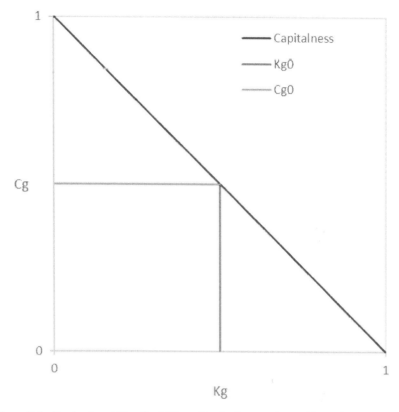

Figure 5.1 Predominant Use (f) of Given Goods. *Source:* Created by author.

that some goods are, by their nature, more suited to being applied as "fixed" capital, while others are more suited, by their nature, to being applied as "circulating" capital. Plotting them along this spectrum, we see the following:

Still in regard to the line separating what at any given time are considered capital goods and what may be considered consumer goods: Although we cannot draw that line other than arbitrarily, the rationale for doing so is given, as I said, by economic agents' subjective evaluation of the profitable prospects of having some goods and not others applied to productive processes. In Lachmann's words: "Something is capital because the market, the consensus of entrepreneurial minds, regards it as capable of yielding an income" (Lachmann, 56: xv).

Whatever resources an economic agent imagines to be a potential instrument for the creation of profits therefore becomes capital, given its application for that purpose. This understanding may be inferred, for instance, from definitions of entrepreneurial activity such as that "profit refers to the added value that results from a redeployment of resources, as a consequence of an insight into their possible uses. In the marketplace, the monetary outcome is a sign of the degree of success of one's insight—that is, the degree of profit" (Den Uyl and Rasmussen, 2016: 299).

In a framework in which the capital structure is functionally differentiated (Lachmann, 2007: 7), it is the application to a given function that defines what capital is, not any intrinsic feature of the goods or processes. Capital resources are scarce and have alternative uses for Lachmann. Capital goods not only must produce goods at prices that consumers are willing to pay, but they must also fit with each other into the capital structure of society (Lachmann, 2007: 8). For Lachmann, "men invest capital in order to have an income. They reshuffle capital goods in order to obtain a higher income than they otherwise would. All capital change is governed by the magnitude of the income thus obtained" (Lachmann, 1956: 74). Perhaps it would be more precise to say that changes in the uses to which all resources are applied are governed, in principle, by the magnitude of the income they may generate, since it is not only the reshuffling of things more obviously perceived as capital goods that may be profitable but also, as I emphasize in this section of the analysis, things that are not so obviously capital goods and yet may perform the function of capital goods if applied to generate income.

A REASONABLE INTERPRETATION OF LACHMANN'S CONCEPT OF CAPITAL

What I have advanced here is that the idea of a continuum of "capitalness" is not only a useful tool to understand the nature of capital on the real side of the economy but also that it is compatible with a strongly subjectivist, Lachmann-style approach to the nature of capital (Lachmann, 2007: xv). That may seem controversial, given the usual, narrower understanding of Lachmann's statements about what capital is; but I would invite the reader to ponder the implications, for the purposes of the current discussion, of statements such as that "the generic concept of capital . . . has no measurable counterpart among material objects; it reflects the entrepreneurial appraisal of such objects" (Lachmann, 2007: xv).[5]

Lachmann's analysis is eminently functionalist. It is, he writes, "from the push and pull of market forces there emerges finally a network of plans which determines the pattern of capital use" (Lachmann, 2007: 10). In other words, what capital is is defined by its use. That cannot be clearer than from Lachmann's very definition of capital: "the (heterogeneous) stock of material resources" (Lachmann, 2007: 11). It is based on Walras's insistence on heterogeneity and Fisher's refusal of the distinction between capital and land. On the other hand, Böhm-Bawerk's definition, as the "produced means of production," is more limited. Some allowance for improvements in the land and efforts to dig minerals out of the ground may be made; still Lachmann's definition is broader, and our claim can be made compatible with it, if not so much with Böhm-Bawerk's.

Making the uses to which resources are put the defining factor in their classification as capital goods is also not compatible with Hayek's definition of capital: "Those non-permanent resources which can be used only . . . to contribute to the permanent maintenance of the income at a particular level" (Hayek, 2014: 75). Hayek is evidently trying there to distinguish capital from "land" in the classical composition of the factors of production. Be that as it may, I trust the reader, by now, to be able to discern the limitations of such a definition.

Let us follow the logical structure of Lachmann's argument: The heterogeneity of capital means heterogeneity in use; heterogeneity in use implies multiple specificity; multiple specificity implies complementarity; complementarity implies capital combinations; and capital combinations form the elements of the capital structure (Lachmann, 2007: 12). In such a structure, the real function of the entrepreneur is to constantly adjust the capital structure to the requirements of an ever-changing world (Lachmann, 2007: 13).

As we have just seen, for Lachmann, "the theory of capital has to start from the fact that the capital goods with which the entrepreneurs operate are heterogeneous." They also need to be used together; there is a complementarity among them, and each "production plan" implies a certain combination of them. For Lachmann, "The theory of capital has to explain why capital goods are being used the way they are." The theory needs to explain why entrepreneurs combine capital goods the way they do and why they rearrange them the way they do when compelled to change their production plans (Lachmann, 2007: 35). However, these changes may be in the use of the goods, not necessarily in the production of different goods.

Böhm-Bawerk's contribution to Capital Theory as developed by Menger (who emphasized the importance of time for production) was to add a quantifiable variable: "average time of production"; but some of his critics considered this innovation meaningless. Böhm-Bawerk concerned himself with how an increase in capital occurs, and with the consequences of increases in capital. Both Böhm-Bawerk and Menger thought that changes in the amount of capital are associated with changes in the time of production, and therefore in the entire structure of production, since the adoption of more capital (additional savings) "happens at the expense of lower order goods and makes possible higher maturities classes (of goods)" (Garrison, 1981: 24). Here we see Böhm-Bawerk and Menger anticipating Lachmann once more in his emphasis that changes in the accumulation of capital imply changes in the structure of production (Lewin, 1996: 114).

Therefore, there is this time dimension to production, and the longer (or more roundabout) the process is, potentially the more productive it is. Menger made clear, however (although Böhm-Bawerk did not follow him in this), that savings (postponing consumption to the future) are neither sufficient nor necessary to increase productivity. For Menger, the time invested in the creation of capital goods is sufficient. He believed, for example, that if a farmer intervenes earlier on in the natural process, he can have better results.

However, I do not think that this explanation is valid. It could be possible to find a way to rearrange the existing capital and make it more productive than the previous combination of capital. A change in the technological level can bring this about. But if the change is a change in time, you need more savings in order to survive while the more roundabout method evolves. For instance, the vintner who rearranges his vines two or three years before they start to bear fruit instead of just pruning his vines at the beginning of the season needs savings to wait for the results of his effort to appear (Lewin, 1996: 112).

Consider another example: a baker. How much of the bread he bakes feeds his family, and how much does he keep as inventory for sale in his bakery? Once a day has passed and some of the bread in the inventory has not been sold, he may even decide to write it off and give it to charity since the possibility of making a profit with what remains of yesterday's bread has disappeared.

In sum, the traditional subjectivism at the core of the Austrian approach to capital is a good mooring for the statement in this chapter that the direction of the trend (*f*) toward a more evident classification of some goods as capital goods is a consequence of a greater conviction among "entrepreneurial minds" about those profits' possibilities, which leads them to apply those goods predominantly, but not always, not necessarily, as intermediary goods.

CAPITAL GOODS HAVE DIFFERENT LEVELS OF "PERMUTABILITY"

The same idea of a continuum between consumer goods and capital goods may be applied to the different levels of "permutability" among different capital goods. The idea here is that there are capital goods that are more "malleable" to different uses (*Kgm*) while others are much more specific for certain uses (*Kgr*). Again, as a function of their greater or lesser malleability

(m), the existing capital goods may be classified along a continuum whose formal statement may be the following:

$$m{:}\left(Kgm, Kgr\right)$$

As seen previously, this discussion of malleable capital is common in the Austrian economics literature, and although it is not particularly novel, it is an important part of the formal model here proposed.

From the perspective of the neoclassical synthesis, statements about the malleability of capital goods will be tantamount to saying that defining capital stock is impossible because of its fluidity. An example of that would be the statement that cars are "consumption good today, investment good tomorrow." What may be seen as a problem may not, from the perspective I am trying to convey here, be a problem at all if cars are classified not only as consumption goods but also as a special category of such goods—that is, durable goods. Under this assumption, car prices reflect not only the net present value of whatever use as an Uber car the owner decides to apply it to, but also the value attributed to it given its availability for personal use.

That is, you may think about the price of a car as simply the cost of buying equity claims to the flow of utility and income from owning that car, regardless of the use to which it will be put. Our neoclassical friends may remind us that durable goods are often included as investment in Real Business Cycle models. They even acknowledge that there is indeed something missing from our measurement of the capital stock, such as the intractable problem of valuing capital when there are not liquid markets for those specific goods. However, they do not think that the malleability of uses poses a problem for the measurement of capital.

My answer to them, regarding the fluidity of what counts as a capital good at any given time, is that this is not something we may learn from the price of any given good. For example, we may think about things like batteries, which may be final or intermediary goods depending on someone's having found a profitable opportunity to employ them in a productive process. My qualm is exactly with the assumption that looking at the goods themselves, you can pronounce upon whether they are capital, like the argument that cars are capital goods to begin with.

To insist on a homogenous treatment of goods, where only quantitative (prices, quantities) differences exist, is to miss the fact that some goods are more malleable than others to different uses and therefore more or less able to be "plugged in" to different structures of production.

Of course, this is not a novel conclusion. We can see already in Lachmann a clear statement that "it is because of these facts that it is impossible to measure capital. Capital has no 'natural' measure, and value will be affected by

every unexpected change." "Only some modes of complementarity are economically significant. These form the basis of the capital order." "The capital
combinations of the various enterprises . . . form the capital structure of
society." "The Theory of Capital is, in the last resort, the morphology of the
forms which this pattern assumes in a changing world" (Lachmann, 2007: 4).

The upshot is that we can see the importance of that feature of Lachmann's
and Lewin's proposed new theoretical framework: Capital is heterogeneous
and complementary, and different entrepreneurial plans take this into consideration. How? Complementarity imposes restrictions on capital allocation.
For the capital composition to change, a reshuffling is necessary, and that
takes time—time, that is, somewhere between the Marshallian "short" and
"long" term. The change in the composition of capital affects complementarity on two levels, the single firm and the market. At the firm level, the need
for changes leads to a reshuffling of the production plan. At the market level,
it leads to (without ever reaching) accommodation and harmonization of the
different plans. Because of the specific character of capital goods, not all of
them can be moved to new second-best uses without losses when they become
redundant (Lewin, 1996: 145); and it is here that the differences in the malleability of the resources make a difference in how we may apply them.

CAPITAL GOODS ARE HETEROGENEOUS

The proper way to describe the stock of capital (Kg) would be to take into
account that it is composed of the sum of many different items. In the model
only, I will continue to describe the stock of capital (Kg) as if it were composed of homogeneous elements with an economic value (Eg) whose sum is
or could be known. I maintain this highly useful simplification for didactic
purposes.

But Ludwig Lachmann said it all when he wrote: "The root of the trouble
is well known: capital resources are heterogeneous." His reference to "the
multiple specificity of capital goods" is apt here. They are heterogeneous
in a way that mere quantitative measurements do not adequately reflect
(Lachmann, 2007: 2).

Capital is heterogeneous in many dimensions: It is at the same time a collection of goods on the real side of the economy and a collection of financial
instruments on the monetary side. On the real side, it is composed of all
possible goods and services that can be put to productive use, as well as
goods which may be used as a store of value without any evident productive
application. On the financial side, it is composed of many different classes
of financial instruments, with varied degrees of liquidity (cash, time deposits,
bonds) and of certainty (stocks, bonds, future contracts).

At this time, I am very skeptical we can understand how all of the permutations of capital take place. Certainly any attempt to treat it as homogeneous, as if it could be understood by quantitative changes of it as an aggregate number, except for the limited purposes of the model, seems to me to be insufficient to capture its significance.

It is noteworthy that this final formulation in regard to actual capital goods (*Kg*), that they are heterogeneous, is already implicit in the previous statement that they have different degrees of malleability; or even more clearly in the claim above that the stock of capital is composed by some goods with physical existence and others which are immaterial. In any case, the proper way to describe more precisely the stock of capital in existence in a given society is to consider such stock of capital (*Kg*) as composed of the sum of many different items, whose formulation may be the following:

$$\Sigma Kg: \left(Kg1, Kg2, Kgn \right)$$

To the extent that the unrealism of treating capital as homogeneous is kept in mind, it should help us avoid the temptation of taking any figure as representative of the stock of capital really in existence in a given society. It was the classical economists who conceived of capital as homogeneous and measurable. I hold, as I said, a contrasting view. Why the classical economists insisted on this, we can learn from Lachmann: "After Ricardo, their main interest was the distribution of incomes, being capital the source of profits, labor the source of wages and land the source of rents" (Lachmann, 2007: 5). For Lachmann, the classical economists thought of capital as homogeneous because the labor theory of value considered labor as divided into homogeneous units and the "wages fund" concept reduced capital goods to consumer goods measurable in labor units.

In the 1870s, the neoclassical economics started to explain the distribution of income by the marginal productive principle: Factors of production were no longer considered to be uniform across society (not measured in labor), but inside each class, and the analysis is still done in equilibrium, although no clear measure of capital exists, given the limitations of applying marginalist reasoning to heterogeneous capital (Lachmann, 2007: 5).

Lachmann also quotes contemporary economists as defining investment as the "net addition to the capital stock." Abba Lerner defines his "marginal efficiency of investment" in terms of present production forgone and future output obtained (Lerner, 1953: 6–9). However, proceeding as if capital were homogeneous and quantifiable handicaps one in registering changes in the composition of the capital stock; the homogeneous/quantifiable approach can only perceive quantitative changes. Keynesian theories display the same infirmity. Contrariwise, if we accept that capital is heterogeneous, we accept that there are problems of compatibility and complementarity between old and new capital that may explain different levels of profitability between them (Lachmann, 2007: 6).

What are the consequences of accepting the terminological distinction that Lachmann makes between capital goods and capital? According to Lewin (Lewin, 1996: 117), for Lachmann (1956: xv) there is a difference between capital goods and capital, the former being physical objects created by man or inherited by nature, which may be used to produce other goods; and the latter being a value estimated subjectively by each entrepreneur and thus unable to be aggregated. The latter cannot be measured unless we were in a static equilibrium, and that is why Lachmann prefers to think in a framework of disequilibrium.

Lewin explains that for Lachmann, "The heterogeneity of capital only matters in disequilibrium." Although Lachmann, according to Lewin, rejects the idea that it is useful to aggregate the value of capital as if capital goods were homogeneous, it is possible to perceive the logic of different combinations of capital goods—hence this should be at the very center of capital studies.

Well, it is good to keep in mind that the structure of capital is not set by caprice and that it is adequate to a certain structure of consumption that it is supposed to serve. Still, I do not think that this insight invalidates the benefit of knowing the aggregate value of capital, although that is clearly not sufficient to have the full picture of capital in society (Lewin, 1996: 117). Lachmann, as understood by Lewin (1996: 143), acknowledges that if you assume homogeneity as Böhm-Bawerk does, the only difference possible is time. But if you accept the heterogeneity of the capital, then questions about its composition arise. So, discussing "beyond homogeneity," both Lachmann and Lewin call attention to the fact that if we accept that capital is heterogeneous, we have to contend with not only the quantity but the composition of the capital that we are planning to add to the stock of capital—and the existing structure of production constrains what capital will be compatible with what other capital.

CAPITAL GOODS ARE COMPLEMENTARY

The complementarity of capital helps to explain some differences in the results of new additions of capital to an existing structure of production, in ways that additions of value to the stock of capital simply cannot.

As stated by Lachmann: "For most purposes, capital goods have to be used jointly. Complementarity is of the essence of capital goods. But the heterogeneous capital resources do not lend themselves to combination in any arbitrary fashion." "Unexpected change, whenever it occurs, will make possible, or compel, changes in the uses of capital goods" (Lachmann, 2007: 3). He even offers as an alternative to Böhm-Bawerk's theory: he offers instead the idea of "exploitable indivisibilities," to explain how the structure of capital becomes more complex and productive (Lachmann, 1956: 81). This aspect of complementarity explains why Lachmann proposed what he called Process Analysis—that is, the method that should replace or complement equilibrium analysis. "It is a causal-genetic method of studying economic change, tracing the effects of decisions made independently of each other by a number of individuals through time, and showing how the incompatibility of these decisions after a time necessitates their revision" (Lachmann, 1956: 38).

Still with complementarity in mind, for Lachmann, "Process analysis, we may say, combines the equilibrium of the decision-making unit, firm or household, with the disequilibrium of the market . . . It is true of course that the market serves to produce interpersonal consistency, but it does so indirectly by modifying the conditions of action of the individuals" (Lachmann, 2007: 40). This form of analysis accounts for capital at two levels: Inside of individual firms, it explains the use of specific capital goods in specific plans of production; at a level above that, it tries to explain the "consistency" of the many different plans that comprise the "plan structure" of the economy.

Capital goods therefore have direct complementarity at times—that is, when by entrepreneurial activity they have plan complementarity—and indirect complementarity at other times, when they have structural complementarity (Lachmann, 1956: 54). For Lachmann, the differences between the two theories, between Process Analysis and Böhm-Bawerk's, as explained on page 83, are first that for Böhm-Bawerk "all capital is circulating capital," while for Lachmann the "layers of specialized capital equipment and their mode of change are the essence of the matter"; and second, Böhm-Bawerk uses time to measure his flow of goods, while Lachmann talks about the changes in capital composition as more stages are added.

NOTES

1. This redefinition of the factors of production as natural resources and human capital serves the purposes of the model proposed with this work for representing economic goods and capital (in particular, in property claims) better than the traditional classification of those factors as land, labor, and capital. Also, there is no point here in commenting on the debate concerning whether human capital is "really" capital. Finally, I understand that it has become clear from the initial explanation of the model that everything that exists in the world that may be appropriated for human purposes is here categorized as "natural resources."

2. In the categories proposed with this model, "knowledge" (Khk) is part of intellectual capital (Ki), and it may or may not be represented by a title on intellectual property, as we will see in Part IV when discussing the abstract side of the model.

3. "Puesto que la naturaleza del objectos adquirido no establece la diferencia entre consumo e inversión es preciso en primer lugar remontarse hasta a la intención de quien compra" (Mathieu, 1990: 166).

4. Another possible classification, a somewhat intermediary one between the one from accounting and the one of relative suitability for productive uses, is the one offered by Professor Carmelo Ferlito, in a recent book, in which he distinguishes "potential capital goods" from "actual capital goods." For Professor Ferlito such distinction happens before and after the moment in which some goods "are thought to be suitable for generating a certain output" (Ferlito, 2016: 14). Such classification, emphasizing the subjective nature of the classification seems compatible with the ones proposed in this work.

5. Professor Carmelo Ferlito also reached a similar conclusion about the possibility of going further by following Lachmann's reasoning to its logical consequences. According to him, Lachmann "failed to develop a definition of capital consistent with his own insights (Ferlito, 2016: 11). That is why he offers his own definition of capital "as the outcome of subjective mental processes, determined by individual intentions and expectations and not by specific physical or economic features" (Ferlito, 2016: xvi).

Chapter 6

The Spatial Dimension of Capital

Although not introduced in the model, instructive with regard to the hetero-geneity and complementarity of capital is the spatial dimension of the capital structure as proposed by Åke E. Andersson and David Emanuel Andersson. In their 2017 book *Time, Space and Capital*, Andersson and Andersson offer a summary of previous contributions to Capital Theory that is also a critical review.[1] They highlight the relevance of location to any meaningful discussion of the capital structure of a society, and in so doing, bring into view a dimension of the capital structure's heterogeneous elements that, with few exceptions in the literature,[2] normally does not receive enough attention. That dimension is space.

The stock of capital in any society is going to be composed, in substantial part, of real estate assets and also of pieces of equipment that are immovable for practical purposes. The implications of what is immovable versus what is movable are many. The authors argue that the very structure of production is shaped spontaneously by the multitude of entrepreneurial agents, who must factor in the constraints of the spatial distribution of factors of production and markets. In the same way that we cannot truly understand investment decisions without taking into consideration the time required for a given capital investment to mature, our authors claim that neither can we understand those decisions without considering the location of the relevant factors about which the entrepreneur, in taking action, needs to be aware.

Their treatment of time as a dimension of production, basically a critical review of the literature on the topic in Capital Theory, is illustrative. They offer valuable charts on "Spatiotemporal theory and modeling choices" (p. 84) and "Types of capital by rate of change and scope of effects" (p. 161).

Their description of "different continuous and interactive timescales" of economic processes (p. 6) makes a difficult concept so easy to understand that it reminded me of the chronology of the 2017 movie *Dunkirk*. It also helps to identify which capital goods are the most relevant ones to consider in regard to location and those are the most durable ones. That is also the criterion for them to emphasize the infrastructure necessary for production in their treatment of capital.

Time, Space, and Capital also brings in related topics, such as the relevance of time for the formation of expectations, among both consumers and entrepreneurs. It covers both static and dynamic economic models of production and the role of different forms of capital in each. Its discussion of real estate properties and infrastructure pays particular attention to the role of transportation in the economy, from both a theoretical and a historical perspective. Our authors argue, in regard to transportation costs, that "trade is advantageous even in the case where production possibilities and consumer preferences are identical in both regions" (p. 12), which statement expands the Ricardian argument of comparative advantages.

Immaterial forms of capital are discussed, as well, with special attention to social capital and creative knowledge. Andersson and Andersson develop a unique approach to understanding capital formation, a signal contribution to the field. But their book is not without its flaws and omissions. Their treatment of material infrastructural capital (p. 165) would have been clearer had they incorporated the concept of the exclusionary use of public goods. Whether a society's institutional framework is deemed part of the non-material infrastructure (p. 174) or is a third form of infrastructure (p. 163) is left ambiguous. On page 179, in discussing what they call "The first logistical revolution in Europe," around the twelfth century, they mention the *Lex Mercatoria*, but there is no reference to the "Papal Revolution" or the Gregorian reforms. The issue of investitures and the establishment of the "peace and truce of God" in many places inaugurated the recognition of private property by the recently institutionalized barbarian kingdoms, as proposed by Harold Berman[3] This has great relevance for their thesis.

In the creative knowledge chapter (chapter 13), the authors offer the dubious statement that knowledge was "rarely" treated by economists before the 1980s. This is disappointing. They omit Hayek's 1945 "The Use of Knowledge in Society," an important and influential contribution well before the last two decades of the twentieth century. More importantly, the chapter lacks any treatment whatsoever of knowledge that is not "scientific."

However, my main problem with the book is how it addresses the value of land. I understand it fits their model to link it to the costs of transportation. But if it is to create a general rule, it is difficult for me to accept any other proposition than that the value of land is a function of its capacity to produce a service, a utility. In formal terms, the value of any real estate property is the present value of the discounted stream of income that is possible to generate with it. Granted, such utility may be (usually is) determined by its location; but there is more to the question, for zoning is also a key element that is not adequately discussed in chapter 11 on real estate capital.

In the section on land-use regulations (p. 223), the authors speak of why urban planning is so anti-market—Marxist influence on the universities, according to them. There is a discussion of negative externalities and the failure of many urban planners to see how entrepreneurship may mitigate them. But again, the relevance of zoning to the determination of real estate value is missing from the equation—even when the topic is the artificial limitation of the supply of urban land (p. 224). Not even in the section on regulations, expectations, and the value of real estate capital (p. 228) we can learn of the impact of regulation on what you can and cannot do with your property, and on that property's market price. There is only a limited example of the impact of regulation on expectations, no discussion of zoning changes, or the uncertainty of permits, or rent-seeking activities that extract rents in and clog up the licensing process. There is, to be fair, an explicit mention of transaction costs created by regulation as driving away new entrants; however, it seems to me that that is a parallel discussion, not the same thing.

Andersson and Andersson do discuss the impact of ideology on transaction costs. They compare the states of Texas and California in that regard. They could have contrasted Texas' two major cities, Dallas with its stringent zoning, and Houston, the biggest American city without a zoning code. This would have enriched their state-to-state comparison. As would references to North on ideology and economic performance,[4] and to Siegan on land use.[5] Those flaws and omissions, though, do not compromise the book's valuable addition to the literature on capital. As I said, that contribution lies in its exploration of the spatial dimension of capital. It helps us to understand the variations in economic value of the same piece of land if subject to different regimes of property, and conversely, the difference in economic value of equal pieces of land with similar regimes of property, but in different locations. Those differences cannot be explained by focusing only on the physical aspects of the land, or only on the elements of the land's property claims. The two elements must be held in view simultaneously to glean the importance of the different kinds of property claims they consider.

NOTES

1. This chapter is based on my review of Andersson and Andersson (Zelmanovitz, 2019a).
2. The exceptions, say the authors, are von Thunen, Launhardt, Weber, Palander, and Losch (p. 10).
3. Berman (1983).
4. North (1992).
5. Siegan (1972).

Part IV

Chapter 7

The Abstract Side

Let us now move to the other side of the equation. All things in the world (Wt) belong either to someone (Pr) or to no one (Rn), as we have said. So far, we've covered those things and combinations of things that are or can be the object of property rights. Now we may begin to develop a deeper understanding of the different forms of property rights, that is, the other side of the equation.

Beginning once again with $Wt = Pr + Rn$, we can now add that, among the things that belong to someone, they may be the private property of some individual or group of individuals (Pp), or they may belong to some political association (Pg). We can express this as:

$$Pr = Pp + Pg$$

Among the things owned by individuals, they may be individual property (Ppi) or property owned in some form of co-ownership—that is, in condominium, such as a share in a social club or in a business enterprise (Ppc). We can formulate this as:

$$Pp = Ppi + Ppc$$

EQUITY CLAIMS AND THEIR DERIVATIVES

In the static model, all the things owned by individuals (Pp) are considered equity claims, while fixed income obligations or "debts" (D), whether or not they are financial instruments, are considered derivatives of the equity claims.

There are many categories in which the total of credit in the economy (*D*) may be classified and, depending on the purpose to which the model is applied, this total may be broken down in more or in less detail. For instance, it may be separated into private (*Dp*) and public debt (*Dg*).

For the purposes of the static model, all the things owned by individuals (*Pp*) are considered equity claims, while fixed income obligations, or "debts" (*D*), regardless of whether or not they are financial instruments, are considered to be derivatives of those equity claims. Public debt may be understood to be a derivative of the government's prerogative of taxation, as we will see below.

THINGS OWNED BY POLITICAL ENTITIES

We cannot explain how claims on goods on the abstract side of the economy are related to actual goods on the real side of the economy if we do not first explain the relation between private property and the taxing and monetary prerogatives of government. That relationship is crucial for the Representational Theory of Capital (RTC) at the center of the present work.

Recurring once again to our basic enunciation (that $Wt = Pr + Rn$), because access to the possession of actual goods in the world (*Wt*) granted by a sovereign's prerogatives (*Pgp*) is essentially a function of claims on part of the private property rights owned by others (*Pp*), the derivative nature of governmental prerogatives requires further elaboration in order for us to make a formal statement about them.

According to the traditional classification of goods owned by political entities (*Pg*) in Continental systems of law, these goods may be things for common use, such as a park or a road with open access for most practical purposes (*Pgc*); things assigned to a specific purpose, such as a military base or a public school, in which entrance is conditioned to the public service performed on the premises (*Pgs*); and things that, despite belonging to the public, supposedly serve as a source of revenue to the fisc, such as offshore mineral rights (*Pgf*).[1]

For the purposes of the model, aside from public property held for fiscal reasons, I will define the fiscal prerogatives of the government (*Pgp*)—respectively, to raise taxes (*Pgpt*) and to regulate money (*Pgpm*)—as kinds of property claims. Bear in mind that such extreme simplification may be confusing; but, like the simplification made earlier in defining "labor" as "human capital," the idea of equating the prerogatives of government to property claims allows us to create a workable model. Another simplification of reality is that, for the purposes of the model, except for the sovereign's prerogatives, we will assume property rights as a single bundle of rights.

For the further purposes of the model, I will assume that the exercise of the sovereign's prerogatives of taxing and of regulating money has an impact on the private property claims held over things that exist in the world as a simple discount at a defined tax rate (tr) and at certain time intervals $(n, n+1, \ldots)$.

Such tax rate (tr) is not necessarily the same as the rate of return (rr) in the economy. The tax rate is a political decision while the rate of return in the economy (rr) is a brute fact; and, in the model, we define it as net of depreciation but still before taxes, and it may be understood as the difference between the total of property claims (Pp) at the initial moment (n) and the total of property claims (Pp) at a second moment $(n+1)$.

$$rr = Pp1 / Pp0 - 1$$

To the extent that the model is presented as static, there is a given amount of property claims that belongs to the government.

To the extent that the model is presented as dynamic, property claims in the following moment $(n+1)$ will reflect a transference of property by the same tax rate of discount (tr) from the distribution of property claims that existed in the initial moment of the analysis (n).

For the sake of simplification, it is assumed in the model that only private property (Pp) generates economic growth; and the rate of return of the entire economy (rr) is defined as a function of private property (Pp). Such simplification means assuming that all governmental property owned for the purpose of generating income (Pgf) has a return of zero in the model.

For the purposes of a dynamic model, the notation of the present value of the future stream of revenues of all titles of fixed income in the model (D) should correspond to a first derivative of the property rights directly exercised over certain goods and productive procedures on the real side of the economy; while the government's prerogatives to raise taxes would be also a competitive claim on that, and, therefore, another first derivative of those rights, or a second derivative of those rights, to the extent that the taxing powers are used to tax fixed income.

In the same way, the public debt, to the extent that it is also a derivative of the taxing prerogatives of government, may be either a second derivative of property rights over things on the real side of the economy or a third derivative of them, to the extent that they are serviced by taxes on fixed income.

As noted earlier, the RTC model requires that government's fiscal prerogatives to raise taxes and regulate money be deemed property claims. Therefore, the complete formal expression of the government's "property" will be:

$$Pg = Pgc + Pgs + Pgf + Pgp$$

and

$$Pgp = Pgpt + Pgpm$$

Property rights are bundles of more specific rights. What are commonly understood as property rights may include the right to transfer property or, in the case of property in land, the right to search for underground mineral deposits. Human societies long ago learned how to unbundle and rearrange the separate elements of what we usually assume to be property rights. Nowadays, they may come in many different combinations, such as the right to own some good separated from the right to the income it may generate (such as with usufructuary rights); the right to benefits from property separated from the fiduciary responsibility to manage the property on behalf of the beneficiary (such as in a trust); and other similar permutations.

For the purposes of this model, except for the sovereign's prerogatives that take a more complex form, we will assume property rights as a single bundle, composed of the rights to dispose of the thing, to possession of the thing itself (that is, to its use), to its fruits, and to transfer it. Such rights are understood to be limited only by local ordinances regarding public health and the obligation to pay taxes to fund the provision of public goods.[2]

Moreover, taxes on equity instruments (that is, on property-rights claims over real goods or Pp) may be equated to taxes on goods and productive processes on the real side of the economy directly (Kn), since in the model, by definition, taxes have as their object the property claims and not the goods themselves. In the model, I have opted to consider taxation as applicable to private property claims (Pp) on all known goods (Kn) and not only on capital goods (Kg). That may seem an arbitrary decision, but it does highlight that taxation may be a way to expropriate unproductive assets.

However, my main reasons for considering tax revenues as derivatives are to emphasize their character, dependent on the existence of actual wealth being produced in the long run; and also, for the purposes of a dynamic model, to avoid double-counting of the same stream of revenues once the income from some productive activity is transferred to pay the equity investors or the fixed income creditors financing that operation, and such financial income is taxed and the product of those taxes used to service the public debt.

NOTES

1. See, for example, the Brazilian Civil Code, Article 98, 2002.
2. I do not think the "bundle" of rights that I have designated as "full" property rights for the sake of simplification is a necessary feature of the model. If the "strongest" rights over what exist in the world are usufructuary rights, the idea of

representation still holds. However, I do not think the only natural rights are rights to use, or that those rights do not include the right to exclude use by others, as already discussed in footnote 19. Personally, I do not think that mere usufructuary rights cre-ate the proper incentives for the conservation of our endowments, be they "land" or man-made tools. And tho reason is simple: without a last claimant, no one is vested in the preservation of the residual value of anything. A society in which there are only rights to "use" things is a society in which the rate of depreciation of goods will be higher and therefore the economic "efficiency" will be lower. One might counter that some inefficiency is a tolerable side effect of greater equality. Without disputing that, I would only say two things:

First, a difference in economic growth of +1 percent per year implies that in one generation, the wealth of that society would be a third higher than otherwise. Imagine having, twenty-five years in the future, an additional one-third more of everything, from porn shops and tattoo parlors to hospitals and schools.

Second, I am not convinced that distribution by coercion—that is, by the political process—brings greater equality. On the contrary; my knowledge of Brazil, in particular, makes me extremely cynical about how much redistribution from the wealthy to the poor can be done by the government. In Brazil, the social security sys-tem, public funding for education, "universal" health care, and programs of economic development are all regressive policies. That is, their net result is to confer income on the beneficiaries of those schemes that gives those beneficiaries higher incomes per capita than the average population. With the aggravation that the actual beneficiaries are not necessarily the needy or the supposedly intended ones.

In the United States, for the little I know, the results are similar: Beneficiaries of public pensions, public functionaries, recipients of subsidies, all receive greater remuneration than the average Joe, the median citizen, with the result that income inequality after redistribution done by the political process is greater than what it would be otherwise. Imagine a less productive society, one in which no one has an incentive to care for the conservation of the things they have received the right to use and, furthermore, one in which the assignation of rights to use is done by Tammany Hall—that would be the end result of the abolition of "full" property rights, in my opinion. But as I said, the concept of representation still would be valid under social-ism, so long as the society is still a monetary society.

Chapter 8

Financial Instruments

To summarize, property rights on the abstract side of the economy take in the following elements:

$$Wt = \left(Ppi + Ppc\right) + \left(Pgc + Pgs + Pgf + \left[Pgpt + Pgpm\right]\right) + Rn$$

Next, let us define what financial instruments ($Ppcf$) are. They are a kind of private property held in common (Ppc) which, for their properties of liquidity and certainty, are traded in financial markets (or capital markets). The kind of market we are talking about is important. In order to be accepted in the more organized variety, those intrinsic properties of a financial instrument are key, marking them as different from other forms of titles to private property held in common which are traded in markets that are less structured ($Ppcn$).

The formula for property held in common is:

$$Ppc = Ppcn + Ppcf$$

And, the complete formal expression of the elements on the abstract side of the economy is:

$$Wt = \left(Ppi + \left[Ppcn + Ppcf\right]\right) + Pgc + Pgs + Pgf + \left[Pgpt + Pgpm\right] + Rn$$

What this formula encapsulates is that all things in the world, material and immaterial, known or unknown, with economic value or not, suitable to final consumption or to be used as intermediary goods, including human capital—if these are not the property of the state (public property) or the property of no one (res nullius)—are either (1) the private property of a single individual or (2) the common property (condominium) of some group of individuals, and in this case, their property claims may be represented by illiquid instruments or by relatively more liquid instruments, the latter being financial instruments.

In regard to public property, some of this property is open to the common use of the people, some is designated for special uses, and some is simply held by one political entity or another with the purpose of getting income, as any private owner would do. I have also classified as "public property" the prerogatives of the government to tax those living under that government and to pursue political goals with the provision and regulation of money.

FURTHER REFINEMENTS, INCLUDING THE FINANCIAL INSTRUMENTS ISSUED BY SOVEREIGN ENTITIES

Financial instruments that are privately issued (*Ppcf*) may be further divided into those that do not have monetary properties (*Ppcfn*), and those that may be considered money substitutes (*Ppcfm*).

There are two other forms of financial instruments issued by political entities that exercise sovereign prerogatives: public debt and money. In the static model, these are considered subcategories, respectively, of the fiscal prerogatives—the taxing prerogative and the monetary prerogative—of government.

Again in the static model, the prerogative of taxation (*Pgpt*) is equivalent to the stock of public debt in a broad sense (*Dg*);[1] and it may be subcategorized as unfunded (*Pgptu*) and as consolidated in financial instruments representative of the public debt (*Pgptd*).

$$Pgpt = Dg$$

Such identity, of course, is not carried over to the dynamic model, where the exercise of the prerogative of taxation at a given rate determines the stock of public debt that may be reasonably served and therefore that debt is able to keep its nominal value.[2]

Back to the static model: In the same way that the taxing prerogative divides into subcategories, the monetary prerogative (*Pgpm*) may be divided into diffuse powers to exercise financial repression (*Pgpmd*) and the power to coin money properly speaking (*Pgpmp*).

$$Pgp = \left(Pgptu + Pgptd\right) + \left(Pgpmd + Pgpmp\right)$$

While the public debt (*Pgptd*) and money proper (*Pgpmp*) are financial instruments, only the former is traded in capital markets.

We can see from the foregoing that financial instruments that are privately issued (*Ppcf*) are just one of the many forms that property claims may take. An additional subclassification to keep in mind is that some privately issued financial instruments, liquid as they are, do not have monetary properties (*Ppcfn*), while others may have monetary properties, and thus may be considered money substitutes (*Ppcfm*). Be that as it may, they are not money proper.

$$Ppcf = Ppcfn + Ppcfm$$

So far, we have discussed the two sides of the equation: the side of natural and social realities, and the abstract side, in which those realities are represented by property claims. I have noted that among the real things (both material and immaterial, both social and natural), there are some that may be used as intermediary goods for enhancing the production of other goods; and those we call capital goods (*Kg*). I have also noted that, among the many different property claims, there are some that are considered financial instruments due to their properties of certainty and liquidity, added to the fact that they are generally transacted in more organized markets—that is, capital markets. Notable exceptions to the general categorization of financial instruments as claims traded in capital markets are money proper and money substitutes. Although they are the quintessential financial instruments (due to their properties), they are also traded outside of financial markets, since they are the counterpart of almost every transaction but barter transactions.

Under modern financial arrangements, government's monetary prerogatives have allowed it substantial discretion to politically allocate resources and to extract rents, generally called *seigniorage* revenue. The importance of these prerogatives becomes clear by the way governments protect them, as we will see from the section below.

WHAT WOULD "THE TREASURY VIEW" OF LIBRA BE?

Teaching us even more about the nature of governments' monetary prerogatives are their reactions to attempts to infringe on those prerogatives. A prominent example in our day is the Libra, the Facebook-backed cryptocurrency first proposed in a white paper released in June 2019 and reviewed in April 2020.[3] Judging from the white paper, Facebook and its partners in this project are seeking to launch a mechanism that, by overcoming the problems facing all previous forms of cryptocurrency, could become a generally accepted medium of exchange on the Internet worldwide.

The intent is to create a privately issued currency that will be backed by a basket of hard currencies issued by major central banks. It is supposed to be similar to a currency issued by a currency board, meaning backed by reserve currencies and assets denominated in those currencies and therefore similarly stable in value.

Libra's architects hope to lower transaction costs for operations in this new currency, thus allowing the free flow of resources worldwide, at less expense. Much more could be said about the details of Libra, but one can already get a sense of the major headwinds its architects will encounter in trying to implement their plan.

What the plan really does is make one wonder how much thought they gave to: (1) the nature of money, and (2) how their creation fits within existing constraints. Not enough—or so it seems at first glance, even in its version 2.0.

According to the proposal, Libra is intended to be "a new decentralized blockchain, a low-volatility cryptocurrency, and a smart contract platform that together aim to create a new opportunity for responsible financial services innovation." As a way to indicate my skepticism about the capacity of Facebook and company to achieve these goals, let me contrast them with what I would call "the Treasury view," that is, considering not the fiscal policy effects on aggregate demand, but the responses to Libra that are likely from the civil servants and politicians in charge of exercising the monetary prerogatives of the U.S. government.

The "Treasury view" (simulated by me as a member of the public with, I want to make clear, no ties to the United States or any other government) entails recognizing that, if the state is to protect the life and property of its citizens, it must be able to use force—either externally, through the armed forces, or domestically, through the police. Monetary prerogatives, in this sense, are just one more weapon in the armory of the Republic. They give the state the capacity to procure stocks of goods beyond the limits of its taxing base at any given time, either by borrowing or, in extremis, by inflating the currency. Notwithstanding the fact that the monetary prerogatives (issuing money and regulating finances) have been applied to uses other than war-finance, the fact is that the original reason for the national state to monopolize them was war-finance. The original reason to hold those prerogatives still remains.

Before addressing Libra's relation to these existing arrangements, let us talk about one of the derivative applications of the government's monetary prerogatives that has become standard nowadays in most countries: the management of capital flows.

First, let us assume the validity of the "impossible trinity" as proposed by the Mundell-Fleming Trilemma, which is that a country cannot simultaneously have a fixed exchange rate, monetary discretion, and free international flows of capital.

Next, let us agree with Facebook and its partners that "global, open, instant, and low-cost movement of money will create immense economic opportunity and more commerce across the world." If we agree with them on that, it makes sense to praise them for stating that "the goal of the Libra Blockchain is to serve as a solid foundation for financial services, including a new global currency, which could meet the daily financial needs of billions of people."

However, something needs to give. It is not realistic to assume that a "global currency" could be created that would allow "open, instant, and low-cost movement of money" around the world when this would infringe with impunity on the monetary prerogatives of those countries who wish to control their own money supply and at the same time keep their foreign exchange rate fixed. I do not see, for instance, India or China going along with that—and if that is the case, it means 36 percent of the world's population will be out.

Another relevant activity performed by a central bank, as mainly responsible for the exercise of the sovereign's monetary prerogatives, is its provision of liquidity (as lender of last resort) to financial institutions issuing claims denominated in the currency the central bank issues. The fact that no single Libra will be minted without the backing of a corresponding reserve in hard currency (as happens with a currency board) does not eliminate the problem that claims denominated in Libras may be issued. A currency board, conceptually, may solve the problem of guaranteeing the monetary base, but it is no solution for problems of liquidity if there is fractional reserve banking.

Are Facebook and its partners prepared to forbid the nodes in their network, such as the managers of digital wallets, from opening credit in Libras to their customers? I doubt they would want to forbid this, and the version 2.0 of the white paper is conspicuously silent about that. Alternatively, would Facebook and its partners accept being regulated as financial institutions by the U.S. government in order to benefit from its umbrella? If so, from where will come the cost reductions they are hoping to realize in comparison with regulated banks?

The main impediment, though, remains the question of the state's monetary prerogatives as a key instrument for the financing of armed conflict. Anything that would reduce the capacity of the U.S. government to float its debt is a security risk for the country. It is as simple as that.

I do not think that reducing the floating of U.S. dollars, and lessening the dollar's role as the reserve currency of the world—which the creation of a leveraged system like the Libra would do—would be acceptable to those holding "the Treasury view." I do not think, either, that a system that would give discretion to Facebook and company to accept, say, Chinese currency as part of their reserves (and therefore to reduce the role of the U.S. dollar) in exchange for a license from the Chinese government to enjoy commercial opportunities in China would be acceptable to those who take "the Treasury view."

To be sure, the Libra's problems might not be insurmountable. And perhaps there is room, between the cracks, to make a lot of money with this project. However, more attention must be paid to the essential nature of monetary arrangements if the Libra is to succeed in becoming a significant part of these arrangements. The roadblocks its architects face become easier to understand, I argue, against the backdrop offered by the present work.

THE RELATION BETWEEN CAPITAL GOODS AND FINANCIAL INSTRUMENTS

Among the things on the real side of the economy, there are (as previously noted) some that may be used as intermediary goods for enhancing the production of other goods. These are capital goods, for which my designation is Kg. A particular relation between things on the real side of the economy and the abstract side deserves further attention. We will now look at how capital goods relate to financial instruments.

Because many capital goods (Kg) are not represented by financial instruments ($Ppcf$) but by other forms of property claims, and some financial instruments are representative of malinvestments in which the capital invested was actually destroyed, there is no necessary identity between those two terms.[4] We could express it this way:

$$Kg \neq Ppcf$$

NOTES

1. This identity is discussed by Robert Barro in his classical "Are Government Bonds Net Wealth?" (Barro, 1974). According to Barro, for the entire private sector, the circumstances in which the issuance of public bonds may represent an increase in the aggregate net worth are limited, since it is assumed that there is this correspondence between new public debt today and future taxation. However, there is no direct relation between all the holders of public debt and their correspondent future tax liabilities. Therefore, it is obvious that for the investors in government bonds, these bonds represent a net wealth, while for the entire private sector, assuming that the identity holds (that is, that the government limits its borrowing activities to its tax-collection capabilities), the net result, in principle, should be zero. Barro nonetheless calls attention to the fact that the monetary prerogatives of the government allow it to

exercise monopoly power over "liquidity services"—that is, monopoly in the supply of money and the exercise of financial repression due to financial regulation. When it exercises that power, it creates a "utility" to the instruments it issues, thus adding to the net wealth in the economy (Barro, 1974; 1998).

2. For an integrated discussion of the dynamics of government debt, inflation, and economic growth, see Fischer and Easterly (1990).

3. This section is based on an article of the same title posted on Law & Liberty, July 31, 2019 (Zelmanovitz, 2019d).

4. "No es en absoluto necesario que un valor sea real para que pueda cotizarse en la Bolsa" (Mathieu, 1990: 99).

Chapter 9

A Dynamic Model

What I will present next is an illustration of what could be a dynamic model of the representational theory of capital (RTC).

The illustration is made with the following three figures.

In figure 9.1, the evolution of the stock of capital (Kg) over time is stated. The stock of capital is assumed to be known at the beginning of the time period ($n= 0$), and although it is shown in the figure as sufficiently homogeneous to be quantifiable, we must once more remember the heterogeneous nature of all its components, as discussed previously in this work.

What figure 9.2 illustrates is that, for a given stock of capital ($Kg0$) at the beginning of the time period ($n= 0$), a given amount of goods with economic value is produced ($Eg0$). This simple counterpoint is meant to show the unequivocal relationship between the two variables; and the curve Eg is shown as growing at a decreasing rate based on the usual hypothesis that the productivity of the production factors decreases over time.[1]

Finally, figure 9.3 illustrates the simple relationship between the gross productivity of capital, here expressed by the general rate of return in the economy (rr), and the rate of return for the investors ($rr*(1-tr)$). Both are departing from the beginning of the same time period ($n= 0$). Also, it is assumed the rate of growth of property claims, both gross and net, is composed of quantifiable elements.

I do not think it is necessary to offer a more complex illustration of the dynamic model here for the purposes of this initial presentation. If we were to add such complexities, however, they might entail a dynamic model where a net variation (after depreciation) is also considered, at a given rate of return

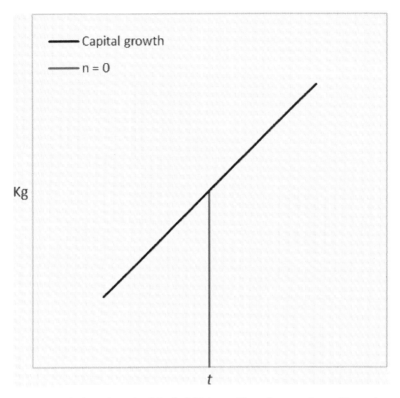

Figure 9.1   Evolution of Stock of Capital (Kg) over Time. *Source:* Created by author.

(*rr*), in the amount of property claims by private individuals (*Pp1*) that is distributed to equity investors (*Pp0-D*) and fixed income creditors (*D0*). Also captured in such a model would be taxation (*Pgpt*) at the given tax rate (*tr*), and the use of some of the tax revenues to service a given stock of public debt (*Dg0*). The sustainable level of public debt (*Dgn*) would, in turn, vary according to the natural interest rate in the economy, which is the same as the net growth in the stock of capital in the economy (*rr*), for the purposes of the model.

These considerations above have built upon the classification of the property rights on the abstract side of the economy in the static model, with the same elements as follows:

$$Wt = \left(Ppi + Ppc \right) + \left(Pgc + Pgs + Pgf + \left[Pgpt + Pgpm \right] \right) + Rn$$

The illustration of a dynamic model, I hope, only helps the reader to understand how these identities, when considered as static, may represent changes observable in the economy with the passing of time.

Figure 9.2 Evolution of Production of Goods with Economic Value (Eg). *Source:* Created by author.

ON THE IMPORTANCE OF TIME

The writers on capital theory in the Austrian school, as we recall, treated time as a factor of production. Such treatment seems straightforward; yet obviously, not all passages of time are productive. Time is a necessary factor for some processes—for most processes, actually. Nonetheless, some more productive processes may consume less time than less productive ones (with the latter being at a different and "lower" level of technology).

Time may be considered as a nonrenewable resource, one that is critical, to some extent, to all productive activity. Still, again, it is worth emphasizing, in a dynamic analysis, one ought not assume that the technological level is

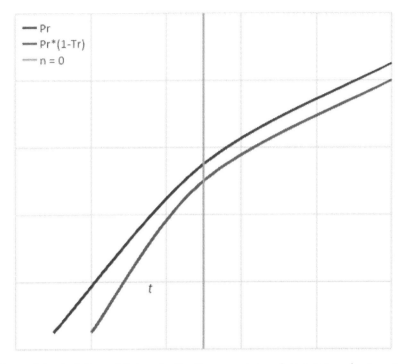

Figure 9.3   Evolution of Return in the Economy (rr) and Net Return for Investors (rr*(1-tr)). *Source:* Created by author.

a given; there is no direct relation between longer productive processes and more productive ones.

This distinction has immense importance for certain discussions of capital theory, although for the purposes of this work, the relevant aspect to consider is the dynamic nature of the economic phenomena under analysis.

NOTE

1. It is in "The Paradox of Saving" that Hayek calls attention to the static assumption that new capital will not increase productivity (Hayek, 2008: 152).

Chapter 10

The Relation between Money and the Structure of Production

The amount of money proper (*Pgpmp*) and money substitutes (*Ppcfm*) are linked to the amount of liquidity that economic agents want to keep at any given time. That is, the intersubjective preference for cash balances is a function of natural and social circumstances on the real side of the economy; and such preference has as its main elements the level of uncertainty about the future, the structure of production, the existence of profitable opportunities for banks to create money substitutes, and the opportunity cost of the economic agents of holding cash (these last two being determined mainly by the interest rate).[1]

The amounts of liquid assets that economic agents would like to hold has a relation to the structure of production to the extent that more predictable expenditures, either in time or in their object, would require lower cash balances for the economic agents than otherwise.[2]

The structure of production—that is, the sum of all capital goods (*Kg*)—for analytical purposes may be divided in fixed capital (*Kf*) and working capital (*Kw*) according to the relative mobility that they may have in relation to the different processes of production which they may be applied to.

But since not everything money can buy is related to production, and therefore not every reason why economic agents need to have cash balances has to do with production, it is another mistake to equate the amount of working capital (*Kw*) in the real structure of production (the sum of inventories of goods and the funds required to compensate the human capital required for production) with the amount of money proper and money substitutes in existence at any given time. Clearly all the working capital not invested in inventories or receivables is held in the form of monetary instruments, but the amount of monetary instruments is higher than the stock of working capital on the real side of the economy:

$$Kg = Kw + Kf$$

$$Kw < Pgpmp + Ppcfm$$

Since the amount of cash balances (*Pgpmp+Ppcfm*) corresponds to how much economic agents want to keep at their disposal to buy things in the real economy about which they are not certain what, when, or where they may want to buy, and those things being mostly in the inventory of some business or other, they are part of what I have defined as working capital (*Kw*). The consequence of that is that, at any given time, the liquidity on the abstract side of the economy (the stock of the most liquid claims over goods on the real side of the economy) is higher than the inventory of goods available for purchase, and this balance is kept only by a preference for holding liquidity in the economy. That preference, in turn, is determined by the above-mentioned factors such as the interest rate and the unpredictability of expenses in the regular course of business, among others.

Yet, there is a proportion, as we said, between inventories and liquidity. The "depth" that may exist in its financial markets serves as a proxy for the economic strength of a society, correlating in fact with the stock of goods and services available on the real side. The above descriptions assume that supply and demand for cash balances will be adjusted spontaneously in a competitive market. But as we know, that is rarely the case in modern, Westernized societies. The political manipulation of money and credit has been the rule for more than 100 years now in Europe, the Americas, and most of the world. Governments' interventions in the supply of money and the regulation of credit through official manipulation of interest rates, although not directly or strictly related to the stocks of available goods or to an economy's capacity to produce more goods, is nonetheless correlated with the structure of production as we have stated above.

That is to say, there is some room for the manipulation of money and credit in a modern, market-oriented economy, but there are definitively real constraints also.

The propriety of manipulating money and credit has been the focus of the study of business cycles. Economists generally believed that when there is idle capacity in the economy, increasing the supply of money and credit may be beneficial. Such increases have been put in practice predominantly by the manipulation of interest rates. It therefore seems relevant to discuss (briefly and by way of illustration) the implications of the model proposed for understanding the equilibrating feature of interest rates in a modern market economy, and its application to the theory of business cycles.

Hayek staked a claim on discerning the cause of business cycles. His claim was that that cause was "to be found in the 'elasticity' of the volume of money at the disposal of the economic system . . . [the] element whose presence forms the 'necessary and sufficient' condition for the emergence of the Trade Cycle" (Hayek, 1999: 120).

BUSINESS CYCLES AND THE EQUILIBRATING ROLE OF INTEREST RATES

In a hypothetical market economy in which the supply of money would be predominantly, if not entirely, endogenous, the creation of credit instruments with monetary properties would be regulated by the existence of opportunities for profitable lending. The marginal cost of financial intermediation would determine the rate of interest on money, bringing it closer to the natural rate of interest in the economy. To see how this idealized model would play out in the world in which we live, we need to add a number of complicating factors:

First, we need to take into consideration that a significant amount of the money supply is created exogenously, that is, by government fiat, outside the market and prompted by political considerations.

Second, politics also determine a substantial part of the lending and borrowing going on in the economy. Funds are thus not being allocated for the most efficient creation of more goods and services as selected by economic agents identifying profitable opportunities for investing. They are allocated as determined by regulatory mandates, and public debt crowds out private finance, in essence, by financial repression.[3]

Third, there are "real" factors outside the market that influence the behavior of economic agents, such as acts of G'd, such as natural disasters, transitory bottlenecks due to the exhaustion of known resources, technological constraints, political instability (such as wars and civil unrest), or as we saw in mid-2020, pandemic disease.

Even in the idealized model, before the addition of these complicating factors, the fact that the structure of production is not perfectly malleable, and that there are transaction costs in financial markets (lower as they may be in relation to other markets), means that "frictions" should still be expected. Moreover, the constant adjustment of the different individual plans among the myriad economic agents would imply the perdurance of at least some idle resources or unsatisfied demand in certain sectors of the economy.[4]

That is the lesson one takes from Hayek's analysis of the economy in equilibrium, and the economy's successfully "traversing" from one stage of equilibrium to another in a context of neutral money and voluntary savings, taking into consideration not only credit creation and credit destruction in the setting of a "monetary economy" but also that the capital structure is not malleable and some friction exists every time an adjustment becomes neces- sary. Such friction accounts in large measure for a crisis, when one happens because of monetary disequilibrium. The specificity and complementarity of capital is what explains labor unemployment and capital idleness during a crisis, not immediate adjustment by changes in relative prices (Hayek, 1999: 30).

According to Hansjörg Klausinger, Hayek's thesis is contingent on the capital structure's being somewhat malleable. If it were totally malleable, there would not be unemployment; if it were totally rigid, any adjustment, even one generated by voluntary savings, would imply unemployment (Hayek, 1999: 33). So, my understanding is that adjustments in the structure of production caused by voluntary savings could indeed generate temporary unemployment. That may well be due to the "rigidity" of the structure of production, but you cannot escape from that just because the "transition" (to a new equilibrium) is triggered by voluntary savings.

Because individual agents' expectations are based on imperfect knowledge, and there are transaction costs even in the most hypothetical scenario if we want to keep a semblance of reality for the model, the demand for liquidity in the economy (defined as the sum of cash balances and liquid investments) would be the counterpart of the inventories of goods readily available for consumption or to be applied in the expected level of production continuously going on in society at any given moment.

Even in this hypothetical situation, depending on the particularities of the existing financial markets, existing modes of production, existing institu- tional and technological factors determining the transaction costs—depend- ing on all that, the amount of resources kept in stock and the demand for liquidity will vary from place to place and from time to time. And the existing "equilibria" will be reached at varying interest rates.[5]

Take, for example, a hypothetical financial system in which there is a 100 percent reserve requirement under a gold standard. That means the supply of monetary instruments is, at any given time, mostly exogenous, as deter- mined by the stock of monetary gold, the marginal cost of mining, and the opportunity cost of converting gold from other uses to monetary ones. It is not that a certain interest rate on money would not equilibrate supply and demand for cash balances; but keeping everything else constant, it is reason- able to assume that, under the arrangements of an almost-inflexible supply of money, credit operations in the economy will happen at a higher interest rate than what it would be possible were the commercial banks allowed to create money substitutes in order to match a demand for credit (as recommended by prudent rules for lending).

So much for the model. Back to the real world, in which there are all those complicating factors mentioned above. We can perceive now how the interest rate on money may diverge from the "natural rate of interest" in the economy, since it results from the sum of all time-preferences held by the individual agents. The ebb and flow of these factors, in addition to the ones existing even in the idealized model, would result in business cycles of both the "real" and the "Austrian" kind. That is, the result would be disequilibrium between the supply and demand for goods and services, both for consumption and investment in the economy as determined by "real" or "monetary" factors—in other words, as determined by factors either "exogenous" or "endogenous" to the market.

A disequilibrium that can only exist in the real world is the one described by Klausinger, for whom "Hayek finds the causes of the deviation of a money economy from this norm of neutral money in the so-called one-sided influence of money, that is, changes in the demand (or supply) of some goods and services that have no counterpart in the system of 'real' demands and supplies, but instead originate from the money side" (Hayek, 1999: 34). According to Klausinger, Hayek "makes a connection between the injection of money (credit creation), false price (in particular a 'false' rate of interest), and the generation of incorrect price expectations" (Hayek, 1999: 35). That is a difference Klausinger sees between Hayek's emphasis on relative prices and the thinking of, for example, Fisher and Keynes, who emphasize the price level.

As pointed out by Lionel Robbins, a "productivity norm" would enhance the neutrality of money, in a way that a constant money supply in the face of changes due to technical progress would not. Klausinger observes: "Looking at the market for loanable funds, in order to keep prices stable in the face of growing output money must be injected into the circulation. In particular, when money is injected by credit creation this constitutes an additional supply of credit beyond that of voluntary saving, and for this additional supply to be absorbed by demand, the interest rate must fall below its equilibrium level. Yet, this is just the situation that will give rise to an unsustainable boom, and thus to the trade cycle" (Hayek, 1999: 36).

If I understand correctly, here Klausinger is saying that, for Hayek, it is not any credit creation by the banks—in the process of their fractional reserve operations, even under competitive banking conditions—that will be inflationary—that is, that will move the interest rate below the natural rate and will lead to a business cycle. Only credit creation that goes "beyond that of voluntary savings" will have this ill effect—that is, an expansion not limited by existing profitable opportunities for investment, but one determined by political intervention in the market.

It seems to me that when banks are operating under competitive arrangements, the marginal cost of their operations (the cost of generating credits) tends to equalize their marginal gains, and therefore it tends toward equilibrium with the natural rate of interest in the economy.[6] That is an endogenous creation of credit—in this sense no different from credit given by the banks based on "existing" deposits. It is a completely different thing if the government, in any shape or form, is supporting the banks to give credit beyond what their prudence under competition recommends.

As Hayek argues, in disregarding the divergences between the natural and the money rate of interest that may happen in the natural development of the current "credit organization" (that is, monetary and banking arrangements of fractional reserve banking with a central bank in place in 1931 at the time of the *Prices and Production* lectures), theorists like Mises, who emphasizes the artificial lowering of the money interest rate, make themselves into defenders of an exogenous theory of the business cycle—whereas in a proper monetary theory of the trade cycle, it should be considered endogenous (Hayek, 1999: 122). Such understanding is reinforced by the following quote from *Good Money*: "It is, of course, a well-known fact that the current supply of money-capital is not necessarily identical with the amount of current savings" (Hayek, 1999a: 237).[7]

Hayek is allegedly saying thereby that all credit creation by the banks is inflationary; but I do not believe that is the correct interpretation. In the absence of a central bank and in competition, credit creation has limiting mechanisms that make it not inflationary. Hayek describes "the actual origin of additional credits" when banks create credits, after explaining that it is not from amounts left idle by the borrowers (Hayek, 1999: 128).

Here, Hayek explains that the effect is perceived not at the level of a single bank, but at the level of the entire banking system, by the multiplication of credits, once the money lent to one borrower increases the deposits in the bank of his supplier. Hayek explains that the officers of a bank do not know whether the origin of its deposits is money saved by its clients or money generated by credit creation by other banks. He also explains that that is why those economists who are also practicing bankers, are the most reluctant to accept the idea that the banks create credits (Hayek, 1999: 131).

Hayek states that, thanks to the creation of credit, the banks can supply more credit to businesses without raising the interest rate (Hayek, 1999: 133). It may well be that the interest rate on money will not be raised as much as it would under 100 percent reserves in the short run. However, the rate of interest on money and the natural rate of interest tend to converge. So, thanks to the maximization of marginal returns by the banks, the rate of interest on money, if the banking system is competitive and without a central bank, tends to be more or less the same in both systems, if the hypothetical banking system with 100 percent reserves is also free of constraints on its maximization of gains

However, if we take into consideration the "friction" caused by the lack of endogenous money in the economy under a 100 percent requirement, Hayek's comment seem unassailable. He is explicit in stating that, as a result of 100 percent reserves ("the complete abolition of all bank-money"), "the rate of interest would be constantly above the level maintained under the existing system" (Hayek, 1999: 144). Fractional reserves, according to Hayek, offer a more efficient allocation of credit than 100 percent reserves. Proposing that the elasticity of the money supply "offers the necessary and sufficient conditions" to have a business cycle is not the same thing as saying that a (monetarily caused) business cycle will happen even if the increase in credit is endogenous. Neither do I think that endogenous changes in the money supply affect the price level.[8]

Specifically about the equilibrating role of interest rates in regard to investment decisions, Hayek explains that the interest rate is what keeps the price of capital goods and consumer goods in equilibrium. That is why, when interest rates are artificially lowered by the inflationary creation of credit, there is an increased investment in capital goods through the phenomenon of "forced savings," since some of the resources that would, absent intervention, be used for consumption would be used by investments (Hayek, 199: 153). Furthermore, Hayek explains that the difference between the rate of interest on money and in capital markets (basically the difference between the interest rate in the money market and in long-term bonds) is open to arbitrage; and that is what drives the differences that one may find between those rates (Hayek, 1999: 159).

Concluding this section on the equilibrating role of interest rates in the business cycle, we should look to Hayek's admonishment that "this idea that changes of relative prices and changes in the volume of production are consequent upon changes in the price level, and that money affects individual prices only by means of its influence on the general price level, seems to me to be at the root of at least three very erroneous opinions."

What are these misconceptions? (1) "that money acts upon prices and production only if the general price level changes"; (2) "that a rising price level tends always to cause an increase of production"; and (3) "that 'monetary theory might even be described as nothing more than the theory of how the value of money is determined'" (Hawtrey, 1930: 64; Hayek, 1999: 197). Here Hayek calls attention to the fact that you may have a stable price level, and still a monetary impact may be felt by the structure of production due to changes in relative prices.

In continuation, Hayek describes three stages of monetary theory. The first one, starting with John Locke, deals with the quantitative theory, the idea that changes in the amount of money change the price level. The second stage, starting with Richard Cantillon's 1755 work, *Essai sur le Commerce*, deals with changes in relative prices and the path by which increases in the money supply reach the market. The third stage, first enunciated by Henry Thornton in his *Inquiry into the Nature and Effects of the Paper Credit of Great Britain* (1802), deals with interest rate changes that result from changes in the quantity of money, and the influence of those changes in the interest rate on the "relative" demand for capital and for consumer goods (Hayek, 1999: 197).

With that we arrive at Knut Wicksell's theory of interest, which became known for what Hayek thought was wrong about it: namely, Wicksell's "attempt to establish a rigid connection between the rate of interest and the changes in the general price level." Hayek summarizes Wicksell's theory as "If it were not for monetary disturbances, the rate of interest would be determined so as to equalise the demand for and the supply of savings." Hayek continues to say that, in a monetary economy, the natural rate may not be the same as the rate of interest on money, since the supply if capital goods and the demand for it meet not in the real "market," but in the "money" market, and in this market, the amount of "capital" available "may be arbitrarily changed by the banks" (Hayek, 1999: 211).

Here one should take a step back and notice the arrangements Hayek had in mind, under which banks can "arbitrarily" change the capital available. As we know, that tends not to be the case if banks are in competition and in the absence of a central bank, since in that case banks react to their marginal profit opportunities. Those opportunities tend to converge at the natural rate of interest.

Hayek states that, to equalize the demand for and supply of capital in the real economy, the banks must operate under 100 percent reserves (Hayek, 1999: 213). I disagree with that. Given the limitations of knowledge each agent has and the price system's role in spontaneous coordination, it seems to me there is no "direct" relation between those quantitates. I would argue that there is always some leeway for price signals to result in changes in the market. Hence such adjustment is constantly done, even when banks create credit, so long and so far as they do that under competition and without privileges or mandates.

Next, Hayek describes how the price signals for capital goods may result from increased savings or from changes in the quantity of money (Hayek, 1999: 229). (We may note that those two possibilities also apply to consumer goods.) Hayek also discusses the increase in production that comes about thanks to credit creation by the banks. He assumes that this produces no impact on the availability of goods, but simply diverts goods from consumption to investment (Hayek, 1999: 234). His assumption is based on the idea of full employment that lies at the foundation of the concept of equilibrium.

However, for me, this starting point seems dubious—necessary for pedagogical purposes but hardly realistic. The economy is always changing, and the rigid assumption that the price elasticity of capital goods is zero, actually of all goods, since they are not distinguished in this model, seems to me a bit strong. Granted, there is some rigidity—the Brazilian economy certainly bears this out—but some of the explanation of how the cycle happens I think is missed when temporary increases in the utilized capacity and new and more productive arrangements brought about by the change in demand for capital goods are not considered.

Finally, lecture three of *Prices and Production* ("The Workings of the Price Mechanism in the Course of the Credit Cycle") starts with a quote from *Theory of Money and Credit* (Mises, 1980: 401) in which Mises states that the first consequence of credit creation by the banks is an increase in the relative price of capital goods in comparison with consumer goods (Hayek, 1999: 242). I disagree that that is always the case. It depends on how the new credit is allocated. Nowadays, most credit is given for the purchase of consumer goods, for instance. I do not think that invalidates Austrian Business Cycle Theory but, as I have said elsewhere, ABCT does need revision.

Over all, Hayek has made clear that some capital goods are very specific in their application while others are of a general nature, mainly the original means of production, raw materials, and several instruments (Hayek, 1999: 243). The general nature of some capital goods is what allows these goods to be used in unpredictable ways, and it is what gives these goods liquidity—speaking here of commodities, for example. Although I disagree with Hayek's hypothesis about how changes in the interest rate will change the relative prices of producers' goods in relation to consumer goods (it doesn't seem that even in his time, new credit creation would go disproportionally to new investments, much less today), I understand that it is a simple model that helps us understand the economic impact of changes in external money by paying attention to those sectors which first receive that new money (Hayek, 1999: 246).

THE KEYNESIAN PERSPECTIVE ON THE REAL AND THE ABSTRACT ECONOMY: A CRITIQUE

Authors in the Keynesian tradition would distinguish themselves from neoclassical economists by stating that for neoclassicals, "investment cannot exceed saving," and because of that, "bank credits appear, in the neoclassical view, as a perturbing element" while for them, the Keynesians, "the close link between saving and investment is cut" (Bortis, 2016: 3). As we can see from the foregoing analysis, the Keynesian authors have left out of the picture the fact that investments in government debt also could create a disequilibrium.

Keynes's followers (see, for instance, Bortis, 2016: 7) refer to chapter 15 of *The Pure Theory of Money* (Keynes, 1998: 217) in claiming that on the real side of the economy, new value is created and money represents real value, but once money moves from industrial to financial circulation, there is no longer a real equivalent to new money and it starts to chase existing wealth and other financial instruments already in existence. Let us accept that this is an accurate description of what Keynes meant with that chapter. What does it mean for money to move from industrial to financial circulation? In my opinion, Keynes is referring to financial claims representative of goods that are part of the capital structure, and financial claims over other forms of existing wealth.

Although in that chapter there is no reference to public debt, it remains the case that public debt would be an important component of what Keynes calls "financial circulation." That is being acknowledged implicitly with the "mention that money creation also takes place if banks buy government bonds to partly finance government deficits" (Bortis, 2016: 11). That is to say, the creation of new money to buy public bonds may be endogenous if the money is created by the banks—or it may be exogenous if the money is created by the central bank.

It is noteworthy that a disequilibrium between real savings and their representation may happen, not only with the purchase of public debt used to raise funds to pay for current expenses but also when the government makes value-destroying investments, such as bailing out insolvent banks (Bortis, 2016: 14). And here we can consult Keynes's admonition that, if investments for speculative purposes are done with money created by the banks, the moment those investments may go sour, the investors may not be able to repay their loans. We can ponder the fact that, if capital is destroyed because it is malinvested, the debtors will not be able to pay either way. It does not matter if the funding is or isn't inflationary.

In the end, what Keynesian authors like the one we have been following in this section (Bortis, 2016: 16) do not perceive is that the decision by individual agents to either invest in new real resources or buy existing assets has to do with the relative marginal returns of those investments. Such decisions are driven by public policies, conjecture, what is in the financial columns of the newspapers, or a host of other influences. So the level of "financialization" depends, among other things, on whether measures taken by policymakers are pro-business and pro-investment, or not. For Bortis, the problem is not the financial sector per se; for him, the financial sector in itself is a morally good activity (p. 17), and the problem arises when its activity becomes relatively larger than that necessary to provide liquidity in the economy.

Well, that can only happen because of government intervention so it should be against that that policymakers should focus their attention. We may conclude this section by highlighting that Bortis does not believe it is possible for monetary production to be self-regulated (Bortis, 2016: 26) and hence for the monetary and the real side of the economy to endogenously trend toward equilibrium. The latter can only happen, for him and authors of his persuasion, through government intervention.

INFLATION AND THE STRUCTURE OF PRODUCTION: COMPARING THE AUSTRIAN AND THE MONETARY DISEQUILIBRIUM APPROACHES

The entire Capital Theory contribution of *Prices and Production* is meant to explain the business cycle, but let me reiterate that my interest is more ample. The RTC can help us understand the business cycle, but it is meant to explain more than that: It is meant to explain the relation between the real goods and services in the economy and their representations on the abstract side of the economy. To amplify this, we recur to Hayek again, where he describes how the increase of credits given by the banks without previous savings alters relative prices and the structure of production. This aspect, while not a precise description of reality, is a useful conceptual description of the relationship between credit creation and the structure of production (Hayek, 1999: 252).

The centrality of monetary equilibrium to mismatches between savings and investments that lie behind some of the aforementioned problems of representation of financial instruments was highlighted by Hayek, when he observed: "The crucial property of a money economy is that, absent neutral money, a divergence of investment from voluntary saving becomes possible" (Hayek, 1999: 19). In Klausinger's introduction to Hayek's *Business Cycles*, he argues that "The basic tenet for interpreting Hayek's writing on money and the cycle in the interwar period is their firm foundation on an equilibrium approach, which served as the benchmark to which cyclical movements are to be related" (Hayek, 1999: 12).

According to Klausinger, Hayek managed to integrate his explanation of the business cycle in a static framework by distinguishing the "dynamics" domain from the "statics" domain, and by distinguishing a "money economy" from a "barter economy." Ideally, a money economy may be imagined in which money, being "neutral," allows the real data to coincide with the values which result in equilibrium in the model (Hayek, 1999: 15).

I understand the importance of stating whether your analysis is dynamic or static, but I think that, in insisting on "intertemporal equilibrium" instead of taking a purely static approach to the business cycle, Hayek has in fact adopted a dynamic approach—and the sweet spot in which money is "neutral" is just a benchmark. (This is noted by Klausinger himself on page 12: "However, due to money ever being prone to generate 'one-sided' changes in aggregate demand, not compensated for by changes in aggregate supply, money generically will become non-neutral.") According to Klausinger, for Hayek, such non-neutrality of (increases in the) money (supply exogenously produced) is not self-correcting; it needs to be reversed, and that dynamic process is what leads to cycles of boom and bust.

Again according to Klausinger, Hayek accepted Johan G. Koopmans' 1933 definition of the "ideal" barter economy in which money is neutral: "The ideal type of a pure barter economy to which the laws of equilibrium theories apply . . . (whose object is) a hypothetical, and in reality unthinkable, state where simultaneously the frictions which prevent full equilibrium due to the lack of a generally accepted medium of exchange are assumed to be absent, as well as those specific changes resulting from the actual introduction of such a medium of exchange" (Hayek, 1999: 16). According to Klausinger, Hayek, in accepting this definition as his point of departure, left his theory "vulnerable to the attacks of critics."

Exploring the concept of the neutrality of money, Klausinger states that, while Hayek at first located the idea of non-neutrality in the existence of indirect instead of direct exchanges, he later assigned a vital role to the interest rate, and therefore to the relevance of money and credit to capital markets. According to Klausinger, Hayek, like others, used Wicksell's concept that money is neutral when the natural rate of interest is the same as the rate of interest on money.

The money rate is defined as the rate at which the banks are willing to lend; for Wicksell, the natural rate may be "the rate that would be determined by supply and demand if real capital goods were lent in kind" or "the rate of interest at which the demand for loan-capital and the supply of savings correspond exactly to each other" (Hayek, 1999: 17). The two definitions are the same if we consider that "savings" for Wicksell means real goods saved from consumption.

Another aspect worth mentioning is that capital goods are not the only goods borrowed in the economy; there is an immense quantity of durable consumer goods, of "human capital," and pure discretionary spending funded by savings in financial markets. On top of that, we of course have the public debt, which is mostly for consumption and capital destruction. So, the equilibrium between "real" goods and their financial representation goes beyond just capital goods, as we have been emphasizing all along in this chapter.

For Horwitz, an important difference between Austrian economics and Monetary Disequilibrium theory when it comes to the micro-foundations of macroeconomics is their disparate treatments of the notion of capital. However, Horowitz, by drawing upon Selgin, shows that the two can be reconciled (Horwitz, 1996: 288).

"The Austrian approach to capital," writes Horwitz, "is to see it not as a homogeneous store of productivity, but rather as an interconnected, intertemporal structure that is reflective of the plans of the various actors in an economic system. . . . For Austrians, the capital structure describes economic actors' current perceptions of the plan-relevance of each of their pieces of capital. . . . The capital structure also reflects the temporal dimension, or 'roundaboutness,' of production. . . . The degree of roundaboutness is linked to the rate of interest" (Horwitz, 1996: 289). Horwitz also explains here why the heterogeneous nature of capital for the Austrians does not allow for a common denominator— not even money—to tabulate it and to consider it a homogenous entity. In addition, he calls attention to the essential aspect of intertemporal coordination of the capital structure for the Austrians: If consumers are not willing to wait during the time it takes to produce goods under a certain structure, waste and misallocation of resources will happen.

Horwitz explains that for Wicksell, there are two rates of interest: the natural and the market rate. "The natural or 'normal' rate of interest is 'the rate of interest at which the demand for loan capital and the supply of savings exactly agree.' The market rate of interest refers to the bank rate, or what is currently being charged for loans in the form of money" (Horwitz, 1996: 291). Here, Horowitz is highlighting the importance of the interest rate for Capital Theory: "The key is that entrepreneurs, basing their capital decisions on the lower market rate[,] lengthen the structure of production, which appears feasible at the lower market rate . . . Eventually it becomes clear that real savings do not exist to finance the remaining parts of the newly undertaken lengthier capital projects and the bust of the business cycle follows."

In a 2015 article, Joshua Hendrickson and Alexander Salter argue that inflation leads people away from cash to bonds (Hendrickson and Salter, 2015: 1). To the extent that bonds have monetary properties, perhaps so, but I would think that investments in equity are the natural tendency with inflation, unless you have confidence that the bonds will yield a positive real interest rate. They argue, moreover, that inflation should lead real interest rates to go down. But given the increased uncertainty, I would bet the opposite would be true. In fact it is more than a hunch—I found from personal experience in Brazil during that country's years of high inflation, that real interest rates rose as inflation rose.

Central to the Hendrickson-Salter analysis of Böhm-Bawerk and Wicksell is that monetary policy—changes in the interest rate—that is, alters the structure of production (Hendrickson and Salter, 2015: 2). The authors want to examine how monetary policy influences a firm's decision to invest, at the "intensive" and the "extensive" margin. To recur to the tree-harvesting example, the "intensive" margin would be the proper time to harvest a tree, and the "extensive" margin would be decisions as to whether to make new investments in forestry (Hendrickson and Salter, 2015: 3).

For the authors, higher inflation causes the real interest rate to decline and the period of production to be extended as a consequence. In their model, lower interest rates mean more goods remaining in the production process and fewer firms exiting the market. The "Friedman Rule" is optimal in their model (Hendrickson and Salter, 2015: 4). Because I doubt, as mentioned, that higher inflation results in lower real interest rates, it does not seem to me that inflation is a factor in increasing the accumulation of capital. This does not affect the fact that reducing real interest rates does explain increases in capital accumulation; furthermore, to assume the Friedman Rule to be optimal, you need to assume that downward prices are uniformly elastic, and therefore, nominal deflation has no allocative consequences or consequences for aggregate demand.

Hendrickson and Salter are right in stating that because of the disagreement between the Mundell-Tobin (Tobin, 1965) and Stockman frameworks,[9] inflation's impact, one way or the other, on capital formation should be answered by empirical evidence (Hendrickson and Salter, 2015: 5).

It is worth keeping in mind, however, that households will only respond to higher inflation by buying bonds if they think they can predict an increase in prices; if not, they will buy "inflation-protection assets." A key variable is whether there are inflation-adjusted bonds available to be bought (Hendrickson and Salter, 2015: 17).

The authors seem to think that it is a good thing to have an opportunity cost of zero for money (Hendrickson and Salter, 2015: 20). I disagree; the purpose of having a positive opportunity cost for holding cash is to make funds available for lending. Otherwise, people who have saved and are able to have financial instruments representative of savings would hold cash instead of buying bonds. Implementing a deflationary monetary policy, which would result from the application of the Friedman Rule, would not "solve" that problem, to the extent that holding cash would "earn" an income "estimated" to be the time preference, the natural rate of interest, and then, the bonds would also earn zero nominal interest. But then, why hold bonds? So, there will be fewer funds available to finance capital formation, not more. Bonds would be required to be indistinguishable from cash for people to hold their liquidity in bonds and in that way to supply funds for capital formation. You can always add commercial banking to the model—then "cash" would be "bank deposits redeemable on demand," and that would solve the problem.

For the authors, as already mentioned, higher inflation *ceteris paribus* makes the demand for bonds go up (Hendrickson and Salter, 2015: 21). However, we need to emphasize that this core assumption only holds water if the future rate of inflation is predictable. One may say that, at the margin, it is better to receive some interest than none and therefore bonds will be marginally preferred. Well, that is true again if the rate of inflation is predictable; if it is unpredictable, other assets and not bonds will be preferred as "inflation protection." The "real world" solution found in Brazil and other countries with high chronic inflation was to find "indexed" investments in order to reduce uncertainty, or, alternatively, to have a nominal rate of interest with a built-in "premium" to bear the risk of unpredictable inflation. In either case, there was no reduction in the real interest rate.

I understand that in the model of the authors we are discussing, the rate of inflation is constant, and therefore, this problem does not appear; but I do not think that the assumption of a constant rate of inflation gives much comfort. Once the rate of inflation becomes predictable, it loses its fiscal "benefit" because it is incorporated into the economic agents' expectations. Only unpredictable inflation brings in inflation "tax" revenue; thus it is to be expected that inflation will always go up and the nominal interest rate will have a risk premium that corresponds to expected future inflation. (It will be the second derivation of the price level; that is, it will imply a positive acceleration of inflation.)

THE "SUPRASECULAR" DECLINE
OF REAL INTEREST RATES

Dr. Paul Schmelzing recently published (Schmelzing, 2020) the results of his research on interest rates, both by "safe" borrowers and global ones, from 1311 to 2018. His general conclusion was that for the last five centuries, the trajectory of interest rates has been a declining one.

His work has many interesting implications, and in his paper he highlights the need to reassess claims of "secular stagnation" by Summers and others, and Piketty's claim of a "constant" return on capital (p. 1).

What Dr. Schmelzing leaves to his readers to hypothesize about are the causes for the decline. Not that he does not raise some candidates, such as "capital accumulation," which he sees as a possible explanation, and "growth and demographics," which he rejects as a direct cause of the downward trend of interest rates.

Another interesting element in his research is that his data demonstrate the independence of the downward trend from the monetary and fiscal regime of governments. What we have in store, if he is accurate, is more and more negative real rates of interests. And I see no reason to doubt his accuracy.

In line with what has been covered in this chapter, and using the theoretical tool kit proposed with this work, it seems that the process described by Dr. Schmelzing of a long-term declining trend in interest rates, both by "safe asset" providers and global financial markets, cannot be considered apart from the constant increase in the accumulation of capital in the leading economies of the world in the last five centuries.

That such reduction in interest rates and increased accumulation of capital has been accompanied by an increase in life expectancy, and therefore, one may assume, a lower time preference and therefore, a lower "natural rate" of interest, should be not surprise anyone, although the author does not discuss them in his paper.

The pattern he discerns, in my understanding, makes for a kind of spiral. Gradually there is accumulation of capital, stronger security of possession (gradually more robust legal protection to private property rights), longer life expectancy, all of which has led to a gradual reduction in interest rates.

At the beginning of his story, in the fourteenth century, the ratio between "non-human" wealth and income was between 150 and 250 percent of Gross Domestic Product (GDP) (p. 2). To give the reader a frame of comparison, the amount of accumulated wealth in any Western society nowadays has easily reached the mark of fifteen times the GDP, albeit "non-human" capital; in the United States, for instance, it is just four times the annual GDP (Lange et al., 2018).

What has happened over time, according to Dr. Schmelzing, is that the accumulation of real productive assets, in spite of all the depredations of the ages, has gradually increased, and with that, their relative scarcity has gone down and the price of money has reflected that accordingly. However, it is not written in the stars that greater accumulation of productive assets will continue, or even that the current ratio between productive assets and processes and population will be kept. So, this trend could reverse itself if its causes, which have been present for the last half millennia, come to fade away.

My favorite historical reference for any deterministic illation from data such as that of Dr. Schmelzing is the decline and fall of the Roman Empire. The Romans' accumulation of material wealth and efficient division of labor on a continental scale, thanks to open borders, free trade, protection of property rights, political stability, social order, resulted in increased income per capital to levels only seen again in modern times. And we know that all of that crumbled, starting in the third century CE, when those institutional conditions started to disappear.

NOTES

1. Eduard Braun and David Howden, in a recent article, describe how Böhm-Bawerk updated the concept of "wage fund" to a "subsistence fund" necessary not only to laborers but also to entrepreneurs and capitalists. Such "subsistence fund," from that moment on, was used as a metaphor for the resource constraint in post-agrarian economies, no longer perceived as a stock of goods but as a constraint on the possible flow of goods. However, Böhm-Bawerk's Austrian followers and mainstream finance theorists failed to establish the link between the resource constraint and the money interest rate, in as much as Wicksell clearly stated the existence of that link and the natural rate of interest (Braun and Howden, 2017: 22).

2. See chapter 6 in Laidler (1993: 62).

3. In the preface to the first edition of Hayek's *Prices and Production* (1931), Lionel Robbins praises the work by saying that the economic theory of equilibrium propounded by others fails to take into consideration changes in "spending power . . . either by the operation of state printing presses or by the credit-creating manipulation of central banks" (Hayek, 1999: 169), whereas Hayek fills this gap by considering changes in the "efficiency" of money, and by limiting his claim in regard to changes in the supply of money to the exogenous ones.

4. Hyman Minsky in his article "Financial Instability hypothesis," operating from within a Keynesian framework, describes the way in which intertemporal economic relations are intermediated by financial markets: "The capital development of a capitalist economy is accompanied by exchanges of present money for future money" (Minsky, 1992: 2), and the effect of changes of expectations in the behavior of economic agents (Minsky, 1992: 8). In my opinion, the factors just mentioned in this paragraph are the ones explaining why Hyman argues that financial instability may occur even without shocks exogenous to the market.

5. That seems to be the understanding of Klausinger when he states in the introduction of Hayek's works on business cycles that "equilibrium in a stationary economy presupposes a distribution of demand between consumers' goods and the means of production just sufficient for sustaining the existing structure of production" (Hayek, 1999: 28), and "Looking at these adjustments from the point of view of an individual firm, the price mechanism works by changing the relation between the expected rate of profit and the rate of interest" (Hayek, 1999: 29).

6. In regard to the natural rate of interest, it is worth mentioning Klausinger's discussion (Hayek, 1999: 39–45) of the Hayek-Sraffa debate. Sraffa criticizes Hayek for the use of the concepts of neutral money, the natural rate of interest, and the viability of forced savings. The concept of neutral money is not a description of a barter economy. Such a thing does not exist, but is a theoretical construct; Sraffa pretended not to see that. Sraffa criticizes Hayek for considering a single rate of interest in an economy with many commodities and therefore many interest rates, since there is no money. That again is disingenuous of Sraffa, because Hayek is describing how all those different rates are bringing equilibrium to their respective markets, or to say differently, as Klausinger does, they are compatible with an intertemporal rate of interest that would allow relative prices to change and adjust. In regard to the possibility of

permanent changes in the structure of production thanks to inflationary credit creation, Sraffa thinks that path dependence is sufficient, when it is not, to guarantee such result. In light of all of that, the traditional interpretation that Sraffa "won" the debate seems unwarranted.

7. Note, in this statement, the imprecision of what Hayek meant by "money-capital" (presumably, bank credit), or "savings" (either inventory of saved goods or bank deposits). It is a perfect example of why those observers who first undertook to study industrial fluctuations "did not have a more lasting success," which "was probably due to the vague meaning of the various capital concepts which they had taken from the City jargon of the time," as Hayek himself decries (Hayek, 1999a: 241).

8. Nor do I think 100 percent reserves are necessarily less efficient in terms of allocation of credit. It seems to me the equilibrium between the natural state of interest and the rate of interest on money under the freedom of contract may find other ways to converge—such as with the increase of time deposits and the use of money market mutual funds (which, granted, did not exist at the time that Hayek wrote). It goes without saying that, if the convergence between a natural and a money rate of interest is allowed to happen at a lower rate that helps coordinate economic activities if it is the result of a better allocation of credit, and not of government fiat.

9. The Mundell-Tobin Effect postulates that nominal interest rates will rise less than one-to-one with higher inflation, because higher inflation incentivizes people to move away from cash to other assets, leading to a decline in the real interest rate. That is, cash and capital are alternatives. Stockman, however, argues that cash is necessary to capital formation, and therefore if people move away from it, the liquidity necessary to fund capital formation diminishes. For Stockman (Alan, 1981, "Anticipated inflation and the capital stock in a cash in advance economy"), cash and capital are complementary, not alternatives.

Part V

Chapter 11

Conclusion

JACQUES RUEFF'S THEORY OF FALSE RIGHTS

As this formal presentation of the RTC draws to a close, it may be beneficial to go back and frame what I have offered here alongside the first statement, by Jacques Rueff, adviser to Charles de Gaulle and cofounder of the Mont Pelerin Society, of the representational character of legal claims.[1] For Rueff, *"La renta tiene una naturaleza doble: económicamente es una cosa; jurídicamente es el derecho que envuelve dicha cosa"* (Rueff, 1964: 97). That is, "Income has a double nature: economically it is one thing; legally, it is the right over such a thing." With these words, Rueff asserts the idea of the representation of something real.

In the manner of theorists discussed earlier (Eugen Böhm-Bawerk, Jesús Huerta de Soto), Rueff is taking a dialectic approach, simultaneously economic and legal, to monetary and financial instruments issued by the government. He has a dialectical explanation for the causes of inflation. One should keep in mind that, although ultimately, the monetary nature of the inflationary process is confirmed for Rueff, he also sees its mediate origin as fiscal. This indirect fiscal origin of inflation is made clear by his many statements to the effect that, whatever expense is properly determined in the budget, and covered with revenue raised with taxation, that expense is not inflationary nor does it create "false rights."

In discussing the effects on property rights of the government's provision of public services, Rueff argues:

El presupuesto, considerado aisladamente, no permite en modo alguno prejuzgar el carácter de los créditos que atribuye. Sin embargo, para todo acreedor del Tesoro es una cuestión esencial saber si su crédito es verdadero

o falso . . . Siendo esto así, si se quiere prever el carácter de los créditos origi-
nados por un presupuesto determinado y, por tanto, de los derechos de terceros
que los contienen, es preciso buscar, bajos de la apariencia del resultado presu-
puestario, la realidad que expresa . . . Cuando el presupuesto está en equilibrio,
los derechos de terceros que forman parte del presupuesto son, todos ellos,
verdaderos derechos. (Rueff, 1964: 125)

He will go on to contrast *"verdaderos derechos"* (true rights) with what he
calls *"falsos derechos"* (false rights).

There is no way for someone who is entitled to some credit attributed to
him by the state and acknowledged in the formal budgetary process (be he the
intended recipient of a pension, wages, a grant, or the repayment of a bond) to
know whether the state is able to honor that claim in money of approximately
constant value, or whether it can only honor that claim in nominal terms,
devaluing the currency because the state's rents and taxing capacity are not
enough to pay in real terms all the claims against it which it has recognized
as legally valid.

We may note that Rueff divides the public budget deficit into two parts:
cash flow problems and problems of net worth. In the case of the latter, the
only way for some creditors to be paid is for them to accept the "false credits"
attributed to them in the budgetary process instead of real wealth. He writes,
*"En este caso, el valor actual de los créditos fiscales que proporciona al
Tesoro la adquisición de una riqueza determinada es inferior al volumen del
derecho que esta adquisición inscribe en su pasivo. Hasta el completo pago
de la diferencia hacen su aparición falsos derechos"* (Rueff, 1964: 129).

If the state still commands credit among investors and is able to float its
debt by collecting savings to fund its expenditures—even though resources
supposedly to be invested in productive endeavors in order to generate an
income sufficient to repay them are actually being destroyed through current consumption, or through unprofitable investments, for that matter—the
destruction of wealth and the creation of rights to nonexistent wealth may be
staved off for long periods of time. But when at last that creditworthiness is
lost, and the only way for the state to honor its debts is by creating monetary
instruments by fiat, the claimants' expectation of being paid in a currency of
some previously real value is frustrated. That is the essence of Rueff's lesson: *"Toda adquisición por el Estado es generadora de falsos derechos, que
no perderán su carácter más que cuando hayan sido satisfechos con riquezas
propiamente dichas mediante el impuesto o mediante el empréstito"* (Rueff,
1964: 133).

It is interesting to note that for Rueff, equity rights are never "false rights"
in that they are limited to the real goods they represent; however, rights of
third parties may be "false" in the sense that they have nominal claims to

goods that no longer exist (Rueff, 1964: 140). Such claims, I would point out, have to be taken with a grain of salt. Consider a situation where an equity investment goes sour and the liquidation of the assets they represent is not sufficient to repay the investors in real/constant value, even if they are equity claims and not debts.

It seems, in other words, that the creation of false claims is not restricted to the arena of public debt. For the same reason mentioned above (bad investment decisions), that may also happen with private debt. Think of the many Mortgage-Backed Securities (MBSs) that were "monetized" by Money Market Mutual Funds (MMMFs) on the eve of the financial crisis of late 2007 to 2009. The reason, however, that the private sector creates false claims relatively less frequently than the public sector is to be found in the mechanisms in private law to assure the rights of third parties; these limit the opportunities for creating "false" rights in the private domain. Contrariwise, in the public domain, the structure of rights is different and, without the right to the forced liquidation of public wealth, claims against the state may easily become "false" claims (Rueff, 1964: 142).

The loss of "monetary properties" of the MBSs held by MMMFs that happened on the verge of the financial crisis twelve years ago, and the deflationary process that it triggered, seem to suggest that Rueff has not explored all the implications of his thesis when he states that "*el nivel general de los precios no podrá variar más que si, en una sesión del mercado, el volumen global de los derechos cedidos de su contenido difiere del volumen de los derechos a satisfacer*" (Rueff, 1964: 174).

We need to remind ourselves, on the other hand, that Rueff wrote his thesis during World War II, and that *L'Ordre Social* was first published in 1946. The institutional framework he had in mind was still one of a gold standard— that is, one in which the difference between "real" and "false" claims could be easily identified (ex post facto) by whether the issuer was able to honor the claims at the gold parity of the time of the issuance of the claim. We can see this from Rueff's statement that

> *Para que el Banco que ha descontado falsos créditos escape a la absorción de su capital y ulteriormente a la insolvencia es preciso que los beneficiarios del descuento no puedan deducir de su activo los verdaderos valore a los que le da derecho el descuento. Para satisfacer esta condición, el Estado, cuando impone a su Banco de emisión la aceptación de falsos créditos, le otorga el privilegio de un régimen sensiblemente equivalente a aquel con el que protege el dominio público: el régimen de la inconvertibilidad.* (Rueff, 1964: 217)

We also may perceive the institutional setting in the background of Rueff's thinking by his statement that "*Un falso crédito, cualquiera que sea su valor nominal, tienen un precio de equilibrio en el mercado: el precio para el cual la oferta y la demanda de moneda a cambio de crédito del tipo a que pertenece tengan el mismo valor"* (Rueff, 1964: 218). That is, an unconvertible claim may be traded at a discount against a convertible claim.

Ultimately, Rueff emphasizes the fiscal nature of the disequilibrium that may be resolved by the inflationary process. He says adherence to fiscal austerity is the only way to prevent it from happening. No doubt his experience with the relatively sound monetary management established by the Vichy regime was in his mind when he wrote that "Las civilizaciones con verdaderos derechos, sean liberales o autoritarias, tienen un carácter común: limitan la amplitud de la intervención gubernamental al volumen de los derechos que ordena el gobierno" (Rueff, 1964: 528).

False rights are used by governments to spend without being required first to tax. In the case of representative and limited governments, such spending is a fraud upon democratic accountability. It deprives the people of one of their controls over government: control of how much it may exact from taxpayers (Rueff, 1964: 561).

Other authors reach similar conclusions. Max Weber, for example, in discussing speculative crises, points out that "In the financial practice of the large states it had long been customary to anticipate revenues by the issue of certificates, to be redeemed later" (Weber, 2003: 286). For Weber, "Law's fall was inevitable simply because neither Louisiana nor the Chinese or East India trade had yielded sufficient profit to pay interest on even a fraction of its capital" (Weber, 2003: 288). He contrasts these situations with that of the Bank of England, which "remained standing in all its former prestige, being the only financial institution based on the rational discounting of exchange and hence possessing the requisite current liquidity. The explanation is that exchange represents nothing but goods already sold, and such a regular and sufficient turnover of goods no place in the world except London at that time could provide" (Weber, 2003: 289).

Another author taking this dialectical approach to capital is Vittorio Mathieu. The University of Turin moral philosopher observes, *"En efecto, parece que la riqueza se presente dos veces; una vez en forma de provisiones, de tierra, de capitales; la segunda, en forma de moneda, de crédito, de trabajo potencial. La utilidad dela primera forma es evidente, la de su reduplicación, mucho menos"* (Mathieu, 1990: 184).

Mathieu claims that this "duplication" does not exist at the individual level, though. His example is of someone buying shares in an existing company with money: the moment that the seller transfers the share representing the company, he receives the money. I think a better example would be a person who incorporates in a firm some assets he held directly until then. At first, he was the owner of the assets, but his property was not substantiated in a financial instrument. The moment he incorporates a business with those assets, the shares in the company are created, and now he owns the shares and the assets now belong to this newly created entity, even if the previous owner of the assets is now the sole proprietor of the new company.

This "duplication" must be understood as an abstract representation of existing wealth in the form of property rights. The instruments representing these claims may be direct (shares or bonds) or indirect (money); they may be more or less liquid; they may be created endogenously in the market and therefore representative of newly created wealth; or they may be claims exogenously created that do not correspond to new wealth (such as inflationary finance).

Mathieu claims that we cannot have an economy without money because we cannot have an economy without the future. The past, present, and future are, he says, represented respectively by assets, work, and money. Since money is what makes possible the convergence of the agents' decisions about the future, it is what allows the establishment of order without violence. Hence in this sense, by definition whoever has money, rules.

Here money is understood as a technology for the ordering of society, replacing direct command. Such an understanding is what prompts collectivists to dream of societies "without money," and to try to exclude as many aspects of social life from the market process as they can—that is, they look to measures that coerce, or that threaten to coerce, to the exclusion of spontaneous cooperation (Mathieu, 1990: 186). Yet Mathieu's understanding of the nature of inflation is remarkably similar to that of Rueff, the "monetary conservative" par excellence, and we can see this from Mathieu's statement that *"el origen de la inflación es una deuda no pagada; una cierta cantidad de trabajo potencial que no retorna bajo la forma de trabajo actual"* (Mathieu, 1990: 265).

Mathieu is less clear when he circles back to Marxism and states that *"El capital real—entendido como utillaje, provisiones, tierra o también capacidades humanas—no es trabajo actual, sino que actualizado. . . . lo que da valor al dinero no son las cosas, que ya existen, sino el trabajo, que no existe todavía, pero se preve que existirá"* (Mathieu, 1990: 266). If I read him right, this is too narrow a way to view the value of money. It may be that among the many things money can buy, you find the potential to get new things done, but that is a very limited part of what money can buy, and the explanation for the "value of money" resides elsewhere.

We can see in Mathieu, however, an implicit understanding not unlike the one we have been arguing for in this work: that the existence of profitable opportunities for investing existing resources is the equilibrating force that limits the endogenous creation of credit in the economy. For, as he writes, *"La inflacion impulsaria a la economia solo si esta se encontrase en una posicion de asentamiento que fuera a la vez una situacion de equilíbrio investable, o de surplace"* (Mathieu, 1990: 288). Here, Mathieu describes what happens to investors when they invest in businesses that cannot sell the goods they produced and therefore experience capital losses: *"A lo que estos acumulan no corresponde ya nada real . . . no correspondiendo a nada, el pretendido ahorro es nulo. Los ahorradores piensan que están ahorrando más, pero en realidad ahorran menos . . . Para que esto no sucediera seria necesario que aquel potencial que los ahorradores acumulan bajo la forma de capital financiero fuera invertido en instrumentos de producción reales"* (Mathieu, 1990: 297).

CONCLUSION

A final word, then, about this first formal elaboration of the RTC. It is important to highlight the difference that exists between the stock of capital in the economy *(Kg)* and the nominal sum of all financial instruments privately issued *(Ppcf)*.

A substantial part of that difference lies in the fact that the stock of capital is represented by property claims *(Pp)*, many of which are not financial instruments.

However, another point of contrast between the two is that the holder of claims issued by the sovereign *(Pgp)*, whether instruments of public debt, money proper, or something else, may not correspond to the capacity of the government to extract from the real sector of the economy to produce the goods necessary to satisfy those claims without frustrating other expectations (as explained by Rueff, with his theory of "false rights") (Rueff, 1964: 129).

In other words, to the extent that property claims correspond to goods on the real side of the economy that they represent, some of the claims issued by the sovereign may be "non-representative"—which is to say, "false rights"—in the sense that they correspond not to real wealth, but to wealth that was already destroyed or extremely difficult to extract or produce.

That allows us to conclude the following: that under current institutional arrangements everywhere around the world, existing goods, ideas, and processes on the real side of the economy are represented imperfectly by property claims that exist on the abstract side of the economy.[2] Such mismatches result in frustrated expectations and wrong economic signals.

Globally, the most egregious cases of misrepresentation are the multiple instances, in almost every country on earth, in which sovereign governments have saddled themselves with future commitments beyond their current capacity to raise sufficient revenues, in constant purchasing parity, to make good on those claims. I of course mean to varying degrees, depending on local circumstances.

It is debatable how much this insufficient capacity, which arguably is common knowledge, has been considered in the pricing of instruments representative of those obligations, to the extent that consensus could be built about measurement and acknowledgement of such insufficient capacity.

Even if adequate pricing could be achieved (something of which I am very skeptical), given all sorts of mandates, misaligned interests, and agency problems plaguing the "market" of public debt, expectations would still be frustrated and some claims would still not be able to be honored in real terms. Many would be honored purely in nominal terms, if honored at all.

The existence of debt obligations that cannot possibly be honored is deleterious to society, given the fact that they are claims on wealth that no longer exists. This is so, even before the arrival of the day of reckoning. The most perverse consequence is the shift toward consumption of part of the wealth produced annually that should have been invested in productive endeavors.

This consumption not only brings the certain and unavoidable frustration of future obligations (such as pensions and health care for the elderly) but also (again, to varying degrees and depending on local circumstances) impedes economic growth, production, and productivity.

Institutional arrangements in Western societies have been criticized by collectivists of the Right and the Left for failing to fulfill promises to various constituencies. Blame has been laid at the feet of free market arrangements in general and financial markets in particular, as we had an opportunity to discuss early in this work. The critics are wrong in their diagnosis of the problem as being one of inequality of wealth, and also in the prescriptions they offer—redistributionism and more government intervention—yet this does not mean they are not right in pointing out that there is a problem.

The patient is feverish; the fever is rising, all right, but the cause is not an imbalance of the four "humors"—blood, phlegm, yellow bile, and black bile. Hence the solution is not bloodletting.

Some of the misguided conclusions they draw—such as that public debt does not matter—are based on faulty analysis, such as the Functional Finance concept originally proposed by Abba Lerner and, more recently, Modern Monetary Theory.

Only a more empirical and commonsensical diagnosis of our problems can yield economic policies that stand a chance of solving them.

With that, I conclude the case I have made herein: that a property rights approach to Capital Theory may be an effective tool to explain much of the current malaise and perceived problems in market economies in general, and financial markets in particular. What I have presented is intended to pave the way for policymakers, and, if it may be summarized in one phrase, the normative stance that may be extracted from this work is a call for the return of the old fiscal religion.

NOTES

1. For a brief biography of Rueff and his main ideas, see Arellano (2019).

2. H. L. Puxley in his 1933 book asks rhetorically, "What, then, are the features characterizing the growth of international indebtedness since 1915, which make of it such an economic 'sore spot' in the eyes of the world?" And he answers: "The outstanding difference between the present large volume of international indebtedness and that to which the world was becoming accustomed before the War is that the latter was mostly contracted by the borrowers for productive purposes. . . . A large part of the new indebtedness, on the other hand, grew up as a result of the unproductive expenses of the War" (Puxley, 2018: 104). If productive investments "such as the building of railroads, or the establishment of a new plant" are represented by the same instruments as "the unproductive expenses of the War," we cannot accept as a representation of the reality the ways by which the representation of wealth under our current institutional arrangements are done.

Epilogue

During the years in which I have been working in this project, one thing that often came to my mind was how I would respond if asked whether this was a work in law, in economics, in law & economics, or in something else. Until I finished it, I was not certain how I would answer this question. Sure, in spite of its recourse to philosophical concepts, the project was mainly an interdisciplinary one firmly located on the intersection between law & economics. However, in my mind, law & economics used to mean law & microeconomics—and into that category, my project did not fit well. It was in conversation with my good friend Bruno Salama that he called my attention to the fact that my work, due to its research topic and methodology, would align well with the studies more recently identified as law & macroeconomics. News to me! As I was reviewing my manuscript, I started to research this "new" subfield, and soon I realized that it was not new but a new label for a vein of scholarship that is a century old.

In 2014, Richard Posner, the "father" of law & economics, which has been traditionally law & microeconomics, in an exchange with Gary Becker (Becker and Posner, 2014), alluded to "the emerging and exciting subfield of macro law and economics." Posner held out hope that the interdisciplinary studies between law & economics could go beyond their previous, micro borders and encompass macroeconomics as well.

Anna Gelpern and Adam J. Levitin edited a book compiled from the proceedings of a September 2019 Georgetown Law conference on the prospects for LawMacro as an area of inquiry. It was an important landmark. In the introduction to that work, Gelpern and Levitin reflected on the object of this new subfield, writing that law and macroeconomics could be approached as "(1) macroeconomic analysis of law, and (2) legal analysis of macroeconomics."

For these authors, "The first is an extension of LawMicro. The second expands on recent legal and interdisciplinary analysis of macroeconomics institutions and phenomena, and explicitly addresses the values and political choices at stake in macroeconomic policy decisions" (Gelpern and Levitin, 2020: iv). Therefore, they saw as one of the possible approaches to the new enterprise that it simply mimic the existing one, which they described as "an application of economic principles to law with the goal of revealing something new about law—not about economics" (Gelpern and Levitin, 2020: vi).

"LawMicro's failure to recognize the many ways in which law constituted economic systems, combined with its focus on static efficiency and neglect of macroeconomics, left it unprepared for the biggest financial crisis since the 1930s," they wrote (Gelpern and Levitin, 2020: vi). According to them, it was only with the financial crisis of twelve years ago that research on law & economics started to trace "crisis transmission channels, identified institutional design fragilities and regulatory failures" (Gelpern and Levitin, 2020: vii). That is, it was only after the financial crisis that research on the intersection of law and economics start to focus "on the design and operation of macroeconomic institutions" (Gelpern and Levitin, 2020: viii). One does not need to agree with their description of recent activity in the field to understand the scope of the research conducted under this new label.

Law professor Gina-Gail Fletcher of Indiana University, in her contribution to their book (Gelpern and Levitin, 2020: 123), argued that private law, such as contract law, could become relevant in macroeconomic terms. This insight is similar to the one proposed in this work—that the legal definition and enforcement of private property rights matter for economic performance and go a long way toward explaining it.

Consider, at a very high level of generalization, the idea that economic efficiency results from the application by individual economic agents of information of particular circumstances that only they possess. If you believe this generalization to be true, as I do, it means that some of the information with economic value is only created when individuals are free to interact with each other, and furthermore, that they will only interact with each other if they have the incentives to do so. In that case, a legal regime of private property rights is best, specifically one that gives individuals the freedom to act, and creates the incentives for them to act, both of which being necessary conditions for economic growth.

Still at this high level of generalization, we can equate the rate of economic growth with the level of confidence economic agents have that they have the freedom to exchange and the right to keep the gains from their exchange. From this reasoning, we are forced to conclude that as authoritarian as the political regime in China has been for the last fifty years, it has granted to its citizens a protection of their private property rights *greater than* the one granted by Western societies to their respective citizenry. A comparison between the licensing process for any major enterprise in the United States and China suffices to prove the point.

The limitations on the uses of private property in the aggregate have macroeconomic consequences. A comparatively lower rate of growth is a best evidence of that.

I understand that such a statement may be challenged by pointing to the different levels of economic development in China versus in the United States. But, although I acknowledge that some consideration should be given to the "low hanging fruit" gleaned on the way to progress, think about the rate of growth that China has had in comparison with middle-income countries in Latin America and Southern Europe. It is pathetic to compare the increase in income per capita in China with those less flourishing countries with *similar* income per capita. Again, based on the premises exposed above, we are forced to consider that private property rights are better protected in China than in most of the world. The alternative is to say that Hayek's insights in his 1945 "The Use of Knowledge in Society" are wrong, but I do not see the evidence suggesting we should do that.

At the core of the new law & macroeconomics subfield is the interrelation between law and development; consideration of the fiscal and monetary policy functions of the law in the present workplaces it very much in that bailiwick. Exploring the LawMacro precincts, so far, are only a few writers, among them Listokin, Salama, Ricks, and Peer. Obviously, works on economics and finance in the developing world abound, although not necessarily with an awareness of the advantages of an interdisciplinary approach that includes law. Again, one does not need to agree with the assumptions, theses, or conclusions of the practitioners I just mentioned to realize the similitude between their and my research interest and methodology.

For instance, Yair Listokin, in his contribution to the Gelpern and Levitin book, argues that the LawMacro lacuna that existed until recently was due basically to two factors: a supposed lack of interest, during the Great Moderation of 1980 to 2007, in macroeconomic issues, since inflation and unemployment were under control; and the supposed "libertarian leanings" of the faculty of the University of Chicago, where most developments in law & economics began (Gelpern and Levitin, 2020: 141). Moreover, "conservative" philanthropies such as the Olin Foundation and Liberty Fund helped the diffusion of LawMicro, and "it is almost impossible to imagine the Olin Foundation or the Liberty Fund providing similar support to law and economics had it been focused on macroeconomics" (Gelpern and Levitin, 2020: 156).

I see major problems with the two factors Listokin adduces.

The first, obviously, is that he is mistaken in saying that the faculty at Chicago did not like macroeconomics. Let us even assume that the majority of that faculty did not like the Keynesian framework for macroeconomics which Listokin favors. That is completely different from saying that some, most, or even all of them eschewed all macroeconomic thinking. However, he does not seem to understand that difference.

Listokin's claim is that the monetarist framework of most Chicago faculty explains why they did not need law. Supposedly they would only need law if they had adopted a Keynesian macroeconomic framework. However, his own research advocates the use of law to regulate the supply of money and credit. An example that he offers is the legal abolition of the "gold clauses" during the Great Depression as more recently pointed out by Edwards (2018). So, if Listokin understands "monetarism" to be a rejection of "Keynesian business cycle management in favor of exclusive reliance on monetary policy" (Gelpern and Levitin, 2020: 142), and changes to the supply of money and credit may have macroeconomic implications under the most orthodox monetarist framework, it follows that his own research may be Exhibit A that that premise of his is false.

In regard to the alleged "veto" of the aforementioned philanthropic institutions to fund LawMacro research, I think that my own affiliation is sufficient evidence to falsify his claim.

Salama, on the other hand, starts his contribution to the volume edited by Gelpern and Levitin by stating: "Efforts to conjoin the disciplines of law and macroeconomics highlight two main challenges: choosing the specific macroeconomic framework that is to be employed, and reconciling macroeconomic interventions with the rule of law" (Gelpern and Levitin, 2020: 181). Indeed those seem to be the main challenges to the enterprise of LawMacro. In regard to the choosing of a framework, one can only point out that any one that is chosen must pass muster as "good economics," such as methodological individualism, a healthy acknowledgement of our limitations of knowledge, and adherence in general to the "economic way of thinking" (Heyne et al., 2013). When it comes to reconciliation of the economics part with the legal part, as already mentioned, a distinction between the constitutional framework of a civil society and state intervention either by legislation or administrative regulation is sufficient to preserve the rule of law and avoid taking "the Road to Serfdom."

Speaking of roads taken or not taken, Salama, in discussing the controversies between Keynesianism and Monetarism in the 1960s and 1970s, highlights other possible theoretical frameworks by stating that "the legal response to inflation is not the addition of a new distortion, but the removal of an existing one." In corroboration, he quotes Hayek's 1976 proposal for the abandonment of legal tender and the introduction of competition in currency (Gelpern and Levitin, 2020: 185).

He notes that "a trend in the field of law and economics that is intimately related to macroeconomics is a concern with economic growth" (Salama,

2020: 186). The discussion of economic development in the present work offers good evidence of that. On the same page, Salama mentions a recent work by Cooter and Edlin (2014) in which these authors describe a "paradox of growth." For Cooter and Edlin, "rapid innovation requires competition for extraordinary profits" and yet perfect competition reduces profits to zero.

There really is no paradox here, for the *model* of perfect competition, given its simplifying assumptions, does not capture the *reality* of the entrepreneurial search for arbitrage that leads to constant innovation—leads in that direction, that is, if the institutional setting provides the proper incentives, such as strong protections for intellectual property, a streamlined process for the licensing of new products, deep financial markets willing to fund new ventures, and the like. Salama understands that Cooter and Edlin's recognition of the *reality* of the market is compatible with the paradigm of endogenous growth theory, under which "growth is primarily the result of investments in innovation by profit-seeking agents."

So, regardless of some discordance I may have with the Cooter-Edlin diagnosis, their approach of examining the market's legal framework for the causes of eventual underperformance, even more so if their reasoning is grounded in a solid understanding of how the market works (as one would expect from these authors), seems similar to our focus in this work on the representation of capital.

Salama also points out that, though many practitioners of LawMacro concerned with "law and development" apply heterodox ideas on economics, such as structuralism and new structuralism, "a non-negligible part of those interested in law and development take the opposite stance and emphasize the role of property and contract law to promote coordination and achieve growth" (Gelpern and Levitin, 2020: 187). Here, Salama refers specifically to the work of Hernando de Soto (1989) and others.

In his article Salama proposes the interesting concept of an "elasticity paradigm" for rule-breaking in order to make sense of "government rule-breaking" in times of macroeconomic crises (Gelpern and Levitin, 2020: 187). Salama acknowledges the problems that governmental rule-breaking poses for the rule of law, but he acknowledges also that political expediency guides governments' decisions in those circumstances. His claim is that rule-breaking is legal in exceptional circumstances (page 188).

The core of Salama's argument in favor of an "elasticity paradigm" is that realities on the ground need to be accommodated by legal dispositions, and those realities are what drive the proper legal response: "Where there are no safeguards in place, governments may have no option other than to break the law. Crucially, this rule-breaking should not be viewed as necessarily a contradiction of the rule of law" (190). Here Salama applies a distinction between proper decisions in normal times and decisions in cases of emergency. That those cases require different moral standards is well known and accepted (Rand, 1964). What Salama is advocating further is that rules created for normal times should not guide our actions in exceptional circumstances and vice versa. The discussions in the literature about emergency powers (the "safeguards" in Salama's nomenclature) help us to understand that.

Let us envision two possible models: In one, the chief magistrate has constitutional powers to decree martial law and suspend the right of habeas corpus. In the other, there is no such provision, but tradition allows the head of the executive branch to suspend individual rights in cases of emergency and have those decisions *ex-post* approved by the legislature, as has been the case with the British. The latter model requires a level of trust among political agents and a restraint in the use of criminal prosecutions in order to uphold the rule of law that are not reasonable to expect in most places at most times. (For more on that see Zelmanovitz, 2019e).

Applying this distinction to the protection of private property in relation to the state's exercise of its monetary prerogatives led Salama to the realization that it is not reasonable to expect the same level of protection of private property under emergencies as in regular times. This idea, in conceptual terms, I had an opportunity to discuss before (Zelmanovitz, 2013), and I am in complete agreement with Salama. His "elasticity paradigm," as I understand it, is the hermeneutical device necessary to apply the law once the reality of the "fiscal proviso" is acknowledged, and in this sense, an important tool for the administration of justice.

Morgan Ricks, in his contribution to the Gelpern and Levitin book, states that "there can be no question that some legal and regulatory frameworks are better than others when it comes to preventing macroeconomic disasters" (Gelpern and Levitin, 2020: 66). That seems a very important insight, as far as it goes, though it prompts us to ask why this should be the case. A question, alas, that Ricks fails to answer.

Yet it seems clear that some legal representations of the structure of production of society offer a more precise representation of what actually exists than others. Following from this, when we assume that legal instruments are representing things that actually exist, as they actually exist, but it's a mistaken assumption, economic agents would make decisions based on the assumption that the legal instruments are adequate representations of the reality when they are not, and therefore, they will take decisions that will not conform with the reality of the structure of production, leading potentially more often to systemic mistakes than to better forms of representation.

Here is an example that might please Ricks, although the lessons to be drawn might from it not so much. If the banks are allowed to create inside money as a counterpart to the actual production of new goods in the economy, there is an equivalence of new claims and new goods, and there is no monetary disequilibrium in the economy. However, if the banks are asked by the government to "monetize" public debt, there is in fact the creation of new claims to wealth without the corresponding creation of new wealth. Monetary disequilibrium will ensue.

The lesson is clear. Fractional reserve banking is an excellent instrument to create inside money and keep the monetary equilibrium in the economy if banks, guided by the prudent management of their lending portfolios, would lend only against good short-term collateral. The moment that there is a government's intervention in financial markets mandating, or nudging banks to give credit to the government represented by monetary instruments, such as banknotes or bank deposits in checking accounts, then, the counterpart between new claims and new wealth no longer holds. Such conclusions are made clear by the discussion we proposed at the beginning of this work about classification of possible banking arrangements (page 47), and about the origins of the Bank of England (page 43), as I have discussed previously elsewhere in a book review of Christine Desan's book (Zelmanovitz, 2015).

Gelpern and Levitin mention the concept proposed by Orian Peer, that of "public purpose finance," which involves "government lending that is macroeconomically significant, but designed to minimize conventional channels of accountability, in the gray zone between government spending, credit, and taxation" (Gelpern and Levitin, 2020: xv). This seems to be a perfect example of obfuscating the actual amount of capital in existence in society when liquid instruments of debt are issued by the sovereign and used to fund current expenses instead of profitable capital investments.

Gelpern and Levitin state that "Microeconomics is about the behavior of people and firms in markets for goods and services" while "macroeconomics is about the behavior of economies, comprising multiple markets interacting in complex ways." So far so good, but they go on to say that "in macroeconomics, government is a central character; even the most politically conservative macroeconomists must contend with its role. Sound governmental intervention is the point." For them, in spite of concerns shared by micro-economists, such as caring about "welfare, incentives, and resource allocation," macroeconomists "operate with different units of analysis. These unites are neither natural nor uniform; they are a function of politics and legal design" (Gelpern and Levitin, 2020: xi).

I see some problems here. First, there is a difference between "law" and "legislation."[1] There is also a difference between "legislation" and "regulations." The fact that a market order can only flourish under a civil constitution with protection of property rights and freedom of contract—that is, the presence of a civil government—does not require government "intervention" in that order, be it by "legislation" or by administrative "regulations" as government "interventions" in the market order are commonly understood. Secondly, macroeconomics, because of the use of aggregation at the level of political units, does not reject methodological individualism, if it hopes to remain a humane science and not fail in a giant fallacy of composition. For more on that, go back to our discussion of abstraction and mild realism, starting on page 101.

Gelpern and Levitin (following Gary Becker's lead in his 2014 discussion with Posner mentioned above) argue that LawMacro as an analysis of law "would study intersections between legal systems and macroeconomic variables, and prescribe law reforms accordingly" (Gelpern and Levitin, 2020: xii). Is this what I am doing with this work? Before answering that, let us consider first the other approach suggested by our authors: LawMacro as legal analysis of macroeconomics. Under this approach, LawMacro "would zoom in on the legal, institutional, and political assumptions behind macroeconomic policies. Beyond this descriptive enterprise, it would strive to broaden the range of plausible institutional designs to satisfy macroeconomic policy and other societal objectives at the same time" (Gelpern and Levitin, 2020: xiii). I would argue that you might find, in the present work, instances of the two approaches. Even if hard-pressed to identify which one is prevalent, I do not think I would be able to.

THE CONSEQUENCES OF THE CHINESE CORONAVIRUS PANDEMIC

Gelpern and Levitin are "cautiously optimistic" about the future of LawMacro. One of the reasons for that is that "substantive questions at the intersection of the two disciplines remain salient even after the 2008 crisis has passed" (Gelpern and Levitin, 2020: xvii). The authors, however, think that "the fact that many of the controversies focus on longer-term structural features of the macroeconomy, and not just the business cycle, expands the potential scope for legal intervention" (Gelpern and Levitin, 2020: xviii). Rather, I would say that it expands the need to better understand the role of existing legal institutions in the current outcomes, that is, the level of long-term economic output, and that may indicate the need for "legal intervention" not in the sense, I think, meant by our authors, but in the sense of a conscious action to reduce regulation, restore some of the freedoms granted to property rights, and to clearly distinguish in public finances what is capital creation and what is capital destruction. The sum of all that seems to be one more argument in favor of the social relevance of the study of Capital Theory applying a Law & Macro approach.

Steve Ramirez, in his article in the book edited by Gelpern and Levitin, argues that LawMacro is just the most recent attempt in a long line of attempts to integrate law and macroeconomics, but that it will ultimately fail if it does not influence lawmaking in the direction of reaffirming law as a force for human development (Gelpern and Levitin, 2020: xvi). I tend to agree with Professor Ramirez, there a need for practical relevance in all fields of social sciences, and the current tragedy that has befallen mankind requires sound responses in order to minimize human suffering, responses that these studies on Capital Theory may help to inform.

Jim Dorn began an April 20, 2020, article on the implications of the Chinese coronavirus pandemic for monetary policy and the independence of the Fed with the following paragraph:

One year ago the U.S. economy was robust with unemployment at historically low levels and real incomes rising. No one would have predicted that a year later the economy would come to a halt and more than 17 million people would be applying for unemployment benefits. This reversal was not due to monetary instability, which has been the primary cause of most recessions, but rather to a decision by government officials to mandate business closures to battle a pandemic. The initial sharp supply-side effect of Covid-19 quickly turned into a strong demand for cash and a corresponding decline in the velocity of money. (Dorn, 2020)

We find in the conclusion of Professor Dorn's piece the following passage:

The Covid-19 pandemic has led to an unprecedented expansion of Fed power and discretion. It has led to the transfer of fiscal responsibility to the Fed and weakened the Fed's independence. The drift into fiscal policy and credit allocation—as opposed to pure monetary policy (i.e., allowing the size of the balance sheet to influence money, prices, and nominal GDP)—places the Fed in a precarious position. The lack of a rules-based monetary regime increases uncertainty and opens the Fed to further politicization. Too much is asked of monetary policy and too little responsibility is placed on Congress for difficult fiscal decisions.

These two passages describe well the economic situation in which we find ourselves in the middle of the pandemic. The implications for our monetary and banking arrangements are dire. As Dorn says, the emergency brought about by World War II led the Fed to become a totally owned arm of the U.S. Treasury, helping the Treasury to fund the war effort by monetizing war bonds and keeping interest rates low. Such de facto subordination of monetary policy to fiscal considerations was only relinquished by the *1951 Accord* that restored the Fed's operational independence.

Before our very eyes we are seeing the elimination of whatever separation between monetary and fiscal policy still existed before the crisis. Not that calls for "Fiscal QE" were not heard before the crisis, as the discussion in this work on MMT (p. 35) and a recent work by George Selgin (2020) made clear.

For the world to experience an economic renaissance after the dislocation created by the responses to the pandemic, we could do worse than take heed of the RTC.

NOTE

1. I am using here Hayek's concepts of "law" as the order which emerges in society from the application of norms of justice to the adjudication of particular cases resulting in jurisprudence and precedents; while "legislation" are norms created by whoever holds the legislative power in a given society (see generally Hayek, 1973).

Glossary

Ad coelum doctrine—It is a principle of property law, from the Latin *"Cuius est solum, eius est usque ad coelum et ad inferos"* which may be translated as "Whoever's is the soil, it is theirs all the way to Heaven and all the way to Hell." With the modern division of property rights over land in rights over the surface (limited by zoning and environmental laws), air rights (limited again by zoning regulations and rights of passage for airplanes and now drones), and rights over the underground (which usually are reserved to the state in most jurisdictions), the *Ad coelum* doctrine ceased to be the default scope of private property rights regulating the ownership of land. (From Wikipedia article, *Cuius est solum, eius est usque ad coelum et ad inferos*.) For a classical statement of the doctrine, see Blackstone's *Commentaries on the Laws of England*, Book II, Chapter 2 (Blackstone, 1979: 18, Volume II).

Capital—The value of the stock of goods in existence at any given moment in terms of a unit of output (Robinson: 53–54, 86).

Capital Market—"The capital market is the market for long term finance—debt and equity" (Kohn, 1999: 4).

Compera—Early (fourteenth century) form of syndicated loans in Northern Italy (Kohn, 99: 12).

Depreciation—"Depreciation refers to the wear capital goods undergo during the production process" (Huerta de Soto, 2006: 280).

Dialectics—The logical study of a given object taking into account its full context (Bissell et al., 2019: 3).

Double-switching—A circumstance in which a given method of production is the most profitable one at different rates of profits. Capital reversing is "the same value of capital moving in the same direction of the rate of interest." (Harcourt, 1969: 388)

Factors of production—"all factors from which we derive income in the form of wages, rent, and interest." (Hayek, 1999: 220).

Fiscal gap—see fiscal sustainability.

Fiscal imbalances—see fiscal sustainability.

Fiscal sustainability—An estimation of the government's capacity to honor its financial commitments in general and to repay the public debt in particular. Usually this estimation is based on objective measurements of fiscal imbalances such as the fiscal gap, which determines the long-term tax revenues necessary, assuming that all fiscal obligations will be paid (Henderson, 2008: 185).

Forced savings—"The effect of credit creation (or inflation) on saving and investment . . . whereby actual saving (and thereby investment) could be increased beyond what would have been forthcoming voluntarily, that is, without the instrument of credit creation" (Hayek, 1999: 21) (Klausinger's introduction). There is also a second meaning that is the effective result of increasing savings over the structure of production. This result, I believe, can only be brought about by coercion, such as mandated pension contributions.

Friedman Rule (FR)—A rule for monetary policy proposed by Milton Friedman (in "The Optimum Quantity of Money") advocating a nominal interest rate equal to zero. The idea is to make the personal cost of the opportunity to hold cash (the nominal interest rate you can get in a bond) similar to the social cost of creating more cash (essentially, zero). To achieve this, a central bank acts to create deflation similar to the real interest rate of treasury bonds. The result, the reasoning goes, is that cash holders would not lose to inflation.

ICOR—Incremental Capital-Output Ratio.

Intermediate products—"producers' goods which are not original means of production." (Hayek, 1999: 220).

Juros—An early (sixteenth century) form of annuities in Castille (Kohn, 99: 10).

Liquidity—Refers to an asset's quality of being easily exchanged without causing a significant movement in the price and with minimum loss of value. The liquidity of a given asset is considered to increase as the spread between its ask and bid prices tends to zero. The essential characteristic of a liquid market is that there are ready and willing buyers and sellers at all times.

Lucas Critique—A theorem published in 1976 that "sparked a genuine methodological revolution in macroeconomic analysis. [Robert E. Lucas, Jr.] emphasized that the underlying coefficients of traditional econometric models are not constant. Hence, these models were inadequate for counterfactual policy evaluation. In other words, these models were inadequate for scientific predictions of the effects of political interventions into the economy, and thus incapable of prognostic comparison of alternative political interventions." From *"The 'Lucas Critique' Is Misesian ui Its Core"* by Karl-Friedrich Israel, posted at https://mises.org, August 31, 2016.

Metallism (or the Commodity Theory of Money)—A conception of the value of money based on the intrinsic value of monetary merchandize (see Zelmanovitz, 2016: 42).

Original means of production—land and labor (Hayek, 1999: 220).

Physical capital—"The stock of goods in existence at any given moment" (Robinson: 53–54, 86).

Producers' goods—"All goods which are directly or indirectly used in the production of consumers' goods" (Hayek, 1999: 220).

Production—"All processes necessary to bring goods into the hands of the consumer" (Hayek, 1999: 220).

Quantity of money—"[The] total of all kinds of media of exchange (including all so-called 'substitutes' for money)" either in a closed economy or the world, depending on the scope of analysis (Hayek, 1999: 269).

Rate of interest—"Excess of repayment over original loan" (Robinson: 53–54, 87).

Ratio factor—"The ratio of real capital to man hour of current employment per annum." (Robinson: 53–54, 86)

Real capital—"Capital valued in terms of wage units" (Robinson: 53–54, 86).

Real wage—"the purchasing power of a wage the worker gets" (Robinson: 53–54, 87).Reification—Literally, "to perceive something immaterial as a thing." In Marxist terminology, reification has a narrower meaning, that is, the specific process by which, in a capitalist society, the relations of production are perceived to be relations between persons and things and not relations between persons. The concept of reification has as its locus classicus Georg Lukács's essay, "Reification and the Consciousness of the Proletariat," part of his book *History and Class Consciousness* (Lukács, 1972).

Rentes—An early (thirteenth century) form of annuities in the Low Countries (Kohn, 99: 8).

Ricardo Effect—As per Joan Robinson, this is what Hayek characterized as the change in the rati of factors in equilibrium given a higher wage rate. Robinson considers that to be an exaggeration and suggests it instead be called, the "Ricardesque effect." For her, "The more the capitalists have been able to take advantage of the Ricardesque effect, the less the workers have benefited from the Wicksell effect" (Robinson, 53–54, p. 96 and *Economica*, Volume 9, May 1942).

Salableness—See "liquidity."

Secular Stagnation—A concept conveying the idea of slow economic growth in the long term. It has been associated with many causes, such as demographic decline, and cultural factors, such as a perception that the society already has "too much," among others. The immediate causes are likely to be changes in the institutional environment that make productive activity not appealing to the economic agents for the foreseeable future and lead them to retrench, retire, or emigrate.

State Theory of Money—A conception that the value of money is the one attributed to it by the state (see Zelmanovitz, 2016: 42).

Structure of production—"Any . . . change from a method of production of any given duration to a method which takes more or less time implies quite definite changes in the organization of production, or, as I shall call this particular aspect of organization, . . . changes in the structure of production" (Hayek, 1999: 221).

Wages—"The cost of labor to the employer in terms of product" (Robinson: 53–54, 87).

Wicksell Effect—For Joan Robinson, "The relation of capital to labor, in an equilibrium position, can be regarded as the resultant of the interaction of three distinct influences: the wage rate, the rate of interest, and the degree of mechanization." Considering that the "Wicksell effect" explains "the influence of the wage rate upon the value in terms of product of a given physical capital"—that is, if capital is considered accumulated savings and savings are considered refrained consumption—the higher the wages, the fewer savings are made and the less physical capital is produced and, consequently, later there will be less employment and less final production than there would have been under other arrangements in which wages were lower (Robinson: 53–54, 95).

Glossary of Terms in the Model

Wt: "Everything that exists" in the world.

Pr: Everything that exists in the world that is "property of someone" human.

Rn: Everything that exists in the world that is "property of no one" (*res nullius*).

Wm: Everything that exists as part of the "material world."

Wi: Everything that exists as social constructs, as part of the "intellectual world."

Nr: The original factor of production "land," in a modern nomenclature, we may classify as "natural resources."

Kh: The original factor of production "labor," in a modern nomenclature, we may classify as "human capital."

Khk: Human capital may be "knowledge"—that is, the knowledge inside each individual of what to do and how to do things.

Khd: Human capital may be "dexterity"—that is, the actual capacity of doing things.

Kt: From the original factors of production, along the evolution of human societies, some utensils and useful tools for production were conceived, produced, and stored, and they are called equipment, that is, "technical capital."

Ki: From the original factors of production, along the evolution of human societies, some processes for production were conceived, their knowledge preserved and transmitted, and we called them "intellectual capital."

Kn: Things classified as "known things."

Ku: Things classified as "unknown things."

Eg: "Things with economic value."

En: "Things with no economic value."

Cg: Among the things with economic value, we find the subcategory of "consumer goods."

Kg: Among the things with economic value, we find the subcategory of "capital goods."

Khs: Among intellectual capital, we find the knowledge already ingrained in social interactions, in processes, for the lack of a better term, we called that "human social capital."

Khc: One part of human capital is the entrepreneurial capacity. It is in part the capacity to do things, in part the skill of becoming aware of the surrounding environment, and in part the "knowledge of particular circumstances" which someone becomes aware.

Khe: The part of human capacity that we called "entrepreneurial skills" is the entrepreneurial capacity to do things, plus the skill of becoming aware of the surrounding environment.

(f):   The "continuum of predominant use" between what we consider a consumer good *(Cg)* and what we consider a capital good *(Kg)*.

(m):   The "continuum of permutability" among different capital goods.

Kgm: Capital goods more "malleable" to different uses at one extreme of *(m)*.

Kgr: Capital goods which are more "specific" for certain uses at the other extreme of *(m)*.

Pp: Among the things that belong to someone, some are "private property of individuals" or group of individuals.

Pg: Among the things that belong to someone, some are "property rights that belong to some political association."

Ppi: Among the things owned by individuals, some are "individual property."

Ppc: Among the things owned by individuals, some are property owned in some form of "co-ownership," that is, in condominium, such as a share in a social club or in a business enterprise.

D: fixed income obligations or "debts," which, regardless of being financial instruments or not, are considered as derivatives of equity claims.

Dp: "private debt."

Dg: "public debt."

Pg: "Things owned by the government."

Pgc: In the traditional classification of things owned by the government *(Pg)*, some are "things for common use."

Pgs: In the traditional classification of things owned by the government *(Pg)*, some are "things assigned to a specific purpose."

Pgf: In the traditional classification of things owned by the government *(Pg)*, some are things that are "sources of revenue to the fisc."

Pgp:	"Fiscal prerogatives of the government."
Pgpt:	Among the fiscal prerogatives of the government (*Pgp*) there are the "prerogatives to raise taxes."
Pgpm:	Among the fiscal prerogatives of the government (*Pgp*) there are the "prerogatives to regulate money."
(tr):	The prerogatives of taxing and regulating money have an impact on private property claims as a simple discount at a defined "tax rate."
(n, n+1, ...):	The impact of taxation and monetary manipulation on private property (*tr*) operates in the model at certain "time intervals."
(rr):	"Rate of return in the economy," defined as the difference between the total of property claims (*Pp*) at the initial moment (*n*) and at a second moment (*n+1*).
Ppcf:	"Financial instruments" are a kind of private property held in common (*Ppc*) which, for their properties of liquidity and certainty, are traded in financial markets.
Ppcn:	"Private property held in common not traded in structured markets."
Ppcfn:	Some financial instruments privately issued (*Ppcf*) are "financial instruments which do not have monetary properties."
Ppcfm:	Some financial instruments privately issued (*Ppcf*) are "money substitutes."
Pgptu:	In the static model, the prerogatives of taxation (*Pgpt*) are equivalent to the stock of public debt in a broad sense (*Dg*); and some may be sub-categorized as "unfunded."
Pgptd:	Some of the prerogatives of taxation (*Pgpt*) are "consolidated financial instruments representatives of public debt."
Pgpmd:	Part of the monetary prerogatives (*Pgpm*) are the "powers to exercise financial repression."
Pgpmp:	Part of the monetary prerogatives (*Pgpm*) is "money proper."

Bibliography

Alchian, Areff. "Un Economista Liberal Injustamente Olvidado," *Procesos de Mercado: Revista Europea de Economía Política*, Volume XVI, Number 1, Primavera 2019, pages 89–139.

Alchian, Armen A. *The Collected Works of Armen A. Alchian*, Two Volumes. Indianapolis, IN: Liberty Fund, Inc., 2006.

Barro Robert J. "Are Government Bonds Net Wealth?" *Journal of Political Economy*, Volume 82, Number 6, 1974, pages 1095–1117.

Barzel, Yoram. *Economic Analysis of Property Rights*. Second Edition. Cambridge: Cambridge University Press, 1997.

Becker, Gary S., and Richard A. Posner. "The Future of Law and Economics," *Review of Law & Economics*, Volume 10, Number 3, 2014, pages 235, 238–240.

Berman, Harold. *Law and Revolution: The Formation of the Western Legal Tradition*. Cambridge, MA: Harvard University Press, 1983.

Bissell, Roger E., Chris Matthew Sciabarra, and Edward W. Younkins (editors). *The Dialectics of Liberty: Exploring the Context of Human Freedom*. Lanham, MD: Lexington Books, 2019.

Blackstone, William. *Commentaries on the Laws of England, a Facsimile of the First Edition of 1765–1769*. Chicago, IL: University of Chicago Press, 1979.

Böhm-Bawerk, Eugen von. "Whether Legal Rights and Relationships are Economic Goods," chapter II, pages 25–138, in *Shorter Classic of Bohm-Bawerk*, Volume I. Spring Mills, PA: Libertarian Press, Inc., 1962 (German original from 1881).

Böhm-Bawerk, Eugen von. *The Positive Theory of Capital*. Translated by William Smart. New York, NY: Cosimo Inc., published under the label Cosimo Classics, 2006 (Original from 1888).

Boianovsky, Mauro. "Beyond Capital Fundamentalism: Harrod, Domar and the History of Development Economics," *Cambridge Journal of Economics*, Volume 42, Number 2, March 2018, pages 477–504.

Boldizzoni, Francesco. *Means and Ends: The Idea of Capital in the West, 1500–1970*. New York, NY: Palgrave-MacMillan, 2008.

Bortis, Heinrich. "The Real and the Financial Section of a Monetary Production Economy in the Perspective of Classical-Keynesian Political Economy," 2016. Available at: https://www.unifr.ch/withe/assets/files/Publikationen/Bortis-Real -Financial-Sector.pdf

Bragues, George. "Towards an Austrian Theory of Finance," in *Prices and Markets*. Canada: Mises Institute, 2016, pages 71–78. Available at: http://pricesandmark ets.org/papers-proceedings-of-the-3rd-annual-international-conference-of-prices-markets/towards-an-austrian-theory-of-finance/

Braun, Eduard, and David Howden. "The Rise and Fall of the Subsistence Fund as a Resource Constraint in Austrian Business Cycle Theory," *Review of Austrian Economics*, Volume 30, 2017, pages 235–249.

Braun, Eduard, Peter Lewin, and Nicolas Cachanosky. "Ludwig von Mises's Approach to Capital as a Bridge Between Austrian and Institutional Economics," 2016. Available at: https://papers.ssrn.com/sol3/papers.cfm?abstract_id=2748937

Cachanosky, Nicolas, and Peter Lewin. "Roundaboutness is Not a Mysterious Concept: A Financial Application to Capital Theory," *Review of Political Economy*, Volume 26, Number 4, 2014, pages 648–665.

Cambreleng, Churchill C. *Examination of the New Tariff by One of the People*. New York, NY: Charles N. Baldwin, 1821.

Cochrane, John H. *Asset Pricing*. Princeton, NJ: Princeton University Press, 2001.

Cohen, Avi J., and G. C. Harcourt. "Retrospectives: Whatever Happened to the Cambridge Capital Theory Controversies?" *Journal of Economic Perspectives*, Volume 17, Number 1, Winter 2003, pages 199–214.

Cooter, Robert, and Aaron Edlin. *The Falcon's Gyre: Legal Foundations of Economic Innovation and Growth*. Berkeley, CA: Berkeley Law Books, 2014. Available at: https://www.law.berkeley.edu/library/resources/cooter.pdf

Cooter, Robert D., and Hans-Bernd Schäfer. *Solomon's Knot: How Law Can End the Poverty of Nations*. Princeton, NJ: Princeton University Press, 2012.

Cowen, Tyler. *Average Is Over*. New York: Dutton, an imprint of Penguin Group, Inc., 2013.

Cowen, Tyler. *Stubborn Attachments: A Vision for a Society of Free, Prosperous, and Responsible Individuals*. San Francisco, CA: Stripe Press, 2018.

Cowen, Tyler. "Transcript from the Podcast Interview with Tyler Cowen, Mark Zuckerberg and Patrick Collison," November 27, 2019. Available at: https://me dium.com/conversations-with-tyler/mark-zuckerberg-interviews-patrick-collison -and-tyler-cowen-on-the-nature-and-causes-of-progress-30de2e2c48f2

Den Uyl, Douglas J., and Douglas B. Rasmussen. *The Perfectionist Turn: From Metanorms to Metaethics*. Edinburgh: Edinburgh University Press, 2016.

Desan, Christine. *Making Money: Coin, Currency, and the Coming of Capitalism*. Oxford: Oxford University Press, 2014.

DesJardins, Jeff. "How Much Government Debt Rests on Your Shoulders?" An article from the Visual Capitalist, November 23, 2016. Available at: http://www .visualcapitalist.com/much-government-debt-rests-upon-shoulders/

Dorn, Jim. "Covid-19: Implications for Monetary Policy and Fed Independence," Posted on the Alt-M website on April 20, 2020. Available at: https://www.alt-m.or g/2020/04/20/covid-19-implications-for-monetary-policy-and-fed-independence/

Dornbusch, Rudiger, and Sebastian Edwards. *The Macroeconomics of Populism in Latin America*. Chicago: University of Chicago Press, 1991.

Dowd, Kevin. "Against Helicopter Money," *Cato Journal*, Volume 38, Number 1, February 2018, pages 147–169.

Edwards, Sebastian. *Left Behind: Latin America and the False Promise of Populism*. Chicago: University of Chicago Press, 2010.

Edwards, Sebastian. *American Default: The Untold Story of FDR, the Supreme Court and the Battle over Gold*. Princeton: Princeton University Press, 2018.

Edwards, Sebastian. "Modern Monetary Theory: Cautionary Tales from Latin America," Economics Working Paper #19106, Hoover Institution, Stanford University, April 25, 2019, pages 1–27.

Eicholz, Hans L. "Ludwig M. Lachmann: Last Member of the German Historical School," *Journal of Contextual Economics*, Volume 137, 2017, pages 227–260. Berlin: Duncker & Humboldt.

Endres, Anthony M., and David A. Harper. "Carl Menger and His Followers in the Austrian Tradition on the Nature of Capital and Its Structure," *Journal of the History of Economic Thought*, Volume 33, Number 3, September 2011.

Endres, Anthony M., and David A. Harper. "Menger on the Nature of Capital and Its Structure: A Reply," *Journal of the History of Economic Thought*, Volume 36, Number 1, March 2014, pages 103–109.

Ferlito, Carmelo. *Hermeneutics of Capital: A Post-Austrian Theory for a Kaleidic World*. New York, NY: Nova Science Publishers, Inc., 2016.

Fernández-Méndez, Daniel. "The Great Capital Controversy: Re-switching, Austrian Economics, and the Misuse of Mathematics in Economics," *Procesos de Mercado: Revista Europea de Economía Política*, Volume XVI, Number 1, Primavera 2019, pages 259–278.

Fischer, Stanley, and William Easterly. "The Economics of the Government Budget Constraint," *World Bank Research Observer*, Volume 5, Number 2, July 1990, pages 127–142.

Fletcher, Gina-Gail. "Macroeconomic Consequences of Market Manipulation," *Law & Contemporary Problems*, Volume 83, Number 1, 2020, page 123.

Frankfurt, Harry G. *On Inequality*. Princeton, NJ: Princeton University Press, 2015.

Friedman, Benjamin M. "Implications of Government Deficit for U.S. Capital Formation," A Working Paper for the Federal Reserve Bank of Boston, 1984, pages 73–111. Available at: https://www.bostonfed.org/-/media/Documents/confer ence/27/conf27c.pdf

Garrison, Roger W. "Austrian Capital Theory," Austrian Economics University 2016, Mises Institute, July 25, 2016. Available at: https://mises.org/library/austrian-capit al-theory-3

Geloso, Vincent, and Phillip Magness. "The Great Overestimation: Tax Data and Inequality Measurements in the United States, 1913–1943," *Economic Inquiry*, Volume 58, Number 2, April 2020, pages 834–855.

Gelpern, Anna, and Adam J. Levitin. "Introduction," in *Considering Law and Macroeconomics*, A *Symposium Issue of Law and Contemporary Problems*, Volume 83, Number I, 2020. Available at: http://lcp.law.duke.edu/

Gibbon, Edward. *Decline and Fall of the Roman Empire.* Everyman's Library, Reprint Edition. New York, NY: Random House, 2010.

Graham, Benjamin, and David L. Dodd. *Security Analysis.* Sixth Edition. New York, NY: McGraw-Hill, 2009.

Hahn, Ludwig Albert. *The Economics of Illusion: A Critical Analysis of Contemporary Economic Theory and Policy.* New York, NY: Squier Publishing Co., Inc., 1949.

Hahn, Ludwig Albert. *Economic Theory of Bank Credit.* Translated by Clemens Matt and with an introduction by Harald Hagemann. Oxford: Oxford University Press, 2015.

Hamilton, Alexander, James Madison, and John Jay. *The Federalist.* Edited by George W. Carey and James McClellan. Indianapolis: Liberty Fund, Inc., 2001.

Harari, Yuval Noah. *Money.* London: Vintage Minis, an imprint of Penguin Random House, 2019.

Harcourt, G. C. "Some Cambridge Controversies in the Theory of Capital," *Journal of Economic Literature,* Volume 7, Number 2, June 1969, pages 369–405. American Economic Association.

Hawtrey, Ralph. "Money and Index Numbers," *Journal of the Royal Statistical Society,* Volume 93, Part I, 1930, page 64.

Hayek, F. A. *Choice in Currency: A Way to Stop Inflation.* London: Institute of Economic Affairs, 1976.

Hayek, Friedrich A. "The Ricardo Effect," *Economica,* Volume 9, May 1942, Reprinted as chapter 9 in *Business Cycles,* part II of the Collected Works of Hayek, Volume 8.

Hayek, Friedrich A. "The Use of Knowledge in Society," *American Economic Review,* Volume XXXV, Number 4, 1945, pages 519–530. American Economic Association.

Hayek, Friedrich A. *Law, Legislation, and Liberty,* Volume 1, Chicago, IL: Chicago University Press, 1973.

Hayek, Friedrich A. *The Constitution of Liberty.* Chicago: University of Chicago Press, 1978.

Hayek, Friedrich A. *The Collected Works of F. A. Hayek, Good Money, Part I: The New World.* Edited by Stephen Kresge. Indianapolis, IN: Liberty Fund, Inc., 1999a.

Hayek, Friedrich A. "The Collected Works of F. A. Hayek," Volumes 7 and 8, in *Business Cycles,* parts I and II. Edited by Hansjörg Klausinger. Chicago, IL: University of Chicago Press, 1999b.

Hayek, Friedrich A. "The 'Paradox' of Saving" (1929/31), in *Prices and Production and Other Works,* F. A. Hayek on Money, The Business Cycle, and the Gold Standard. Auburn, AL: Ludwig von Mises Institute, 2008.

Hayek, Friedrich A. "The Collected Works of F.A. Hayek," Volume XII, in *The Pure Theory of Capital.* Chicago, IL: University of Chicago Press, 2014.

Henderson, David R. *The Concise Encyclopedia of Economics.* Indianapolis, IN: Liberty Fund, Inc., 2008.

Hendrickson, Joshua R., and Alexander William Salter. "Money, Liquidity, and the Structure of Production," Working Paper, 2015. Available at: http://ssrn.com/abstract=2567014

Heyne, Paul L., Peter J. Boettke, and David L. Prychitko. *The Economic Way of Thinking.* Thirteenth Edition. London: Pearson Education, Inc., 2013.

Hicks, John. *Capital and Time: A Neo-Austrian Theory.* London: Clarendon Press, Oxford University Press, 1973.

Horwitz, Steven. "Capital Theory, Inflation and Deflation: The Austrians and Monetary Disequilibrium Compared," *Journal of the History of Economic Thought,* Volume 18, Fall 1996, pages 287–318.

Horwitz, Steven. "Language, Monetary Exchange, and the Structure of the Economic Universe: An Austrian-Searlean Synthesis," chapter 5, pages 75–88, in *Economics and the Mind.* Edited by Barbara Montero and Mark D. White. New York, NY: Rutledge, 2009.

Huerta de Soto, Jesús. *Money, Bank Credit, and Economic Cycles.* Auburn, AL: Ludwig von Mises Institute, 2006.

Hume, David. "Essays, Moral, Political, and Literary," Part II, Essay I, in *Of Commerce (1752).* Indianapolis, IN: Liberty Fund, Inc., 1987.

Jones, Charles I., and Dietrich Vollrath. *Introduction to Economic Growth.* Third Edition. New York, NY: W. W. Norton & Company, Inc., 2013.

Keynes, John Maynard. "A Treatise on Money, Volume I, on the Pure Theory of Money," in *The Collected Writings of John Maynard Keynes,* Volumes V and VI. Cambridge: Cambridge University Press, published for the Royal Economic Society, 1998 (First Edition, 1930).

Klausinger, Hansjorg (1999) "Introduction," in *The Collected Works of F. A. Hayek,* Volumes 7 and 8, *Business Cycles,* Parts I and II. Edited by Hansjörg Klausinger. Chicago, IL: University of Chicago Press.

Kohn, Meir. "The Capital Market before 1600," Working Paper 99-06, 1999. Available at: http://www.dartmouth.edu/~mkohn/Papers/99-06.pdf

Kohn, Meir. "Payments and the Development of Finance in Pre-Industrial Europe," Working Paper 01-15, November 2001. Available at: http://www.dartmouth.edu/~mkohn/Papers/01-15.pdf

Lachmann, Ludwig M. *Capital and Its Structure.* London: Bell & Sons, Ltd., on behalf of the London School of Economics and Political Science, 1956, reprinted by the Ludwig Von Mises Institute, Auburn, Alabama, 2007.

Lachmann, Ludwig M. *Capital, Expectations, and the Market Process: Essays on the Theory of the Market Economy.* Edited by Walter E. Grinder. Mission, KS: Sheed Andrews and McMeel, Inc., a subsidiary of Universal Press Syndicate, 1977.

Laidler, David. *The Demand for Money: Theories, Evidence & Problems.* Fourth Edition. New York, NY: HarperCollins College Publishers, 1993.

Lange, Glenn-Marie, Quentin Wodon, and Kevin Carey. *The Changing Wealth of Nations, 2018: Building a Sustainable Future.* Washington, DC: World Bank. Available at: https://openknowledge.worldbank.org/handle/10986/29001

Lawson, Tony. *Economics & Reality.* Abingdon: Routledge, 1997.

Lawson, Tony. "Ontology and the Study of Social Reality: Emergence, Organization, Community, Power, Social Relations, Corporations, Artefacts and Money," *Cambridge Journal of Economics,* Volume 36, Number 2, 2012, pages 345–385.

Lemieux, Pierre. "An Open and Enlightened Libertarianism," *Regulation*, Volume 42, Spring 2019, page 46. Available at: https://object.cato.org/sites/cato.org/files/serials/files/regulation/2019/3/regulation-v42n1-9_4.pdf#page=12

Lerner, Abba. "Functional Finance and the Federal Debt," *Social Research*, Volume 10, Number 1, February 1943, pages 38–51. Johns Hopkins Press.

Lerner, Abba P. "On the Marginal Product of Capital and the Marginal Efficiency of Investment," *Journal of Political Economy*, Volume 61, Number 1, February 1953, pages 1–14. Chicago, IL: University of Chicago Press.

Lewin, Peter. "Knowledge, Expectations, and Capital: The Economics of Ludwig M. Lachmann: Attempting a New Perspective," *Advances in Austrian Economics*, Volume 1, 1994, pages 233–256. Greenwich: JAI Press.

Lewin, Peter. "Time, Change, and Complexity: Ludwig M. Lachmann's Contributions to the Theory of Capital," *Advances in Austrian Economics*, Volume 3, 1996, pages 107–165.

Lewis, Paul, and Jochen Runde. "Subjectivism, Social Structure and the Possibility of Socio-economic Order: The Case of Ludwig Lachmann," *Journal of Economic Behavior & Organization*, Volume 62, Number 2, February 2007, pages 167–186. Elsevier.

Listokin, Yair. "Law and Macro: What Took so Long?" *Law & Contemporary Problems*, Volume 83, Number 1, 2020, pages 141–156.

Locke, John. *Two Treatises of Government*. Cambridge: Cambridge University Press, 2000.

Lucas, Robert E., Jr. "Econometric Policy Evaluation: A Critique," *Carnegie-Rochester Conference Series on Public Policy*, Volume 1, 1976, pages 19–46.

Lukács, Georg. *History and Class Consciousness*. Second Printing. Cambridge, MA: MIT Press, 1972.

MacLeod, Henry Dunning. *Elements of Political Economy*. London: Longman, Brown, Green, Longmans, and Roberts, 1858, reprinted in New York, NY, by Cosimo Inc. under the label Cosimo Classics (December 1, 2007).

Marx, Karl. *Capital: A Critique of Political Economy*, Volume 3. Translated by David Fernbach. London: Penguin Classics, Paperback, 1993.

Mathieu, Vittorio. *Filosofía del Dinero*. Madrid, Spain: Ediciones RIALP, S.A., 1990.

Meacci Ferdinand. "Fictitious Capital and Crises," in *Marxian Economics: A Reappraisal*. Edited by Riccardo Bellofiore. London: Palgrave Macmillan, 1998.

Meacci, Ferdinand. "The Distinction Between Relative and Positive Profit: Sir James Steuart after Adam Smith and the Classics," in *The European Journal of the History of Economic Thought*, Volume 27, Number 1, 2020, pages 66–85, a revised version of "Positive Profit, Relative Profit and Capital as Command of Productive Labour," paper presented at the Annual Meeting of the European Society for the History of Economic Thought, Paris, January 30–February 2, 2003.

Menger, Carl. *Investigations in the Method of Social Sciences with Special Reference to Economics*. Edited by L. White. New York, NY: New York University Press, 1985.

Menger, Carl. *Principles of Economics*. Grove City, PA: Libertarian Press, 1994 (Original from 1871).

Menger, Carl. "Sobre La Teoría Del Capital," *Procesos de Mercado: Revista Europea de Economia Política*, Volume IV, Número 1, Primavera 2007, pages 177 228 (Original from 1888).

Meyerhof Salama, Bruno. "Macroeconomic Analysis of Law Versus Law and Macroeconomics," *Law & Contemporary Problems*, Volume 83, Number 1, 2020, pages 181–194.

Minea, Alexandru, and Patrick Villieu. "Borrowing to Finance Public Investment?: The 'Golden Rule of Public Finance' Reconsidered in an Endogenous Growth Setting," *Fiscal Studies*, Volume 30, Number 1, 2009, pages 103–133.

Minsky, Hyman P. "The Financial Instability Hypothesis," Working Paper 74, May 1992, pages 1–9. Downloaded from the Levy Economics Institute Working Paper Collection. Available at: http://www.levyinstitute.org/pubs/wp74.pdf

Mises, Ludwig, von. *The Theory of Money and Credit*. Indianapolis, IN: Liberty Fund, Inc., 1980.

Mises, Ludwig von. "Mexico's Economic Problems," in *Selected Writings of Ludwig von Mises*, Volume 3. Indianapolis, IN: Liberty Fund, Inc., 2000.

Mises, Ludwig von. *Human Action: A Treatise on Economics*. Indianapolis, IN: Liberty Fund, Inc., 2007.

Mises, Ludwig von. *The Anti-Capitalistic Mentality*. Auburn, AL: Ludwig von Mises Institute, 2008.

Mitchell, William, L. Randall Wray, and Martin Watts. *Macroeconomics*. London: Red Globe Press, an imprint of Springer Nature Limited, 2019.

Nersisyan, Yeva, and L. Randall Wray. "How to Pay for the Green New Deal," Working Paper #931, Levy Economics Institute of Bard College, Annandale-on-Hudson, NY, May 2019, pages 1–56.

Nimark, Kristoffer P. "Private and Public Information," 2015. Available at: http://www.kris-nimark.net/Info_2015/Lecture_Notes_Public_and_Private_Info.pdf

North, Douglass C. "Institutions, Ideology, and Economic Performance," *Cato Journal*, Volume 11, Number 3, Winter 1992, page 477.

Orian Peer, Nadav. "Public Purpose Finance," *Law & Contemporary Problems*, Volume 83, Number 1, 2020, page 101.

Osborne, Evan W. "Captive of One's Own Theory: Joan Robinson and Maoist China," in *Econ Journal Watch*, Volume 17, Number 1, March 2020, pages 191–227.

Piketty, Thomas. *Capital in the Twenty-First Century*. Cambridge, MA: The Belknap Press of Harvard University Press, 2014.

Pipes, Richard. *Property and Freedom*. New York, NY: Vintage Books, a division of Random House, Inc., 2000.

Pistor, Katharina. *The Code of Capital: How the Law Creates Wealth and Inequality*. Princeton, NJ: Princeton University Press, 2019.

Popper, Karl. "Three Words," in *The Tanner Lecture on Human Values*, delivered at the University of Michigan, April 7, 1978, page 1420167. Available at: https://fdocuments.in/document/popper-three-world.html

Puxley, H. L. *A Critique of the Gold Standard.* Abingdon: Routledge, 2018, first published in 1933 by George Allen & Unwin, Ltd.

Ramirez, Steve. "The Emergence of Law and Macroeconomics: From Stability to Growth to Human Development," Volume 83, in *Law & Contemporary Problems*, Volume 1, 2020, page 219.

Rand, Ayn. "The Ethics of Emergencies," in *The Virtue of Selfishness.* Centennial Edition. New York, NY: A Signet Book, published by the New American Library, a division of Penguin Group, first printing 1964.

Rasmussen, Douglas B. "Rothbard's Account of the Axiom of Human Action: A Neo-Aristotelian-Thomistic Defense," in *Philosophy, Politics, and Austrian Economics.* Edited by Adam Martin and Daniel D'Amico. forthcoming, UK: Emerald, Bingley, 2020, 35-page typescript.

Rasmussen, Douglas B., and Douglas J. Den Uyl. *Norms of Liberty: A Perfectionist Basis for a Non-perfectionist Politics.* University Park, PA: Pennsylvania State University Press, 2005.

Reinhart, Carmen M., Vincent R. Reinhart, and Kenneth S. Rogoff. "Public Debt Overhangs: Advanced-Economy Episodes since 1800," *Journal of Economic Perspectives*, Volume 26, Number 3, 2012, pages 69–86.

Ricks, Morgan. "Money, Private Law, and Macroeconomic Disasters," *Law & Contemporary Problems*, Volume 83, Number 1, 2020, pages 65–81.

Robinson, Joan. "The Production Function and the Theory of Capital," *Review of Economic Studies*, Volume 21, Number 2, 1953–1954, pages 81–106.

Rueff, Jacques. *El Órden Social.* Madrid, Spain: Aguilar Publicaciones, 1964.

Salsman, Richard M. *The Political Economy of Public Debt: Three Centuries of Theory and Evidence.* Cheltenham: Edward Elgar Publishing Limited, 2017.

Sarjanovic, Ivo A. *En Desequilibrio – Ensayos sobre procesos de Mercado.* Madrid, Spain: Unión Editorial, 2020.

Schmelzing, Paul. "Eight Centuries of Global Real Interest Rates, R-G, and the 'Suprasecular' Decline, 1311–2018," Staff Working Paper 845, Bank of England, January 2020. Available at: https://www.bankofengland.co.uk/working-paper /2020/eight-centuries-of-global-real-interest-rates-r-g-and-the-suprasecular-dec line-1311-2018

Searle, John R. *The Construction of Social Reality.* New York, NY: The Free Press, a division of Simon & Schuster, Inc., 1995.

Selgin, George. *The Menace of Fiscal Q.E.* Washington, DC: Cato Institute, 2020.

Sen, Amartya. "On Some Debates in Capital Theory," *Economica*, Volume 41, Number 163, August 1974, pages 328–335.

Siegan, Bernard H. *Land Use Without Zoning.* Lanham, MD: Lexington Books, 1972.

Skidelsky, Robert. "Why We Should Take Corbynomics Seriously," *Guardian*, August 19, 2015. Available at: https://www.theguardian.com/business/2015/aug /19/corbynomics-why-we-should-take-it-seriously

Skidelsky, Robert. *Money and Government: The Past and Future of Economics.* New Haven, CT: Yale University Press, 2019.

Skidelsky, Robert, and Edward Skidelsky. *How Much is Enough?: Money and the Good Life.* New York, NY: Other Press, 2013.

Smith, Adam. *An Inquiry into the Nature and Causes of the Wealth of Nations*. The Glasgow Edition of the Works and Correspondence of Adam Smith. Indianapolis, IN: Liberty Classics, Liberty Fund, Inc., 1981.

Smith, Barry, David M. Mark, and Isaac Ehrlich (editors), *The Mystery of Capital and the Construction of Social Reality*. Peru, IL: Open Court Publishing, 2008.

Smithin, John. *Rethinking the Theory of Money, Credit, and Macroeconomics: A New Statement for the Twenty-First Century*. Lanham, MD: Lexington Books, 2018.

Smithin, John, and Jeffrey Lau. "The Role of Money in Capitalism," *International Journal of Political Economy*, Volume 32, Number 3, Fall 2002, pages 5–22.

Solow, Robert M. "A Contribution to the Theory of Economic Growth," *Quarterly Journal of Economics*, Volume 70, Number 1, February 1956, pages 65–94.

Soto, Hernando de. *The Other Path: The Economic Answer to Terrorism*. New York, NY: Basic Books, 1989.

Soto, Hernando de. *The Mystery of Capital*. New York, NY: Basic Books, 2000.

Spitznagel, Mark. *The Dao of Capital: Austrian Investing in a Distorted World*. Hoboken, NJ: John Wiley & Sons, Inc., 2013.

Streissler, Erich. "Structural Economic Thought on the Significance of the Austrian School Today," *Zeitschrift für Nationalökonomie/Journal of Economics*, Volume 29, Number 3/4, 1969, pages 237–266. Springer.

Strigl, Richard von. *Capital & Production*. Auburn, AL: Ludwig von Mises Institute, 2000, first edition in German (1934).

Summers, Larry. "Larry Summers's 4-Point Plan for Saving the Economy," *The Atlantic*, July 2, 2014. Available at: https://www.theatlantic.com/business/archive/2014/07/larry-summerss-4-point-plan-for-saving-the-economy/373849/

Tobin, James. "Money and Economic Growth," *Econometrica*, Volume 33, Number 4, 1965, pages 671–684, published by the Econometric Society.

Tupy, Marian L. "We Work Less, Have More Leisure Time and Earn More Money," Article posted in HumanProgress, November 15, 2016. Available at: http://humanprogress.org/blog/we-work-less-have-more-leisure-time-and-earn-more-money

Vasak, Karel. "Human Rights: A Thirty-Year Struggle: The Sustained Efforts to Give Force of Law to the Universal Declaration of Human Rights," in *UNESCO Courier*, Volume 30, page 11. Paris, France: United Nations Educational, Scientific, and Cultural Organization, November 1977.

Waddilove, D. P. "Credit Before Banks: Suretyship in Early-Modern England," Draft October 29, 2018, paper presented at the 23rd British Legal History Conference, London, July 2017.

Weber, Max. *General Economic History*. New York, NY: Greenberg, Publisher, Inc., 1927, this edition, first published in Mineola, NY, by Dover Publications Inc., in 2003.

White, Lawrence H. *The Theory of Monetary Institutions*. Oxford: Blackwell Publishers, Inc., 1999.

Whitman, Martin J. *Value Investing: A Balanced Approach*. New York, NY: John Wiley & Sons, Inc., 1999.

Woolf, Schoomaker H. "Life Expectancy and Mortality Rates in the United States, 1959–2017," *Journal of the American Medical Association*, Volume 322, Number 20, 2019, pages 1996–2016. Available at: https://doi.org/10.1001/jama.2019.16932

Wray, L. Randall. *Modern Money Theory: A Primer on Macroeconomics for Sovereign Monetary Systems*. New York: Palgrave McMillan, 2015.

Young, Michael. *The Rise of the Meritocracy*. New Brunswick: Transaction Publishers, 2008 (Original from 1958).

Zelmanovitz, Leonidas. "The Fiscal Proviso," *Criterio Libre*, Volume 11, Number 19, July–December 2013, pages 23–49. Bogota, Colombia.

Zelmanovitz, Leonidas. "Designing Capitalism," *Law & Liberty*, September 8, 2015. Available at: https://www.lawliberty.org/book-review/designing-capitalism/

Zelmanovitz, Leonidas. *The Ontology and Function of Money: The Philosophical Fundamentals of Monetary Institutions*. Lanham, MD: Lexington Books, 2016.

Zelmanovitz, Leonidas. *Editorial Review of Rethinking the Theory of Money, Credit, and Macroeconomics: A New Statement for the Twenty-First Century by John Smithin*. Lanham, MD: Lexington Books, 2018a.

Zelmanovitz, Leonidas. "A Model for a Representational Theory of Capital," *Perspectivas en Inteligencia*, Volume 10, Number 19, 2018b, pages 141–161.

Zelmanovitz, Leonidas. "Review of Time, Space and Capital by Åke E. Andersson and David Emanuel Andersson," *Journal of the History of Economic Thought*, Volume 41, Number 2, 2019a.

Zelmanovitz, Leonidas. "The Baleful Consequences of Robert Skidelsky's Keynesianism," *Law & Liberty*, March 12, 2019b. Available at: https://www.law liberty.org/2019/03/12/the-baleful-consequences-of-robert-skidelskys-keynesianism/

Zelmanovitz, Leonidas. "Modern Monetary Theory and the Moral Equivalent of War," *Law & Liberty*, November 20, 2019c. Available at: https://www.lawliberty .org/2019/11/20/modern-monetary-theory-and-the-moral-equivalent-of-war/

Zelmanovitz, Leonidas. "What Would 'the Treasury View' of Libra Be?" *Law & Liberty*, July 51, 2019d. Available at: https://www.lawliberty.org/2019/07/31/what -would-the-treasury-view-of-libra-be/

Zelmanovitz, Leonidas. "Liberty in the Political Institutions of the 21st Century," *Laissez-faire*, Number 50–51, March–September 2019e, pages 36–52. Guatemala City, Guatemala.

Zelmanovitz, Leonidas. "A Representational Theory of Capital," in *Procesos de Mercado*. Madrid, Spain: Union Editorial, 2020.

"Brazil: Law No. 10.406 of January 10, 2002 (Civil Code)." Available at: www.wipo .int/wipolex/en/details.jsp?id=9615

Congressional Budget Office (CBO) "The 2018 Long-term Budget Outlook," Congress of the United States, June 2018. Available at: www.cbo.gov/publications /53919

"Wikipedia Article: Cuius est solum, eius est usque ad coelum et ad inferos." Available at: https://en.wikipedia.org/wiki/Cuius_est_solum,_eius_est_usque_ad _coelum_et_ad_inferos

Index

About the Author

Dr. Zelmanovitz has a law degree earned from the Federal University in Porto Alegre, Brazil, a Master degree in Austrian economics, and a PhD in applied economics from the Universidad Rey Juan Carlos in Madrid, Spain. After a business career in real estate and finances in Brazil, Dr. Zelmanovitz joined Liberty Fund, where he is currently a senior fellow.